The Institute of Mathematics
and its Applications
Conference Series

Volumes in the previous series were published by Academic Press to whom all enquiries
should be addressed. The following and all forthcoming titles are published by Oxford
University Press throughout the world.

NEW SERIES

Continued overleaf

Mathematics of Dependable Systems II

Based on the proceedings of a conference organized by the Institute of Mathematics and its Applications on the Mathematics of Dependable Systems, and held at the University of York in August 1995.

Edited by

V. STAVRIDOU
Queen Mary and Westfield College, London

CLARENDON PRESS · OXFORD · 1997

Oxford University Press, Great Clarendon Street, Oxford OX2 6DP

Oxford New York
Athens Auckland Bangkok Bogota Bombay
Buenos Aires Calcutta Cape Town Dar es Salaam
Delhi Florence Hong Kong Istanbul Karachi
Kuala Lumpur Madras Madrid Melbourne
Mexico City Nairobi Paris Singapore
Taipei Tokyo Toronto Warsaw

and associated companies in
Berlin Ibadan

Oxford is a trade mark of Oxford University Press

Published in the United States
by Oxford University Press, Inc., New York

© Institute of Mathematics and its Applications, 1997

A catalogue record for this book is available from the British Library

Library of Congress Cataloging in Publication Data
(Data available)

ISBN 0 19 852382 3

Typeset using LaTeX
Printed in Great Britain by
Bookcraft (Bath) Ltd

PREFACE

This volume contains proceedings of the second international IMA conference
on the "Mathematics of Dependable Systems" which took place at the University of York, England, in September 1995 (MDS 95). The conference, as its title
implies, is a forum for discussing the role of mathematics in the construction
of dependable systems, that is systems with stringent safety, reliability, security
and availability requirements. The conference theme is unique in that it is not
confined to applications of one kind of mathematical theory. Instead it celebrates all innovations in the theory and practice of dependable systems which
come about through the use of mathematics. The long term objective of the
conference is the harmonisation and cross-fertilisation of mathematical theories
for the development of safe, secure, reliable and available computing systems.

The conference programme included ten regular and six invited papers. In his
invited paper, Parnas discusses the difference between descriptions of programs,
specifications of programs and models of programs and he suggests that these
important differences are often neglected by the formal methods community.
Moser and Melliar-Smith present a methodology for modular composition and
hierarchical refinement of specifications and proofs for dependable systems which
involves the interesting concept of independence predicates, a notion related to
non-interference in security. Mukherjee demonstrates how system level reasoning
about VDM-SL specifications can be achieved by considering the specification
as a labelled transition system. Piper's invited paper gives a perspective and an
introduction to the problems and techniques of key management for secure communication. Musyoka and Morgan describe a repeatable, structured verification
methodology for fault tolerant processors. In his invited paper, Sennett describes the historical origins of computer security notions and critically discusses
the impact of formal methods on the subject. Chapman, Burns and Wellings
present a new approach to the static analysis of non functional properties of
programs such as worst-case execution time, which is based on regular expressions. Nissanke demonstrates the application of deontic logic to the specification
of non-functional system requirements using railway signalling as an illustration.
Harman and Tucker present a generalised algebraic method for modelling microprocessors in a modular way at different levels of abstraction. The invited
paper by Chapront reports on GEC-Alsthom's pioneering industrial application
of formal verification in railway control systems. Knight, in his invited paper,
reviews some significant issues in software development which are not currently
tackled and examines the role of mathematics in each. Bridal presents a methodology based on a time homogeneous, continuous time Markov chain model, which
allows symbolic evaluation of the reliability of complex, repairable fault tolerant systems. Perkins and Tyrell present a new reliability model for hard real
time systems which is based on Markov chains complemented with ideas from
Petri nets. Haines and Longshaw propose the use of space based modelling, a
technique based on Rough Sets, to the validation of safety properties of depend-

able systems. Finally, the invited paper by Littlewood and Wright presents a Bayesian model that combines disparate evidence for the quantitative assessment of system dependability. All in all, a truly outstanding, thought provoking and diverse collection of papers.

MDS 95 was a remarkably friendly and vibrant conference. In closing, I would like to thank the people who made it such an enjoyable and useful event, including the conference participants, the authors, the invited speakers, the programme committee members (D. Gollmann, M. Ingleby, J. Jacob, B. Littlewood, R. Shaw and B. Wichmann), the York organisers, as well as our sponsor, Nuclear Electric. May we have lots more like it.

Dr. V. Stavridou
Queen Mary and Westfield College, University of London

ACKNOWLEDGEMENTS

The Institute thanks the authors of the papers, the editor Dr. Victoria Stavridou (Royal Holloway, University of London), Debbie Brown and Karen Jenkins for typesetting the papers, and Simon Byles for proof reading them.

CONTENTS

CONTRIBUTORS

O. BRIDAL; Department of Computer Engineering, Laboratory for Dependable Computing, Chalmers University of Technology, S-412 96 Gothenburg, Sweden.

A. BURNS; British Aerospace Dependable Computing Systems Centre, Department of Computer Science, University of York, Heslington, York, YO1 5DD.

R. CHAPMAN; Praxis Critical Systems, 20 Manvers Street, Bath, BA1 1PX.

P. CHAPRONT; GEC Alsthom, 33 rue des Bateliers, 93404 Saint Ouen Cedex, France.

S. HAINES; DRA Malvern, St. Andrews Road, Malvern, Worcestershire, WR14 3PS.

N.A. HARMAN; Department of Computer Science, University of Wales Swansea, Swansea, Wales, SA2 8PP.

J.C. KNIGHT; Department of Computer Science, University of Virginia, Charlottesville, VA 22903, USA.

B. LITTLEWOOD; Centre for Software Reliability, City University, Northampton Square, London, EC1V 0HB.

T. LONGSHAW; DRA Malvern, St. Andrews Road, Malvern, Worcestershire, WR14 3PS.

P.M. MELLIAR-SMITH; Department of Electrical and Computer Engineering, University of California, Santa Barbara 93106, USA.

G. MORGAN; Department of Computer Science, University of York, Heslington, York, YO1 5DD.

L.E. MOSER; Department of Electrical and Computer Engineering, University of California, Santa Barbara 93106, USA.

P. MUKHERJEE; School of Computer Studies, University of Leeds, Leeds, LS2 9JT.

G.M. MUSYOKA; Institute of Computer Science, University of Nairobi, P.O. Box 30197, Nairobi, Kenya.

N. NISSANKE; Department of Computer Science, University of Reading, P.O. Box 225, Whiteknights, Reading, Berkshire, RG6 6AY.

D.L. PARNAS; Department of Electrical and Computer Engineering, McMaster University, Hamilton, Ontario, Canada, L8S 4K1.

C.S. PERKINS; Department of Electronics, University of York, Heslington, York, YO1 5DD.

F. PIPER; Department of Mathematics, Royal Holloway, University of London, Egham, Surrey, TW20 0EX.

C.T. SENNETT; Defence Research Agency, St. Andrews Road, Malvern, Worcestershire, WR14 3PS.

J.V. TUCKER; Department of Computer Science, University of Wales Swansea, Swansea, Wales, SA2 8PP.

A.M. TYRRELL; Department of Electronics, University of York, Heslington, York, YO1 5DD.

A. WELLINGS; British Aerospace Dependable Computing Systems Centre, Department of Computer Science, University of York, Heslington, York, YO1 5DD.

D. WRIGHT; Centre for Software Reliability, City University, Northampton Square, London, EC1V 0HB.

Precise Description and Specification of Software

D.L. Parnas

*Department of Electrical and Computer Engineering, McMaster University,
Ontario, Canada*

Abstract

Precise descriptions and specifications of software products can be very
useful if they are simpler than the products that they describe. No new
mathematical concepts are needed for this task; we can use old math in
new ways. This paper discusses the difference between descriptions of programs, specifications of programs, and models of programs suggesting that
these important distinctions are being neglected by the "formal methods"
community. We also discuss the distinction between programs, modules,
objects, and real-time systems and the descriptive methods appropriate to
each.

1 On foundational research

As an engineer, I recognise the importance of having a solid foundation for
practical work and note with dismay that most software developers work in an
ad hoc way, without solid foundations. At the same time, I harbour great doubts
about the directions taken by foundation research in general and formal methods
reseach in particular.

An analogy[1] may be the best way to illustrate these doubts. Suppose that
we wish to erect a house in a marsh; we need a foundation. One approach would
be to wade around in the marsh until we stumble over some solid rocks. An
alternative would be to sketch the shape of the house we wish to build and then
look for ways to erect foundations where they are needed for the house. Often it
seems to me that computer scientists swarm around the solid rocks in the marsh
without asking if these are in the appropriate places for the structures that we
are trying to erect.

In formal methods, we see many researchers focusing on the problems of
proof. While nobody can deny the attractiveness of the idea of program verification, examination of the needs of practitioners reveals that, in most cases,
there are interesting research problems that must be solved before formal program verification could be of any help at all. For example, until we can write
mathematical descriptions of program requirements that can easily be read by

---

[1] The analogy is due to Professor Donald Loveland, logician and computer scientist.

those who know the requirements, proof will be of little value. We would end up proving the wrong theorems.

Denotational semantics of programming languages is another area where we see swarms of academic researchers trying to sharpen a "rock" that is in the wrong place. Rather than solve the problem of defining the semantics of languages that developers find useful, they work on the definition of languages whose semantics is easier to define. Although this work is interesting and potentially useful, it has resulted in a growing gap between theory and practice.

Although this paper discusses the problem of mathematical description of software it is neither about verification nor about language semantics. We focus on the very practical problem of documenting programs. Rather than present a set of axioms for a programming language fragment, we assume that the programmer understands the available tools and ask how a creator's understanding of a program can best be recorded for future use. Rather than concern ourselves with formal proof, the problem for the next century, we ask only how program documentation can be organised so that it facilitates systematic inspection of programs.

Our goal is to be able to write program documentation that is sufficiently complete and precise that programmers can use the programs on the basis of the documentation alone, i.e. without needing to read the code itself. Of course the descriptions we produce must be easier to read than the programs; otherwise the documentation will not be used. We also want to be able to describe requirements for programs that have yet to be written and to do so without unnecessarily restricting the set of acceptable solutions.

2   Language is not the issue

Discussions of mathematical methods for software developers have a tendency to degenerate into discussions of specification languages. Language is not the issue that needs to be discussed first. In fact, the use of the term "language" seems to be something that has seriously misled our field. A *language* is a set of signals, symbols and conventions for formulating, communicating, and recording facts, or ideas, about the world, between people. Algol-60 was originally intended to fit this definition, but things like FORTRAN, C, Modula, ADA, have another purpose. They are the input to program generation tools, not conventions for discussing the world. Natural languages grow by an exception handling process; we add features when we need them. Program construction tools, should not grow that way. Restrictions must be removed before features are added. Current computer "languages", have grown like natural languages and we suffer for it. The so called "specification languages" seem to grow the same way.

Before we talk about language or notation, it is essential to agree on the information that should be presented in our documents. Once we have done that, we can turn our attention to the relatively simple issues of notation.

The use of the term "language" has led computer scientists to discuss "semantics". I find it useful to note that electrical engineers do not use that term to explain their use of differential equations in the analysis of circuits. They recognise that the equations are simply abstract descriptions of physical objects. Rather than talk about semantics, in this paper we try to show how mathematics can be used to describe programs in the same way that differential equations can describe a large class of circuits.

Just as engineers have long recognised that it takes several drawings to describe their products, we recognise that we will not seek complete descriptions of programs. Instead we shall look at a set of partial descriptions, each showing one aspect or view of the programs.

3 A polemic about four words

Engineers distinguish between <u>descriptions</u>, <u>specifications</u>, <u>models</u>, and <u>prototypes</u> of their products.

- A *description* is a statement of some of the <u>actual</u> attributes of a product, or a set of products. A description is considered faulty if it contains information that is not true of the actual product.

- A *specification* is a statement of some of the properties <u>required</u> of a product, or a set of products. A product is considered faulty if the statements made in its specification are not true of that product.

- A *model* is a simplified or reduced size version of a product. Models have some, but not all, of the properties of the "real product" and are used because they are easier to study than the actual product. Discrepancies between models and products are normal and neither the model nor the product is necessarily faulty. The relation of the model to the product, i.e. which properties of the model are also properties of the product must be clearly stated; otherwise the model may be misused.

- A *prototype* is an early (often the first), full-scale, version of a product. A prototype can actually be used to perform the functions that the future (production version) product will be intended to perform. Prototypes, unlike models, are expected to have *all* the essential properties of the real product.

We often speak of "mathematical models", which are not actually models in the sense described above. *Mathematical models* are sets of mathematical equations or axioms that are simplified descriptions of a mechanism that might be present in a system or product. Like models and prototypes, mathematical models can be used to predict the behaviour of a proposed product. Like physical models, they have some properties of the actual product but may not be completely accurate. With the aid of an interpreter (usually a computer, but possibly a human), mathematical models may be used as models. Mathematical models may also be used to construct physical models, for example, using analog computing techniques.

A description may include attributes that are not required, i.e. incidental properties. For example, a description of a program may include the number of ones in its binary representation; usually there is no requirement to have any particular ratio of zeros to ones. A specification may include attributes that a (faulty) product does not possess. The statement that a product satisfies a given specification constitutes a description of the product. Perhaps it is this fact that leads some to confuse descriptions and specifications.

Any list of attributes can be interpreted <u>either</u> as a description or as a specification. "A volume of more than 1 cubic meter" may be either an observation about a specific box that has been measured, or a requirement for a box that is about to be purchased. While a specification may allow a choice of attributes, a description of a specific object will contain only the actual attributes. It follows that a list of attributes, should be accompanied by a statement of intent to indicate whether it is to be interpreted as a description, or as a specification.

When talking about aircraft and other physical products, we seldom have trouble distinguishing between "model", "prototype", "specification", and "description". A model 747 fits on my desk and is unable to fly. In contrast, a prototype 747 would have held more than 350 people and would have been able to fly. A specification of the 747 would tell us, among other things, that it must be able to carry 350 persons a certain distance. The statement "has a funny looking bump on top at the front" could be part of a description, but I doubt that it was part of a specification. When talking about mathematical products, such as programs, the distinction seems to get lost. Specifications, descriptions, models, prototypes, and even the final product are all abstract, mathematical in nature, and usually represented as text. Consequently, many tend to forget the distinction between real things and their descriptions.

We often try to use models as descriptions or specifications by accompanying a model with a statement such as, "It looks like this but is 100 times larger" or "Make it look like this". Before Floyd's paper [3], several researchers proposed using one program to specify another and thus to accomplish proofs of correctness by proving equivalence. In discussions of communication protocols, researchers and developers often present finite state machines that conform to a protocol as if they were specifications of the protocols. In fact, these are simply mathematical models, descriptions of mechanisms that purportedly satisfy unstated requirements. I see the same tendency to use models as if they were specifications in most current work on "formal methods".

These distinctions are important because we want software developers to be able to distinguish between incidental and required properties of products. If we use models or descriptions as specifications, they will be unable to do so.

4 Four types of software products

Just as it would be unrealistic to expect that chemicals would be described using the same notation as hardware, it is unrealistic to expect that we could describe all kinds of software products in same way. In this paper, we distinguish four types of computer system products.

4.1 Real-time and interactive systems

These computer systems, sometimes called real-time systems, are controlled by non-terminating programs, observe an effectively infinite sequence of inputs, and produce an effectively infinite sequence of outputs. We have found that models based on those used in control theory are useful in describing these systems. Further discussion of the documentation of these systems can be found in [11,12]. We will not describe them further in this paper.

4.2 Terminating programs

These programs, often used as components of larger programs, are initiated, run for some time and then terminate leaving their results as part of the data state of the invoking program. We will describe them by describing their effect on the state of a data structure.

4.3 Modules

We use the term "module" to describe a collection of programs, usually a work assignment for a programmer or a group of programmers, that hides (abstracts from) the details of a shared (internal) data structure [9]. Because we wish to avoid describing that data structure, the methods that can be used for individual terminating programs are not appropriate. Instead we will have to describe the set of observable event sequences (traces) observable at the interface of the module. We discuss these further in Section 11.

4.4 Objects (created by modules)

In recent years, it has become popular to use modules to produce many copies of its data structure, each of these known as an object. The descriptions of the creating modules describe the essential properties of those objects, but we must allow for the fact that some operations will affect several objects. We discuss this further in Section 10.

5 Programs and executions

This section presents a treatment of terminating programs that allows us to write useful descriptions and specifications of such programs. This approach was most heavily influenced by the work of Mills [6,7] as well as private communications with N.G. de Bruijn, but there have been many similar approaches. Many of these ideas were developed some years ago and presented in [8,13], but there are some valuable refinements and clarifications in this version.

A digital computer can usefully be viewed as a finite state machine and a program as a description of a behaviour pattern for that machine. In this paper we have no need to exploit the fact that the number of states is finite, but in any practical application of these ideas the user must bear the finiteness in mind and be sure that this limitation is reflected in the descriptions of the programs and objects of interest. Otherwise, the descriptions will be inaccurate and it could be dangerous to use them.

Definition 1. *A finite state machine is a machine that is always in exactly one of a finite set of stable states, S, and whose operation consists of a sequence of state changes, i.e. transitions from state to state. These machines have a finite set of input symbols, called the input alphabet, and a finite set of output symbols, the output alphabet.*

It would be a mistake to confuse the physical machine with its description, for example, by saying "a machine is an n-tuple".

Definition 2. *An execution is a sequence (either finite or infinite) of states.*

Definition 3. *A program is an initial state of a machine that determines a set of executions, sometimes called the executions of that program. The set of all executions of P is denoted Exec(P,S).*

Definition 4. *The subset of Exec(P,S) that begin with the state x, $(x \in S)$, is denoted by $e_P(x)$, and x is called the starting state of those executions.*

Definition 5. *If there exists an execution in $e_P(x)$ that is finite and its last state is z, then we may write $<x,...,z> \in e_P(x)$, say that this execution terminates (in z), and call z the final state (of this execution). We will also say that the program P may start in x and terminate in z.*

Definition 6. *An infinite sequence in $e_P(x)$ $(<x,...>)$ is called a non-terminating execution.*

Definition 7. *If there exists a state x, $(x \in S)$, such that $e_P(x)$ contains two or more distinct executions, then P is called a non-deterministic program.*

Definition 8. *If for a given state x, $(x \in S)$, every member of $e_P(x)$ is finite, x is called a safe state of P. The set of safe states of P is denoted S_P.*

6　A mathematical interlude: LD-relations

Definition 9. *A binary relation R on a given set U is a set of ordered pairs with both elements from U, i.e. $R \subseteq U \times U$. The set U is called the Universe of R. The set of pairs, R, can be described by its characteristic predicate, $R(p,q)$, i.e. $R = \{(p,q): U \times U \mid R(p,q)\}$. The domain of R is denoted $Dom(R)$ and is $\{p \mid \exists q\,[R(p,q)]\}$. The range of R is denoted $Range(R)$ and is $\{q \mid \exists p\,[R(p,q)]\}$.*

Below, "relation" means "binary relation".

Definition 10. *A limited-domain relation (LD-relation) on a set, U, is a pair, $L = (R_L,\ C_L)$, where:*

- *R_L, the relational component of L, is a relation on U, i.e. $R_L \subseteq U \times U$, and*

- *C_L, the competence set of L, is a subset of the domain of R_L, i.e. $C_L \subseteq Dom(R_L)$.*

7　Program construction tools

We treat compilers as program construction tools. For each such tool, we can identify two components: primitive programs and constructs (or constructors).

Definition 11. *A program is a primitive program with respect to a program-construction tool if it was produced without the tool. Primitive programs cannot be constructed using the tool but are used as building-blocks to construct programs with the tool.*

In conventional programming tools, (for example, Pascal compilers) the primitive programs include assignment of values to variables, arithmetic computations, tests of boolean variables, access of variables, etc. Some interesting tools contain unusual primitive programs, for example list processing languages have primitive programs deemed useful for working with symbolic lists.

Definition 12. *Constructs are "templates", strings with one or more places to insert programs, that take one or more programs and produce new programs from them. Each construct is a function mapping from a tuple of programs to a program. There is one function argument for each of the "program places" in the templates.*

For example, " **if** ... **then** ... **else** ..." is a construct that takes three programs, and combines them to produce a single program. Each construct can be defined by saying how to determine a description of the constructed program from descriptions of the component programs.

8 Describing programs

Engineers have been describing their products precisely for centuries. In their work:

- They use mathematics, not just words, to describe their products.

- They use a variety of descriptions rather than attempt one "complete" description.

- There is never a complete description of a product. Each product description is intended for a different purpose and each is an accurate description of some aspects of the product. However, even taken together, these descriptions need not constitute a complete description.

8.1 Constructive descriptions of programs

The texts that we conventionally call programs are constructive descriptions of programs.

Definition 13. *For a given program construction tool, a constructive description of a program is either the name of a primitive program or a construct with the program places filled with constructive descriptions of programs.*

In other words, we can get a constructive description of a program by taking a construct, and putting primitive programs, or constructive descriptions of programs, in its places. Simple programming languages are defined in this way in [8,13].

Constructive descriptions are the primary product of the people that we call programmers. However, for larger programs, we need other kinds of descriptions because the constructive descriptions are hard to understand.

8.2 Behavioural descriptions of programs

Definition 14. *Behavioural descriptions describe some aspects of the executions of a program; they generally do not describe how the program is constructed from component programs.*

For example, performance models are behavioural descriptions.

Those who are going to use, not inspect or modify, a program need behaviour descriptions far more than they need constructive descriptions of programs. They do not want to know the details of program construction; they want to know what the program will do. Even programmers need behavioural descriptions of programs when they are trying to debug or modify a program. They need them to be able to change one part of a program without understanding the constructive details of the other parts.

8.2.1 Before/after descriptions

Before/after descriptions are behavioural descriptions that are used when the intermediate states of an execution are not important. For each state, s, they must describe (a) whether or not s is safe and (b) the final states of executions in $e_P(s)$.

8.2.2 Using LD-relations as before/after descriptions

Definition 15. *Let P be a program, let S be a set of states, and let $L_P = (R_P, C_P)$ be an LD-relation on S such, that $(x,y) \in R_P$ if and only if $<x,...,y> \in Exec(P,S)$, and $C_P = S_P$. L_p is called the LD-relation of P[2].*

By convention, if C_P is not given explicitly, it is, by default, Dom(R_P).
The following are some of the consequences of this definition:

- If P starts in x and $x \in C_P$, P always terminates; if $(x,y) \in R_P$, y is a possible termination state when P is started in state x.

- If P starts in x and $x \in ($Dom(R_P) - $C_P)$, the termination of P is non-deterministic; in this case, if (x, y) R_P, when P is started in x, y is one of the possible termination states, but the program may not terminate.

- If P starts in x, and $x \notin$ Dom(R_P), then P will not terminate.

- If P is a deterministic program, the relational component, R_P is Mills' program function and C_P (which will be the same as Dom(R_P)) need not be written. Hence, our approach is "upward compatible" with Mills [6,7].

LD-relations have practical advantages over some more popular before/after descriptions.

- They provide complete before/after descriptions of non-deterministic programs.

- They can be described by giving the characteristic predicates of R_P and C_P; those predicates can be expressed in terms of values of program variables. Illustrations can be found in [1,10].

8.2.3 Other kinds of behavioural descriptions of programs

The before/after descriptions offered by LD-relations are not complete descriptions or suitable for all purposes. For example, they do not describe whether or not certain conditions were "invariant" in an execution of a program, or the length of an execution. This section discusses a few of the more popular alternatives and explains our choice.

---

[2]Please note that C_P is not the same as the precondition used in VDM [4]. S_P is the safe set of P.

8.2.4   The VDM alternative

VDM is also based on a model that represents programs by a set and a relation
but the set is a precondition rather than the set of safe states. VDM [4] does
not describe the behaviour of a program if the precondition does not hold. Consequently, the VDM model does not allow one to distinguish certain programs
that have distinct before/after behaviour.

8.2.5   The "pure" relational alternative

Many people, have suggested representing programs by a relation alone, using a special symbol to denote non-termination. These models are theoretically equivalent[3] to LD-relations, but introducing an element that is not a state
means that the sets cannot be characterised in terms of variable values alone.
The non-state requires special treatment and complicates the use of this model.
N.G. de Bruijn used such a model when representing programs in his Automath
system [2]. Another well written paper that uses such a model is [5], which gives
precise definitions of Dijkstra's predicate transformers in relational terms.

Since most of the programs encountered in practice are deterministic, we
value the fact that Mills' model, which has been found practical for deterministic
programs, is compatible with this more general model. The competence set is
very convenient when dealing with non-deterministic programs.

9   Specifying programs

When writing specifications for programs, we want to be able to allow behaviour
that need not actually be exhibited by a satisfactory program. For example, if
we want a square root program we may be willing to accept either the positive
or the negative root, but would be satisfied with a program that always gave the
positive root. We may want to require termination for certain starting states, but
do not care about what happens in some of the others. The following definitions
allow us to write such specifications.

9.1   Before/after specifications

When we are only concerned about the starting and stopping states of the executions, we should write before/after specifications.

9.2   Using LD-relations for before/after specifications

We can use LD-relations to specify programs. The conditions under which a
program satisfies an LD-relation used as a specification differ from those under
which an LD-relation can be said to describe a program.

---

[3]It is always possible to determine the pure relation corresponding to the LD-relation and
vice-versa.

Definition 16. *Let $L_p = (R_P, C_P)$ be the LD-relation of a program P. Let S, called a specification, be a set of LD-relations on the same universe, and let $L_S = (R_S, C_S)$ be an element of S. We say that (1) P satisfies the LD-relation L_S, iff $C_S \subseteq C_P$ and $R_P \subseteq R_S$, and (2) P satisfies the specification S, iff P satisfies at least one element of S. Often, S has only one element.*

If $S = \{L_S\}$ is a specification, then we can informally call L_S a specification. The following are implications of Definition 16.

- An acceptable program must not terminate if started in states outside $\mathrm{Dom}(R_S)$.

- An acceptable program must terminate if started in states in C_S ($C_S \subseteq \mathrm{Dom}(R_P)$).

- An acceptable program may only terminate in states that are in $\mathrm{Range}(R_S)$.

- A deterministic program can satisfy a specification that would also be satisfied by a non-deterministic program.

It is important to note the following differences between the description and the specification of a program.

- There is only one LD-relation describing a program, but that program may satisfy many distinct specifications described by different LD-relations.

- An acceptable program need not exhibit all of the behaviour allowed by R_S ($R_P \subseteq R_S$).

- An acceptable program may be certain to terminate if started in states that are outside C_S but are in $\mathrm{Dom}(R_S)$ ($C_S \subseteq C_P$).

9.3 Constructive specifications of programs

One may want to put restrictions on the way that programs are constructed. For example, one may want to restrict the use of certain constructs, or primitive programs. It should be clear that constructive specifications are quite different from constructive descriptions; constructive specifications restrict the way that programs can be constructed, but do not describe the way a particular program has been constructed.

10 Objects vs. programs

It is wise to design software by designing a set of objects. Each object is implemented by a *module* (a set of programs) using a data structure that is "hidden from" (never accessed directly by) programs outside the module. Changing the state of the object, or getting information about the object's state, is always done by invocations of programs from the module. For example, a stack is an object implemented by a module that includes accessible programs. PUSH, POP, TOP, and DEPTH might be programs in the module that are accessible in external programs and PUSH(x,3), PUSH(x,5), and POP(x) are operations on an objected named x, created by that module.

Definition 17. *An object is a finite state machine. The input alphabet of the object is the set of operations that one can perform upon the object. The output alphabet of the object is the set of values that can be returned by such operations.*

Describing or specifying objects is very different from describing or specifying programs. It is best to provide "black box" descriptions of objects, descriptions that do not reveal the hidden data structure used to represent the state. For such descriptions, LD-relations on the data structure that is changed by the program would be inappropriate as would be any method that describes an internal data structure for the module.

11   Descriptions and specifications of objects

There are many possible descriptions of objects. One can describe them by giving the next state and output functions or by describing their data structure and programs. For black box descriptions of finite state machines, the only information that we should mention is the externally visible events, i.e. sequences of inputs and outputs. We call such sequences *traces*.

Definition 18. *A trace of a finite state machine is a finite sequence of pairs, each containing a member of the input alphabet and a member of the output alphabet. A trace, T, is considered possible for machine M, if M could react to the sequence of inputs in T by emitting the sequence of outputs in T.*

Descriptions and specifications of objects can both be written as predicates on classes of traces. LD-relations are not needed if we can assume that operations on objects always terminate.

12   Conclusions

The mathematics of program descriptions can be kept quite simple without losing utility. However, the definitions must be done very carefully. We have seen that "minor" changes can remove descriptive power. The difference between program description and program specification can be made precise, even though the same mathematical formalism can be used for both. As most programs encountered in practice are deterministic, this special class of programs can be described using a special class of LD-relations. The simplicity of these ideas must be viewed as a feature. In many years of participation in practical software development, I have seen many places where "theory" or mathematics was useful, but it was *always* simple theory. When theories get complex, they are not likely to be useful or used.

13 Acknowledgements

Work with Wm. Wadge, Jan Madey and Michal Iglewski has strongly influenced this paper. Comments by Dennis Peters, Yabo Wang, Jim Horning, Jeff Zucker, and John Tucker on earlier drafts were very helpful. Anders Ravn and Victoria Stavridou made very helpful suggestions when editing the final version.

References

1. Bauer, B. and Parnas, D.L. (1995). Experience with the use of precise documentation. *Proc. of the Tenth Ann. Conf. on Computer Assurance*, 273–285.

2. de Bruijn, N.G. Computer program semantics in space and time. *Selected Papers on Automath Series - Studies in Logic and the Foundations of Mathematics*, Editors: R.P. Nederpelt, J.H. Geuvers and R.C. de Vrijer, **113**, North-Holland.

3. Floyd, R.W. (1968). Assigning meanings to programs. *Proc. of the Sym. of Applied Maths.*, **19**. Also in *Mathematical Aspects of Computer Science*, (1967), Editor: J.T. Schwartz, American Mathematical Society, 19–32.

4. Jones, C.B. (1986). *Systematic Software Development Using VDM*, Prentice-Hall.

5. Majster-Cederbaum, M.E. (1980). A simple relation between relational and predicate transformer semantics for nondeterministic programs. *Information Processing Letters*, **11**, 190–192.

6. Mills, H.D. (1975). The new math of computer programming. *Comm. ACM*, **18**, 43–48.

7. Mills, H.D. (1980). Function semantics for sequential programs. *Proc. of the IFIP Congress*, North Holland, 241–250.

8. Parnas, D.L. (1983). A generalised control structure and its formal definition. *Comm. ACM*, **26**, 572–581.

9. Parnas, D.L., Clements, P. and Weiss, D. (1985). The structure of complex systems. *IEEE Transactions on Software Engineering*, **SE-11**, 259–266.

10. Parnas, D.L., Madey, J. and Iglewski, M. (1994). Precise documentation of well-structured programs. *IEEE Transactions on Software Engineering*, **20**, 948–976

11. Parnas, D.L. and Madey, J. (1995). Functional documentation for computer systems engineering. *Science of Computer Programming*, **25**, Elsevier, 41–61.

12. van Schouwen, A.J., Parnas, D.L. and Madey, J. (1993). Documentation of requirements for computer systems. *Proc. of '93 IEEE Int. Sym. on Requirements Engineering*, San Diego, CA, 198–207.

13. Parnas, D.L. and Wadge, W.W. (1986). Less restrictive constructs for structured programs. *Technical Report 86-186*, Queen's, C&IS, Kingston, Ontario, Canada, **16**.

Consistent Composition and Refinement for Dependable Systems

Louise E. Moser and P.M. Melliar-Smith

*Department of Electrical and Computer Engineering, University of California,
USA*

Abstract

We present a methodology for modular composition and hierarchical refinement of specifications and proofs for dependable systems. Composition and refinement have long been regarded as the method of choice for the specification, verification, and implementation of safety-critical fault-tolerant systems and of multi-level secure systems. To ensure validity, composition of specifications that share predicates requires a demonstration of their consistency. Such a demonstration of consistency is, however, seldom provided and may be computationally infeasible using existing verification systems.

To facilitate the demonstration of consistency, we introduce the notion of independence predicates. An independence predicate asserts that a specification does not constrain the value of the predicate that is asserted to be independent. These independence predicates, together with demonstrations of validity, are used to show the consistency of composite specifications. We give examples of the use of independence predicates, as well as algorithms for checking consistency of specifications based on these independence predicates.

Keywords: Formal specification and verification, hierarchical refinement, modular composition, consistency, independence, non-interference.

1   Introduction

Verification of the design of large-scale dependable systems is inherently difficult and is feasible only if a methodology of composition and refinement is employed. Compositional methodologies have been widely used for the specification, verification, and implementation of safety-critical fault-tolerant systems and of multi-level secure systems [1–5].

A compositional methodology requires that the specifications for several components be combined together into a single specification. Refinement involves two specifications, a concrete specification and an abstract specification, and a mapping between them such that the concrete specification implements the abstract specification under the mapping. Composition and refinement are sometimes considered to be orthogonal, but are usually applied together in constructing specifications for complex systems from specifications of simpler components.

In designing complex dependable systems, verification can be used to confirm that the properties (be they reliability, safety, or security properties) defined by the abstract specification are substantiated by the detailed concrete specifications. The verification is performed in many small steps, each of which establishes validity of a proof that a small subset of the concrete specifications implies a property of the abstract specification. Such a verification methodology is sound only if the set of concrete specifications is consistent.

The consistency of a large set of specifications, viewed as an axiom system, is difficult to establish with existing verification technology. Demonstration of consistency requires consideration of the entire set of specifications simultaneously, typically as a demonstration of satisfiability in a model theory. Such a demonstration may exceed the storage capacity of the computer and may involve excessive computation time. In contrast, demonstration of validity of a proof of refinement is easier because such a proof can be broken into a sequence of small proof steps. Each proof step can be mechanically verified in isolation without exceeding the capabilities of the computer. Thus, for safety-critical fault-tolerant systems and for multi-level secure systems, it is not unusual for proofs of validity to be exhibited even though no proofs of consistency are demonstrated.

In this paper, we introduce a method for demonstrating the consistency of large sets of specifications by including independence predicates in the specifications and by employing a sequence of demonstrations of validity. The method is not complete, but appears to be applicable to a wide range of specifications, particularly if the limitations of the method are considered when developing the specifications. Like other verification techniques, the method is expensive but, unlike other techniques for establishing the consistency of a set of specifications, the method is feasible using existing computers.

2   Related work

The concepts of refinement and abstraction have existed in the design of programs, at least informally, since the earliest days of computing, but much of the credit for promoting refinement and abstraction as a design methodology is due to Dijkstra [6].

Subsequent work by Parnas [7] applied hierarchical design to specifications rather than program code and led to SRI's Hierarchical Development Methodology (HDM), one of the earliest attempts to support the methodology with mechanical tools [8] and to apply hierarchical specification and verification to a non-trivial problem [3,4]. Similar work by other researchers in developing Larch [9], CLU [10], and ALPHARD [11] has also influenced our approach.

Much of the formal justification for development methodologies based on composition and refinement is due to Lam and Shankar [12,13], who developed a method of projections for reasoning about complex systems. Their technique involves projecting onto one system component, abstracting away other system components, and reasoning about the remaining image.

Lynch and Tuttle [14] have devised I/O automata, which define the input/ output interaction between a module and its environment. Their formalism allows modules to be composed, and checks a composition for consistency, but requires a static definition of inputs and outputs for each component module.

Abadi and Lamport [15] have produced a theory of composition which, like the approach of Lynch and Tuttle, requires a static definition of inputs and outputs. In their investigation of refinement mappings [16], they demonstrated the input/output equivalence of two state machines, assuming consistency. Like other methodologies, Abadi and Lamport methodology employs overriding assumptions to indicate the conditions under which the behavior of the component is constrained by the specification. If the assumptions are not satisfied, the behavior is not constrained.

It is important to be able to constrain the behavior of a component even when its assumptions are not satisfied so that it will not interfere with the operation of some other component whose assumptions are satisfied. Thus, in our methodology, assumptions are represented as implications within specifications and explicit independence predicates are used. Moreover, in many specifications a predicate is regarded as an input under some conditions and as an output under other conditions. Static assignment of inputs and outputs is, therefore, likely to be quite constraining for the specification of complex dependable systems.

3   Independence predicates

Given a specification S, we let P_S be the set of predicates that occur in S. To specify that a predicate p is independent in a specification S, i.e. that the value of p is not determined by S, we include the independence predicate $\mathrm{Ind}_S(p)$ in the specification S.

To specify that a predicate p is independent of a predicate q in a specification S, i.e. that the value of p is not determined by the value of q in the specification S, we include the independence predicate $\mathrm{Ind}_S(p, q)$ in the specification S.

3.1   Syntax

The syntax of propositional calculus with independence predicates for a specification S is defined relative to the set P_S in terms of its well-formed formulas (wff) as follows:

> *true* and *false* are wff.
> If $p \in P_S$, then p is a wff.
> If f is a wff, then so is $\neg f$.
> If f and g are wff, then so is $f \wedge g$.
> If $p \in P_S$, then $\mathrm{Ind}_S(p)$ is a wff.
> If $p \in P_S$, $q \in P_S$ and $p \neq q$, then $\mathrm{Ind}_S(p, q)$ is a wff.

A formula is a wff only if it is obtained by finite application
of these rules.

Here $p, q, r, \ldots$ represent elements of P_S and $f, g, h, \ldots$ represent arbitrary well-formed formulas. The derived operators $\vee$, $\Rightarrow$, and $\equiv$ are defined as usual. In the following, we let $P_S' = P_S \cup \{\mathrm{Ind}_S(p) \,|\, p \in P_S\} \cup \{\mathrm{Ind}_S(p, q) \,|\, p \in P_S, q \in P_S, \text{and } p \neq q\}$.

3.2 Semantics

The semantics of propositional calculus with independence predicates for a specification S are defined in terms of a model M, the models relation $\models$, and a valuation function $v \colon P_S' \to \{true, false\}$.

$$M \models true \text{ and } M \not\models false$$
$$M \models p \quad \text{iff} \quad v(p) = true$$
$$M \models \neg f \quad \text{iff} \quad M \not\models f$$
$$M \models f \wedge g \quad \text{iff} \quad M \models f \text{ and } M \models g$$
$$M \models \mathrm{Ind}_S(p) \quad \text{iff} \quad v(\mathrm{Ind}_S(p)) = true$$
$$M \models \mathrm{Ind}_S(p, q) \quad \text{iff} \quad v(\mathrm{Ind}_S(p, q)) = true.$$

As usual, a well-formed formula f is *satisfiable* in a model M if and only if $M \models f$. A formula f is *satisfiable* if and only if there exists a model M such that f is satisfiable in M. A formula f is *valid* if and only if, for all models M, f is satisfiable in M.

The semantics of independence predicates are given in Definition 1. Intuitively, q is independent in S means that, for every satisfying model M of S, there exists a satisfying model M' of S in which the value of q is the negation of its value in M and the value of every other predicate r that is independent in S is unchanged. From this, it is easy to see that there exist models for every combination of values of the predicates that are independent in S, i.e. these predicates may be regarded as inputs.

To demonstrate consistency, we define a finer grain of independence, that is the value of one predicate is independent of the value of another predicate in a specification. Intuitively, p is independent of q in S means that, for every satisfying model M of S, there exists a satisfying model M' of S in which the value of q is the negation of its value in M, the value of p is unchanged, and the value of every other predicate r of which p is not independent is unchanged.

Definition 1. *A specification S respects independence if and only if*

- *For every predicate $q \in P_S$, for every model M such that $M \models S$, $M \models \mathrm{Ind}_S(q)$ and $M \not\models S'(q)$, where $S'(q)$ is S with $\mathrm{Ind}_S(q)$ replaced by $\neg\mathrm{Ind}_S(q)$, there exists a model M' such that*

* $M' \models S$

* $M' \models \neg q$ *if and only if* $M \models q$

* *For all* $r \in P_S$, $r \neq q$, *such that* $M \models \mathrm{Ind}_S(r)$,
  $M' \models r$ *if and only if* $M \models r$.

- *For every pair of predicates* $p \in P_S$, $q \in P_S$ *and* $p \neq q$, *for every pair of models* M *and* N *such that* $M \models S$, $M \models \mathrm{Ind}_S(p,q)$, $M \not\models S'(p,q)$, $N \models S$, $N \models \neg q$ *if and only if* $M \models q$, *where* $S'(p,q)$ *is* S *with* $\mathrm{Ind}_S(p,q)$ *replaced by* $\neg\mathrm{Ind}_S(p,q)$, *there exists a model* M' *such that*

  * $M' \models S$

  * $M' \models \neg q$ *if and only if* $M \models q$

  * $M' \models p$ *if and only if* $M \models p$

  * *For all* $r \in P_S$ *such that* $M \not\models \mathrm{Ind}_S(p,r)$,
    $M' \models r$ *if and only if* $M \models r$.

An independence predicate can be contingent on the value of other predicates as, for example, in $r \Rightarrow \mathrm{Ind}_S(p,q)$.

4 Modular composition and decomposition

Our objective is to show that, if we have a set of specifications S_i, $1 \leq i \leq N$, each of which is satisfiable, then their composition $\bigwedge_{i=1}^{N} S_i$ is satisfiable. We use the notions of independence predicates and respects independence to achieve this objective.

Definition 2. *The specification* $\bigwedge_{i=1}^{N} S_i$ *is a consistent composition of the specifications* S_i, $1 \leq i \leq N$, *if and only if*

- $\bigwedge_{i=1}^{N} S_i$ *is satisfiable.*

Of course, a necessary condition for $\bigwedge_{i=1}^{N} S_i$ to be satisfiable is that each S_i is satisfiable, as Example 3 shows.

Example 3.

$S_1 : \mathrm{Ind}_{S_1}(standby) \wedge primary \equiv true$
$S_2 : \mathrm{Ind}_{S_2}(primary) \wedge standby \equiv false$

The composition $S_1 \wedge S_2$ *has the satisfying model*

$M : v(\mathrm{Ind}_{S_1}(standby)) = true,\ v(\mathrm{Ind}_{S_2}(primary)) = true,$
$\quad v(standby) = false,\ v(primary) = true$

This model is a satisfying model for S_1 and a satisfying model for S_2.

Definition of each predicate by at most one specification and independence in all other specifications, as in Example 3, may appear to be sufficient for the existence of a satisfying model for the composition but is not, as Example 4 shows. Here, there is a circular dependency between the predicates *primary* and *standby*, and there is no model that satisfies both specifications even though each predicate is defined by only one specification and is independent in all other specifications.

Example 4.

$$S_1 : \mathrm{Ind}_{S_1}(standby) \wedge primary \equiv standby$$
$$S_2 : \mathrm{Ind}_{S_2}(primary) \wedge standby \equiv \neg primary$$

The methodology for establishing a consistent composition presented below checks for the existence of such circular dependencies.

4.1   The algorithm for checking non-interference

Given specifications S_i with predicate sets P_{S_i}, $1 \le i \le N$, we let $S = \bigwedge_{i=1}^{N} S_i$ and $P_S = \bigcup_{i=1}^{N} P_{S_i}$. We define a directed graph, the nodes of which are labeled with predicates $p \in P_S$ and the edges of which are labeled with indices $i, 1 \le i \le N$. If $p \in P_{S_i}$ and $q \in P_{S_i}$, then the graph contains an edge labeled i from the node labeled p to the node labeled q.

The steps of the algorithm for checking non-interference are as follows:

Order the predicates of P_S into an order $p_1, p_2, \ldots, p_K$, where $K = |P_S|$.

For $i = 1$ to K, using the formulas of S that only involve predicates p_j, $j < i$, such that $\mathrm{Ind}_{S_n}(p_j)$ or $\mathrm{Ind}_{S_n}(p_j, p_k)$, $i < k \le K$ and $1 \le n \le N$, demonstrate for the node labeled p_i

1. For every pair of edges (p_i, q) labeled l and (p_i, r) labeled m, either $l = m$ or $\mathrm{Ind}_{S_l}(p_i)$ or $\mathrm{Ind}_{S_m}(p_i)$ or $\mathrm{Ind}_{S_l}(p_i, q)$ or $\mathrm{Ind}_{S_m}(p_i, r)$.

2. For every cycle in the graph involving p_i with nodes labeled $q_1, q_2, \ldots, q_L, q_1$ and edges labeled $l_1, l_2, \ldots, l_L$
   (for all $u, v : 1 \le u, v \le L : l_u = l_v$) or
   (for some $u : 1 \le u \le L : \mathrm{Ind}_{S_{l_u}}(q_{u+1})$ or $\mathrm{Ind}_{S_{l_u}}(q_{u+1}, q_u)$).

We refer to Property (1) as the *locality* property and Property (2) as the *acyclic* property. Together, they comprise the *non-interference* property.

In Property (1), specification S_l cites both p_i and q and specification S_m cites both p_i and r, but the property demonstrates that either p_i is independent of q or p_i is independent of r, thus precluding inconsistency. In Property (2), the cycle of potential dependencies must be broken at some point by an independence predicate, again precluding inconsistency.

Theorem 5. *If for each i, $1 \leq i \leq N$, S_i has a satisfying model and respects independence and if S_i, $1 \leq i \leq N$, satisfies the non-interference property, then $\bigwedge_{i=1}^{N} S_i$ has a satisfying model.*

Proof. The non-interference property ensures that the value of each predicate is determined by only one specification (the locality property) and also ensures that the dependency relations between predicates are acyclic (the acyclic property). Since each specification respects independence and has a satisfying model, a value is determined for each predicate. Thus, a satisfying model exists for the composition.

In Example 4, the algorithm for establishing non-interference determines that the acyclic property is not satisfied and, consequently, rejects the composition. If we replace *standby* in S_1 by $\neg standby$ (except in $\mathrm{Ind}_{S_1}(standby)$ which would be syntactically incorrect), then a satisfying model for the composition exists; however, the algorithm still rejects the composition. Thus, the algorithm is conservative; only a full semantic analysis performed by a satisfiability checker can determine in all cases whether or not a composition is satisfiable. For large systems, such an analysis will generally exceed the capabilities of the human and of the computer.

In Example 6, the algorithm for checking non-interference determines that the locality and acyclic properties are satisfied. Since S_1 and S_2 each have a satisfying model and respect independence, it follows that the composition $S_1 \wedge S_2$ has a satisfying model by Theorem 5.

Example 6.

$S_1 : \mathrm{Ind}_{S_1}(primary_2) \wedge \mathrm{Ind}_{S_1}(standby_2) \wedge$
$\quad \mathrm{Ind}_{S_1}(primary_1, primary_2) \wedge \mathrm{Ind}_{S_1}(primary_1, standby_1) \wedge$
$\quad \mathrm{Ind}_{S_1}(primary_1, standby_2) \wedge \mathrm{Ind}_{S_1}(standby_1, standby_2) \wedge$
$\quad primary_1 \equiv true \wedge standby_1 \equiv primary_2$

$S_2 : \mathrm{Ind}_{S_2}(primary_1) \wedge \mathrm{Ind}_{S_2}(standby_1) \wedge$
$\quad \mathrm{Ind}_{S_2}(primary_2, standby_1) \wedge \mathrm{Ind}_{S_2}(primary_2, standby_2) \wedge$
$\quad primary_2 \equiv \neg primary_1 \wedge standby_2 \equiv \neg standby_1$

The locality property is satisfied since $\mathrm{Ind}_{S_1}(primary_2)$, $\mathrm{Ind}_{S_1}(standby_2)$, $\mathrm{Ind}_{S_2}(primary_1)$, and $\mathrm{Ind}_{S_2}(standby_1)$ and thus each predicate is defined in at most one specification. To check that the acyclic property is satisfied, note that the node labeled $primary_1$ cannot be involved in a cycle with another node since $\mathrm{Ind}_{S_1}(primary_1, primary_2)$, $\mathrm{Ind}_{S_1}(primary_1, standby_1)$, $\mathrm{Ind}_{S_1}(primary_1, standby_2)$, and $\mathrm{Ind}_{S_2}(primary_1)$ hold. Thus, the node labeled $primary_2$ cannot be involved in a cycle containing the node labeled $primary_1$; moreover, it cannot be involved in a cycle containing the nodes labeled $standby_1$ or $standby_2$ since $\mathrm{Ind}_{S_2}(primary_2, standby_1)$, $\mathrm{Ind}_{S_2}(primary_2, standby_2)$, and $\mathrm{Ind}_{S_1}(primary_2)$

hold. Consequently, the node labeled $standby_1$ cannot be involved in a cycle containing the nodes labeled $primary_1$ or $primary_2$; moreover, it cannot be involved in a cycle containing the node labeled $standby_2$ since $\text{Ind}_{S_1}(standby_1, standby_2)$ and $\text{Ind}_{S_2}(standby_1)$ hold. Therefore, the node labeled $standby_2$ cannot be involved in a cycle with any other node. The above argument shows that it is not necessary to consider all cycles in Step 2 of the algorithm and, thus, that the algorithm can be implemented more efficiently.

In Example 7, the algorithm for checking non-interference determines that the locality property is satisfied since each of the predicates is independent in either S_1 or S_2. In the case split, if $operational$ has the value $true$, then $\text{Ind}_{S_1}(enabled, monitoring)$, $\text{Ind}_{S_2}(controlling, enabled)$, and $\text{Ind}_{S_2}(controlling, monitoring)$ hold. Alternatively, if $operational$ has the value $false$, then $\text{Ind}_{S_1}(enabled, controlling)$, $\text{Ind}_{S_2}(monitoring, controlling)$, and $\text{Ind}_{S_2}(monitoring, enabled)$ hold. In either case, the algorithm determines, as in Example 6, that the acyclic property is satisfied. Since S_1 and S_2 each have a satisfying model and respect independence, the composition has a satisfying model by Theorem 5.

Example 7.

$$S_1 : \text{Ind}_{S_1}(controlling) \wedge \text{Ind}_{S_1}(monitoring) \wedge$$
$$\text{Ind}_{S_1}(operational, controlling) \wedge$$
$$\text{Ind}_{S_1}(operational, enabled) \wedge$$
$$\text{Ind}_{S_1}(operational, monitoring) \wedge$$
$$operational \Rightarrow (enabled \equiv controlling \wedge$$
$$\text{Ind}_{S_1}(enabled, monitoring)) \wedge$$
$$\neg operational \Rightarrow (enabled \equiv monitoring \wedge$$
$$\text{Ind}_{S_1}(enabled, controlling))$$

$$S_2 : \text{Ind}_{S_2}(operational) \wedge \text{Ind}_{S_2}(enabled) \wedge$$
$$operational \Rightarrow (controlling \equiv operational \wedge$$
$$monitoring \equiv enabled \wedge$$
$$\text{Ind}_{S_2}(controlling, enabled) \wedge$$
$$\text{Ind}_{S_2}(controlling, monitoring)) \wedge$$
$$\neg operational \Rightarrow (controlling \equiv enabled \wedge$$
$$monitoring \equiv operational \wedge$$
$$\text{Ind}_{S_2}(monitoring, controlling) \wedge$$
$$\text{Ind}_{S_2}(monitoring, enabled))$$

4.2   The algorithm for establishing independence

Let $K = |P_S|$. Let $S'(p_i)$ represent S with all instances of $\text{Ind}_S(p_i)$ replaced by $\neg \text{Ind}_S(p_i)$, and let $S'(p_i, p_j)$ represent S with all instances of $\text{Ind}_S(p_i, p_j)$ replaced by $\neg \text{Ind}_S(p_i, p_j)$.

The steps of the algorithm for establishing independence are as follows:

1. For all j, $1 \leq j \leq K$, such that $\mathrm{Ind}_S(p_j)$ occurs in S

   Demonstrate validity of

   $$(\exists p_1 \exists p_2 \ldots \exists p_K\colon S \,\wedge\, \mathrm{Ind}_S(p_j) \,\wedge\, \neg S'(p_j) \,\wedge$$
   $$\bigwedge_{k=1}^{K}((p_k \equiv r_k) \,\wedge\, ((\mathrm{Ind}_S(p_k) \,\wedge\, \neg S'(p_k)) \equiv t_k)))$$
   $$\Rightarrow (\exists p_1 \exists p_2 \ldots \exists p_K\colon S \,\wedge\, (p_j \not\equiv r_j) \,\wedge$$
   $$\bigwedge_{k=1}^{K}((t_k \wedge k \neq j) \Rightarrow (p_k \equiv r_k)))$$

2. For all i, $1 \leq i \leq K$,

   For all j, $1 \leq j \leq K$, $i \neq j$, such that $\mathrm{Ind}_S(p_i, p_j)$ occurs in S

   Demonstrate validity of

   $$(\exists p_1 \exists p_2 \ldots \exists p_K\colon S \,\wedge\, \mathrm{Ind}_S(p_i, p_j) \,\wedge\, \neg S'(p_i, p_j) \,\wedge$$
   $$\bigwedge_{k=1}^{K}((p_k \equiv r_k) \,\wedge\, ((\mathrm{Ind}_S(p_i, p_k) \,\wedge\, \neg S'(p_i, p_k)) \,\vee$$
   $$(\mathrm{Ind}_S(p_k) \,\wedge\, \neg S'(p_k)) \equiv t_k)))$$
   $$\Rightarrow (\exists p_1 \exists p_2 \ldots \exists p_K\colon S \,\wedge\, (p_i \equiv r_i) \,\wedge\, (p_j \not\equiv r_j) \,\wedge$$
   $$\bigwedge_{k=1}^{K}((t_k \wedge k \neq j) \Rightarrow (p_k \equiv r_k)))$$

We refer to Properties (1) and (2) as the *independence* property.

Property (1) demonstrates that, if we have a model with a particular value of p_j, then we also have a model with the negated value of p_j, showing that the specification does not constrain p_j. Note that the expression $\mathrm{Ind}_S(p_k) \wedge \neg S'(p_k)$ selects a value of k such that p_k is truly independent in S and that t_k carries this information from one model to the other and, similarly, that r_k carries the value of the predicate p_k between models. Property (2) performs a similar demonstration, showing that the value of p_i is unaffected by negating the value of p_j.

Theorem 8. *If a specification S satisfies the independence property, then S respects independence.*

Proof. The proof of Theorem 8 follows directly from the statement of the independence property and the definition of respects independence.

An example application of the algorithm for establishing the independence property is given below.

Example 9.

S: $\mathrm{Ind}_S(enabled) \,\wedge\, \mathrm{Ind}_S(monitoring, enabled) \,\wedge$
   $((enabled \,\wedge\, operational) \Rightarrow controlling) \,\wedge$
   $(operational \Rightarrow monitoring)$

To demonstrate that S respects independence, we substitute the given predicates into the above formulas for the independence property and simplify to obtain the following implications, both of which are easily shown to be valid.

$$(\forall enabled: (\exists monitoring\, \exists operational\, \exists controlling:$$
$$\text{Ind}_S(enabled) \wedge \text{Ind}_S(monitoring, enabled) \wedge$$
$$((enabled \wedge operational) \Rightarrow controlling) \wedge$$
$$(operational \Rightarrow monitoring) \wedge$$
$$\text{Ind}_S(enabled) \wedge$$
$$\neg(\neg\text{Ind}_S(enabled) \wedge \text{Ind}_S(monitoring, enabled) \wedge$$
$$((enabled \wedge operational) \Rightarrow controlling) \wedge$$
$$(operational \Rightarrow monitoring)))$$
$$\Rightarrow (\exists monitoring\, \exists operational\, \exists controlling:$$
$$\text{Ind}_S(enabled) \wedge \text{Ind}_S(monitoring, enabled) \wedge$$
$$((\neg enabled \wedge operational) \Rightarrow controlling) \wedge$$
$$(operational \Rightarrow monitoring)))$$

$$(\forall monitoring\, \forall enabled: (\exists operational\, \exists controlling:$$
$$\text{Ind}_S(enabled) \wedge \text{Ind}_S(monitoring, enabled) \wedge$$
$$((enabled \wedge operational) \Rightarrow controlling) \wedge$$
$$(operational \Rightarrow monitoring) \wedge$$
$$\text{Ind}_S(monitoring, enabled) \wedge$$
$$\neg(\text{Ind}_S(enabled) \wedge \neg\text{Ind}_S(monitoring, enabled) \wedge$$
$$((enabled \wedge operational) \Rightarrow controlling) \wedge$$
$$(operational \Rightarrow monitoring))) \wedge$$
$$\Rightarrow (\exists operational\, \exists controlling:$$
$$\text{Ind}_S(enabled) \wedge \text{Ind}_S(monitoring, enabled) \wedge$$
$$((\neg enabled \wedge operational) \Rightarrow controlling) \wedge$$
$$(operational \Rightarrow monitoring)))$$

5   Hierarchical abstraction and refinement

We now formalize the concepts of abstraction and refinement. The intent of abstraction and refinement is that a lower-level concrete specification S_L should provide an implementation of a higher-level abstract specification S_H. A mapping S_M relates the predicates of S_L and S_H. We let P_{S_L} be the set of predicates of S_L, P_{S_H} the set of predicates of S_H, and P_{S_M} the set of predicates of S_M. The set P_{S_H} is a subset of the set $P_{S_L \wedge S_M}$.

Definition 10. *A specification S_L is a consistent refinement of a specification S_H under a mapping S_M (equivalently, S_H is a consistent abstraction of S_L under a mapping S_M) if and only if*

- $S_L \wedge S_M$ *is a consistent composition*

- $S_L \wedge S_M \Rightarrow S_H$ *is valid.*

The first condition is required because, if there is no satisfying model for $S_L \wedge S_M$, then the second condition is trivially established. The second condition, that the lower-level specification and the mapping imply the upper-level specification, is the usual idea of a refinement.

Theorem 11. *If S_L is a consistent refinement of S_H under a mapping S_M, then S_H is satisfiable.*

Proof. The proof of Theorem 11 follows directly from the definition of a consistent refinement.

An example of a consistent refinement and a mapping is given below.

Example 12.

$$S_H : \mathrm{Ind}_{S_H}(alive) \wedge (alive \Rightarrow functioning)$$

$$S_M : \mathrm{Ind}_{S_M}(alive) \wedge \mathrm{Ind}_{S_M}(controlling) \wedge$$
$$(alive \Rightarrow (operational \wedge enabled)) \wedge (controlling \Rightarrow functioning)$$

$$S_L : \mathrm{Ind}_{S_L}(operational) \wedge \mathrm{Ind}_{S_L}(enabled) \wedge$$
$$((operational \wedge enabled) \Rightarrow controlling)$$

We now present the methodology for establishing consistency that combines composition and refinement.

5.1 The methodology for establishing consistency

The methodology for establishing consistency comprises the following steps:

1. The user must establish that

   - S_L is satisfiable and respects independence.
   - S_M is satisfiable and respects independence.
   - $S_L \wedge S_M$ satisfies the non-interference property.

   By Theorem 5, it then follows that $S_L \wedge S_M$ is satisfiable.

2. The user must also establish that

   - $S_L \wedge S_M \Rightarrow S_H$ is valid.

   By Theorem 11, it then follows that S_H is satisfiable.

Note that the mapping S_M is treated as a specification in its own right and must be shown to be satisfiable and to respect independence. This may require that the mapping itself be constructed by composition and refinement.

To show that S_L or S_M respects independence, the user can apply the algorithm for establishing the independence property. To show that $S_L \wedge S_M$ satisfies the non-interference property, the user can apply the algorithm for establishing that property. Typically, it will be convenient to perform in a single step the composition of the several specifications that form S_L with the specifications of the mapping S_M.

The observant reader will have noticed that the algorithm for establishing the independence property requires demonstration of the existence of a satisfying model, and may wonder how that demonstration can be achieved since it is a premise of this work that the set of specifications may be too large to permit such a demonstration.

Note that respects independence is required only to justify a composition and, thus, is not needed at the top level specification. At the lowest level, the specifications for a component are small and, thus, respects independence can readily be demonstrated for each component. At intermediate levels, demonstration of the independence property requires demonstration of the existence of a satisfying model with particular properties. This can be achieved by demonstration of the existence of a satisfying model at the lower level, using Theorem 5, which can be mapped into the required model at the higher level. Demonstration of the existence of a satisfying model at the lower level may be easier since independence predicates and non-interference at that level can be exploited, but it may depend upon the existence of satisfying models at still lower levels.

6   Conclusion

We have introduced the notion of independence predicates to facilitate the verification of large-scale dependable systems using a methodology of composition and refinement. These independence predicates ensure consistency as specifications are composed by guaranteeing that a satisfying model for the composition exists. We have given examples of the use of independence predicates, and have presented algorithms for checking consistency of specifications based on these independence predicates.

Currently, we are extending the formulation of independence predicates presented here to first-order predicate calculus in which formulas of the base logic contain quantification. We are also extending the methodology to linear-time temporal logic with composition and refinement based on sequences of states instead of a single state. In addition, we are developing methods for carrying independence predicates through composition and refinement so that the independence property does not need to be reestablished after each step.

References

1. Neumann, P.G., Feiertag, R.J., Robinson, L. and Levitt, K.N. (1976). Software development and proofs of multi-level security. *Proc. of the 2nd IEEE Int. Conf. on Software Engineering*, 421–428.

2. Spitzen, J.M., Levitt, K.N. and Robinson, L. (1978). An example of hierarchical design and proof. *Communications of the ACM*, **21**, 1064–1075.

3. Melliar-Smith, P.M. and Schwartz, R.L. (1982). Formal specification and verification of SIFT: A fault-tolerant flight control system. *IEEE Transactions on Computers*, **C-31**, 616–630.

4. Moser, L.E. and Melliar-Smith, P.M. (1990). Formal verification of safety-critical systems. *Software–Practice and Experience*, **20**, 799–821.

5. Owre, S., Rushby, J., Shankar, N. and von Henke, F. (1995). Formal verification for fault-tolerant architectures: Prolegomena to the design of PVS. *IEEE Transactions on Software Engineering*, **21**, 107–125.

6. Dijkstra, E.W. (1968). The structure of The multiprogamming system. *Communications of the ACM*, **11**, 341–346.

7. Parnas, D.L. (1972). A technique for software module specification with examples. *Communications of the ACM*, **15**, 330–336.

8. Melliar-Smith, P.M. and Rushby, J. (1985). The Enhanced HDM system for specification and verification. *Proc. of VerkShop III, ACM Software Engineering Notes*, **10**, 41–43.

9. Guttag, J.V., Horning, J.J. and Wing, J.W. (1985). The Larch family of specification languages. *IEEE Software*, **2**, 24–36.

10. Liskov, B., Synder, A., Atkinson, R. and Shaffert, C. (1977). Abstraction mechanisms in CLU. *Communications of the ACM*, **20**, 564–576.

11. Wulf, W., London, R. and Shaw, M. (1981). Abstraction and verification in ALPHARD: Introduction to language and methodology. *ALPHARD: Form and Content*, Editor: M. Shaw, Springer-Verlag, Germany.

12. Lam, S.S. and Shankar, A.U. (1984). Protocol verification via projections. *IEEE Transactions on Software Engineering*, **SE-10**, 325–342.

13. Lam, S.S. and Shankar, A.U. (1989). Refinement and projection of relational specifications. *Proc. of the REX Workshop on Stepwise Refinement of Distributed Systems, Lecture Notes in Computer Science*, **430**, Springer-Verlag, Germany, 454–486.

14. Lynch, N. and Tuttle, M. (1987). Hierarchical correctness proofs for distributed algorithms. *Proc. of the 6th ACM Sym. on Principles of Distributed Computing*, 137–151.

15. Abadi, M. and Lamport, L. (1989). Composing specifications. *Proc. of the REX Workshop on Stepwise Refinement of Distributed Systems, Lecture Notes in Computer Science*, **430**, Springer-Verlag, Germany, 1–41.

16. Abadi, M. and Lamport, L. (1988). The existence of refinement mappings. *Proc. of the 3rd IEEE Sym. on Logic in Computer Science*, 165–175.

System Specification in VDM-SL

Paul Mukherjee

School of Computer Studies, University of Leeds

Abstract

Formal specifications in model-based languages such as VDM-SL and Z often suffer from only being able to describe a system at the operation level. In this paper, by considering a VDM-SL specification as a labeled transition system, we show that describing the computations generated by the labeled transition system allows us to reason about a system at both the operation level and the system level. To illustrate the method, we show how to specify properties involving termination, priority and fairness – properties not normally associated with model-based specifications.

1 Introduction

The formal specification language VDM-SL [1] now has many converts and is established as one of the foremost formal techniques. Evidence of this is provided by the growing number of case studies in the literature (for example [2,3]), the availability of tools for the language (for example [4,5]) and the fact that due to popular demand the language is being standardized [6]. Indeed, for the systems developer looking to use formal techniques, these factors contrive to make VDM-SL an extremely attractive candidate.

Yet previous examples of the use of VDM-SL have only described systems at the operation level; little attention has been paid to system level descriptions, that is, how operations may be combined and the power of expression that such combinations give rise to. In the few cases where such combinations are considered, informal reasoning is employed or a different formalism is used. Neither solution is satisfactory. Unless it is clear that correctness of such combinations is significantly less important than correctness of the components, the use of informal reasoning cannot be justified; moreover many of the advantages of using formal methods are negated if several formalisms are used concurrently.

The ideal scenario would be one where we are able to specify properties and requirements at both the operation and system level. This would allow a clean system description while retaining a formal meaning for the specification. Moreover for pragmatic reasons it would be most desirable if such a description could be framed without recourse to semantic extensions to the specification language, thus allowing existing tools and proof techniques to be used unaltered.

In this paper we describe precisely such a scenario, namely a method of describing both operation-level and system-level requirements in a uniform VDM-SL framework with no semantic extensions.

As noted in [7], a VDM-SL specification may be considered as a labeled transition system [8], with operations corresponding to atomic transitions that may be performed upon the state. We may extend this analogy further by considering the computations (i.e. sequences of transitions) generated by the labeled transition system. This allows us to reason at both the operation level and the system level within the VDM-SL framework.

In fact, as we shall see, we can think of the collection of computations generated by a specification as a specification itself; we refer to the underlying specification as the operation-level specification, and the generated specification as the system specification.

Therefore, our objectives in this paper are

- to describe how the system specification may be systematically constructed from the operation-level specification, and

- to illustrate the expressive power available in the system specification by describing properties not normally associated with model-based specifications.

The paper is organized as follows. We begin by constructing the system specification corresponding to a simple operation-level specification. We then use this system specification to describe termination, priority and fairness of computations generated by the specification. We conclude by considering the system specification in the context of different specification formalisms.

2   Construction of system specification

In this section we give a simple example of how to construct a system specification from an operation-level specification. The operation-level specification that we use is the specification of a simple sender-receiver system. Although this specification employs operations specified in pre/post form, there is no reason in principle why the construction will not proceed similarly for operations defined explicitly.

2.1   Operation-level specification

The sender-receiver system consists of two streams of data, *send* and *receive*, which transmit data by means of a channel *chan*. We assume the channel operates a First-In-First-Out discipline. Clearly, *send*, *receive* and *chan* will be represented by state variables. We also assume the existence of some constant value *init-send*, representing the initial stream of data to be sent. Thus our state specification is:

$$Sender\ ()$$
ext wr *send* : *Data**
  wr *chan* : *Data**

pre *send* $\neq$ []

post *chan* = $\overleftarrow{chan}$ $\frown$ [hd $\overleftarrow{send}$]

  $\wedge$ *send* = tl $\overleftarrow{send}$

$$Receiver\ ()$$
ext wr *receive* : *Data**
  wr *chan* : *Data**

pre *chan* $\neq$ []

post *receive* = $\overleftarrow{receive}$ $\frown$ [hd $\overleftarrow{chan}$]

  $\wedge$ *chan* = tl $\overleftarrow{chan}$

Figure 1. The sender-receiver system

state Σ *of*
  send : *Data**
  receive : *Data**
  chan : *Data**
  inv $mk\text{-}\Sigma(s, r, c) \underline{\triangle}\ init\text{-}send = r \frown c \frown s$
  init $mk\text{-}\Sigma(s, r, c) \underline{\triangle} s = init\text{-}send\ \wedge r = [] \wedge c = []$
end.

In our state invariant we require that collectively, *send*, *receive* and *chan* contain precisely the same information as *init-send*, and it is also stored in the same order as *init-send*. Such an invariant is only possible because the communication history is (unrealistically) known in advance. (Later when we introduce an operation that produces data, we remove *init-send* from the specification.)

We specify two operations, one for sending data to the channel, and one for receiving data from the channel. The former operation is called *sender* and is shown in Figure 1. Provided *send* is non-empty, this moves data from *send* to *chan*, while preserving the state invariant.

Similarly, provided *chan* is non-empty, the operation *receiver* shown in Figure 1 moves data from *chan* to *receive*, again preserving the state invariant in the process.

Thus in the operation-level specification, we have specified the system state and the operations on that state. However we can say little about computations of the labeled transition system arising from this specification, or about the effect that changes in the operation-level specification have on this labeled transition system. This is the objective of constructing the system specification.

2.2 System specification

The system specification describes the valid computations of an operation-level specification. A computation is a finite, non-empty sequence of states, as defined by the operation-level specification, such that for each such sequence $\sigma_1 \ldots \sigma_n$, for any i in $\{1, \ldots, n-1\}$, σ_i satisfies the pre-condition of some operation Op defined

                                P. *Mukherjee*

by the operation-level specification, and (σ_i, σ_{i+1}) satisfies the post-condition of
Op.

As we are constructing a new specification with its own state definition[1], we
need to rewrite the state definition of the operation-level specification as a type
definition:

Σ :: $send$: $Data^*$
$\quad$ $receive$: $Data^*$
$\quad$ $chan$: $Data^*$
inv mk-$\Sigma(s, r, c) \triangle$ $init$-$send = r \frown c \frown s$.

Therefore we also have to rewrite our operation definitions. It will be convenient to refer to these operations numerically, so we define two maps from
natural numbers to operation pre-conditions and post-conditions respectively:

$$pre\text{-}Ops : \mathbb{N} \to (\Sigma \to \mathbb{B}) = \{1 \mapsto (\lambda\sigma : \Sigma \cdot \sigma.send \neq [\,]),$$
$$2 \mapsto (\lambda\sigma : \Sigma \cdot \sigma.chan \neq [\,])\}$$

$$post\text{-}Ops : \mathbb{N} \to (\Sigma \times \Sigma \to \mathbb{B}) =$$
$$\{1 \mapsto (\lambda mk\text{-}(\overleftarrow{\sigma}, \sigma) : \Sigma \times \Sigma \cdot$$
$$\sigma.chan = \overleftarrow{\sigma}.chan \frown [\,\mathsf{hd}\ \overleftarrow{\sigma}.send\,] \wedge \sigma.send = \mathsf{tl}\ \overleftarrow{\sigma}.send\,),$$
$$2 \mapsto (\lambda mk\text{-}(\overleftarrow{\sigma}, \sigma) : \Sigma \times \Sigma \cdot$$
$$\sigma.receive = \overleftarrow{\sigma}.receive \frown [\,\mathsf{hd}\ \overleftarrow{\sigma}.chan\,] \wedge$$
$$\sigma.chan = \mathsf{tl}\ \overleftarrow{\sigma}.chan)\}.$$

Note that we have to simulate our operations in this relational style to avoid
losing nondeterminism, since Σ is now a type.

In our state definition we formalize our notion of a computation, informally
described above. A computation of the operation-level specification Σ is an
element of the state Σ-$Comp$, defined

state Σ-$Comp$ of
$\quad$ $comp$: Σ^+
$\quad$ inv mk-Σ-$Comp(\sigma s) \triangle$
$\qquad$ len $\sigma s > 1 \Rightarrow \forall j \in \{1, \ldots, \text{len } \sigma s - 1\} \cdot$
$\qquad\quad$ $\exists i \in \{1, \ldots, num\text{-}ops\} \cdot$
$\qquad\qquad$ $pre\text{-}Ops(i)(\sigma s(j)) \wedge post\text{-}Ops(i)(\sigma s(j), \sigma s(j + 1))$
$\quad$ init mk-Σ-$Comp(\sigma s) \triangle$
$\qquad$ len $\sigma s = 1 \wedge (\mathsf{hd}\ \sigma s).send = init\text{-}send \wedge$
$\qquad$ $(\mathsf{hd}\ \sigma s).receive = [\,] \wedge (\mathsf{hd}\ \sigma s).chan = [\,]$
end

where num-ops is a constant representing the number of operations defined in the
operation-level specification (here taking value two). The initialization condition

---

[1]This would not be necessary if we used a (non-standard) modular scheme such as that in
[5].

here is derived from the initialization condition of Σ. The invariant states that any Σ-computation may only be generated by operations in Σ.

This essentially completes our construction of the system specification. However we find it convenient to define a couple of auxiliary functions.

The function *is-enabled* takes a Σ sequence and a Σ state predicate, and returns true iff the final state in the sequence satisfies the predicate:

$$is\text{-}enabled : \Sigma^+ \times (\Sigma \to \mathbb{B}) \to \mathbb{B}$$
$$is\text{-}enabled\,(\sigma s, p)\underline{\triangle}$$
$$p(\sigma s(\mathsf{len}\ \sigma s)).$$

The function *enabled*, takes a Σ sequence and a map from the natural numbers to Σ state predicates, and returns the subset of the domain of the map corresponding to state predicates satisfied by the argument state:

$$enabled : \Sigma^+ \times (\mathbb{N} \xrightarrow{m} (\Sigma \to \mathbb{B})) \to \mathbb{N}\text{-set}$$
$$enabled(\sigma s, ps)\underline{\triangle}\{i | i \in \mathsf{dom}\ ps \cdot is\text{-}enabled(\sigma s, ps(i))\}.$$

Having constructed this system specification, in the following sections we use it to describe properties of the sender-receiver system which we cannot capture in the operation-level specification. We begin by considering termination.

3 Termination

In a traditional VDM-SL specification, the term "termination" is usually used in the context of operations. In the case of explicit operations (statements), termination proof obligations arise. In the case of implicit operations (pre/post), the meaning of the operation is that whenever it is executed in a state satisfying the pre-condition, it terminates in a state satisfying the post-condition, so termination is represented by the satisfiability proof obligation. However, in the context of a system specification, since we consider operations as atomic transitions, we can consider termination as a property generated by the operation-level specification.

For instance, consider the sender-receiver specification described in the previous section. If we assume computations are maximal i.e. at any stage during the computation, if the set of enabled operations is non-empty, then one such operation is executed (the feasibility of this assumption is considered below), then we see that any such computation $\sigma s : \Sigma\text{-}Comp$ must have a final state $\sigma s(\mathsf{len}\ \sigma s)$ in which no operation is enabled. This is intuitively obvious as we are moving a fixed amount of data from *send* to *receive*.

Consider what happens if we add another operation *Producer* to the specification, which just creates more data to be sent. Introducing such an operation means that the previous invariant of Σ no longer holds. To overcome this, we introduce a new state variable *hist*, that represents the communication history. This gives us the specification shown in Figure 2.

$$
\begin{array}{ll}
\textsf{state } \Sigma \textsf{ of} & Sender\;()\ldots \\
\quad send : Data^{*} & \\
\quad receive : Data^{*} & \\
\quad chan : Data^{*} & Receiver\;()\ldots \\
\quad hist : Data^{*} & \\
\quad \textsf{inv } mk\text{-}\Sigma(s, r, c, h) \triangleq & Producer\;() \\
\qquad h = r \frown c \frown s & \textsf{ext wr } send : Data^{*} \\
& \quad\;\; \textsf{wr } hist : Data^{*} \\
\quad \textsf{init } mk\text{-}\Sigma(s, r, \dot{c}, h) \triangleq & \\
\qquad s = init\text{-}send \wedge & \textsf{pre } send = []\, \\
\qquad r = [] \wedge c = [] & \textsf{post len } send = 1 \wedge \\
\textsf{end} & \qquad hist = \overleftarrow{hist} \frown send
\end{array}
$$

Figure 2. Sender-Receiver after addition of *Producer*

In the modified design, in any state we must have an operation enabled, since *pre-Sender* and *pre-Producer* partition true. Thus, if we assume computations are maximal as we did before, we find there are no finite computations satisfying the specification. Since VDM-SL requires all sequences to be finite, this means that the system specification is not satisfiable, even though the operation-level specification *is* satisfiable. This is clearly an unsatisfactory state of affairs, so we must drop our assumption that computations are maximal and reconsider how we are to treat termination.

The problem outlined above occurs because a non-terminating computation corresponds to an infinite sequence of states, which cannot be captured in VDM-SL. Therefore we consider termination as a property of a system specification, rather than as a property of an individual computation. This leads us to three distinct notions, which we consider separately.

3.1   Strong termination

Consider once more the sender-receiver system described in Section 2. Since we no longer assume maximality of computations, valid computations need not have final states that are not enabled; indeed the single computation $[mk\text{-}\Sigma(init\text{-}send, [], [])]$ is a valid model for the specification. However, given such a computation, we know that only finitely many further transitions are possible before we reach a state in which no transition is enabled. Thus the property that distinguishes this specification from, for instance, the specification in Figure 2, is that any computation in this specification may be extended to one with a final state in which no transition is enabled.

Formally, we say a system specification is *strongly terminating* (or deadlock guaranteed) iff any computation is a prefix of a computation whose final state has no enabled transitions.

$$strong\text{-}term \underline{\triangle} \forall \sigma s : \Sigma\text{-}Comp \cdot \exists \sigma s' : \Sigma\text{-}Comp \cdot$$
$$prefix(\sigma s, \sigma s') \wedge \neg\, enabled(\sigma s', pre\text{-}Ops)$$

$$prefix : \Sigma^* \times \Sigma^* \to \mathbb{B}$$
$$prefix(\sigma s, \sigma s')\underline{\triangle}$$
$$\exists \sigma s'' : \Sigma^* \cdot \overline{inv\text{-}\Sigma\text{-}Comp}(\sigma s'') \wedge \sigma s \frown \sigma s'' = \sigma s'.$$

We can then easily prove that our sender-receiver system is strongly terminating, since we can do at most len *init-send* sender transitions and receiver transitions, after which neither is enabled.

3.2 Weak termination

The situation described above is clear-cut: every computation may be extended to one which is not enabled. However we will not always have such a clear-cut situation. For instance, suppose we modify the specification of Figure 2 by including an extra state variable *can-produce* $:\mathbb{B}$, which is initially true, and by replacing the operation *Producer*, by the following operation:

$Producer'()$
ext wr *send* : $Data^*$
   wr *hist* : $Data^*$
   wr *can-produce* $:\mathbb{B}$
pre *send* $= []\ \wedge\ can\text{-}produce$
post len *send* $= 1 \wedge\ hist = \overline{hist} \frown send\ \wedge$
   let $x \in \{$true, false$\}$ in *can-produce* $= x$.

Thus, *Producer'* acts as *Producer* except that it may nondeterministically choose the final value of *can-produce*; if it chooses the value true, *Producer'* may be executed again, but if it chooses false, since this falsifies the pre-condition, no further executions of *Producer'* may be made.

Thus, if whenever *Producer'* is executed, it leaves *can-produce* unchanged, then that computation is essentially a computation of the system in Figure 2. However, if it changes *can-produce*, thereafter the only operations available are *sender* and *receiver*. Thus in this system specification, we get computations which can be extended finitely to be non-enabled, as well as computations that are always enabled. We call such a specification *weakly-terminating* (or deadlock possible).

$$weakly\text{-}term \underline{\triangle} \neg\, strongly\text{-}term \wedge$$
$$\exists \sigma s : \Sigma\text{-}\overline{Comp} \cdot \neg\, enabled(\sigma s, pre\text{-}Ops).$$

3.3   Non-termination

Non-termination is now straightforward to characterize – if every computation in a specification is enabled, then the specification is non-terminating:

$$non\text{-}term \triangleq \forall \sigma s : \Sigma\text{-}Comp \cdot enabled(\sigma s, \ pre\text{-}Ops).$$

So it is clear that the system in Figure 2 is non-terminating. In fact, it is obvious from the definition of *enabled* that whenever the operation pre-conditions in a specification partition true, the corresponding system specification is non-terminating.

Since *strong-term* $\land$ *weak-term* $\land$ *non-term* $\Leftrightarrow$ true, these three notions represent the spectrum of possibilities with regard to termination of system specifications.

4   Priority

Another property that can be difficult to capture in a normal VDM-SL specification is *priority*. Informally, we say an operation Op_1 has priority over operation Op_2 if, whenever we have a state satisfying the pre-conditions of both operations, we prefer to execute Op_1.

Priority requirements may occur in a number of guises. The most simple example of such a requirement is a straightforward functional requirement. For instance, in our sender-receiver system we might require the receiver to have priority over the sender (in the presence of an unreliable channel, say). Priority requirements may also arise as part of the environment which we are trying to model. For instance, in the sender-receiver system, performance might deteriorate badly if the channel has to store more than a certain number of data items, so in such a situation the receiver should have priority over the sender. Finally, priority may manifest itself as a safety requirement of a system. For instance, in a vehicle control system, reducing the speed of the vehicle may take priority over sending data to the operator display.

In all these situations it is not immediately clear how we can capture the notion of priority, without introducing further state variables, which leads to an artificial, inelegant specification. In this section we consider how the notion of priority may be described in the system specification.

4.1   Strict priority

The simplest form of priority is strict priority – if Op_1 has strict priority over Op_2, then in any state where both operation pre-conditions are satisfied, Op_1 is executed rather than Op_2. For instance, suppose we wish to assert that in the sender-receiver system, *receiver* has priority over *sender*. We specify this requirement in the state invariant; in any computation, each state in the computation must satisfy the requirement stated above. This leads to the following state definition:

```
state Σ-Comp of
    comp : Σ⁺
    inv mk-Σ-Comp(σs)△
        len σs > 1 ⇒ ∀j ∈ {1,..., len σs − 1}·
            ∃i ∈ {1,..., num-ops}·
                    pre-Ops(i)(σs(j)) ∧ post-Ops(i)(σs(j), σs(j + 1))∧
                enabled(σs(1,...,j), {1,2} ◁ pre-Ops) = {1,2}
                    ⇒ post-Ops(1)(σs(j), σs(j + 1))
    init mk-Σ-Comp(σs)△
        len σs = 1 ∧ (hd σs).send = init-send ∧
        (hd σs).receive = [] ∧ (hd σs).chan = []
end
```

Note here that we have only defined a priority relation between two operations. If more than these two operations are enabled in a particular state, no priority applies. However, strict priority need not be a binary relation, so we could equally have *receiver* taking strict priority over both *sender* and *Producer* in the specification shown in Figure 2.

The effect of asserting strict priority of Op_1 over Op_2 is equivalent to including $\neg pre\text{-}Op_1 \wedge pre\text{-}Op_3 \ldots pre\text{-}Op_{num-ops}$ as a conjunct in $pre\text{-}Op_2$. However this is essentially an abuse of the pre-condition; the rôle of the pre-condition is to state the requirements on the environment for the post-condition to be satisfiable. In most cases priority does not affect the satisfiability of the post-condition, and so it is inappropriate to include it in the pre-condition. This demonstrates that strict priority does not need the system specification in order to be expressed. Nonetheless, consideration of strict priority leads to the notion of non-strict priority, considered next, which does require the system specification to be expressed.

4.2 Non-strict priority

A disadvantage of strict priority is that it can significantly reduce the amount of choice available to the implementor of the system. An alternative technique for specifying priority is to make an assertion of the form "if both Op_1 and Op_2 are enabled for n states in a computation, Op_1 must be executed more than $n/2$ times". This clearly specifies that Op_1 is preferred to Op_2, but nonetheless gives the implementor some flexibility in how the preference is to be implemented. We call this form of priority, "non-strict priority".

Again, we illustrate this using our sender-receiver system. Suppose that we have an unreliable channel which is capable of duplicating the next element to be received by *receiver*. Assuming that *init-send* contains no duplicates, we first modify our state definition in the operation-level specification:

```
state Σ of
    send : Data*
    receive : Data*
    chan : Data*
    inv mk-Σ(s, r, c)△ init-send = r ⌢ remove-dupls(c) ⌢ s
    init mk-Σ(s, r, c)△ s = init-send ∧ r = [] ∧ c = []∧
        init-send = remove-dupls (init-send)
end.
```

$$remove\text{-}dupls : Data^* \to Data^*$$
$$remove\text{-}dupls\ (ds)\triangle$$
$$[ds(i)\,|\,i \in \mathsf{inds}\ ds \cdot \forall j \in \{i+1,\ldots,\mathsf{len}\ ds\} \cdot ds(j) \neq ds(i)].$$

Then we introduce another operation to our specification that represents an unreliable channel.

```
Channel-Error ()
ext wr chan : Data*
pre chan ≠ []
post chan = (hd  chan) ⌢ chan .
```

And we assume that $pre\text{-}Ops(3) \equiv pre\text{-}Channel\text{-}Error$ and $post\text{-}Ops(s) \equiv post\text{-}Channel\text{-}Error$.

In this case we require of each computation that, if we restrict our interest to those states in which *sender* and *receiver* are both enabled, then in any contiguous sub-sequence of ten of these states, *receiver* must not have been executed fewer times than *sender*. As before, we specify this requirement in the system state invariant

```
state Σ-Comp of
    comp : Σ⁺
    inv mk-Σ-Comp(σs)△
        len σs > 1 ⇒
            (∀j ∈ {1,…, len σs − 1} · ∃i ∈ {1,…, num-ops}·
                pre-Ops(i)(σs(j)) ∧ post-Ops(i)(σs(j), σs(j + 1))∧
            let σs-m = {i ↦ σs(i)| ∈ inds σs·
                pre-Ops(1)(σs(i)) ∧ pre-Ops(2)(σs(i))} in
            ∀s ∈ 𝓕 dom σs-m·
                (card s = 10 ∧ {min(s),…, max(s)} ∩ dom σs-m =
                    {min(s),…, max(s)})
                ⇒ (card{i|i ∈ s · post-Ops(2)(σs(i), σs(i + 1))} ≥
                    card{i|i ∈ s · post-Ops(1)(σs(i), σs(i + 1))})
    init mk-Σ-Comp(σs)△
        len σs = 1 ∧ (hd σs).send = init-send∧
        (hd σs).receive = [] ∧ (hd σs).chan = []∧
        init-send = remove-dupls (init-send)
end.
```

Such non-strict priorities are attractive as they are less committal than the strict priority described earlier. However care must be taken when using them, as such conditions have the potential to yield complex, intractable proof obligations.

4.3 Priority and termination

It is interesting to consider how priority affects termination. It has been stated elsewhere [9] that priority does not affect logical behaviour, and that remains the case here. This becomes evident when priority is considered as a device for restricting the state definition i.e. any computation satisfying the priority specification also satisfies the original system specification. However, it is not clear how introducing priority impinges on the termination behaviour of the specification.

If we consider a non-terminating system specification, every computation in the specification is enabled, by definition of non-termination. Introducing priority merely has the effect of removing some computations from the specification. Thus those remaining computations must still be enabled. Therefore priority preserves non-termination. In the case of strong termination, similar reasoning leads us to the conclusion that it also is preserved by priority. What then, of weak termination?

Suppose we specify priority of some operation Op_1 over another operation Op_2. We distinguish two categories:

- Asserting priority is equivalent to excluding Op_2 completely;

- Op_2 may still be executed, albeit in fewer cases than previously.

Considering the first category, suppose that before introducing priority the specification is weakly terminating. With priority, there are three different possibilities. The specification remains weakly terminating, the specification becomes strongly terminating or the specification becomes non-terminating. The first of these may trivially occur, and therefore needs no further consideration. To achieve the second, Op_2 must be an operation that prevents termination of the system specification. The operation *Producer'* described in Section 3.2 is an example. Suppose we add the operation *Disable* shown in Figure 3 to the specification. Without priority the specification is still weakly-terminating since *Disable* need never be executed. However, if we assert strict priority of *Disable* over *Producer'*, *Producer'* can no longer be executed. *Disable* may be executed once, after which both *pre-Disable* and *pre-Producer'* are falsified. Thus we get a strongly-terminating specification. In fact, this is also the case if we assert non-strict priority of *Disable* over *Producer'* – only one execution of *Disable* is needed to prevent *Producer'* being enabled.

Suppose now that introduction of priority renders the specification non-terminating. This means that priority must inhibit the partial termination mechanism. In the case of *Producer'*, this mechanism is the falsification of *can-produce*. So if we add the operation *Producer"* shown in Figure 3 to the specification, then

P. Mukherjee

$Disable$ ()
ext wr $can\text{-}produce$: $\mathbb{B}$
  rd $send$: $Data^*$
pre $send = [\,] \wedge$
  $can\text{-}produce$
post $\neg\, can\text{-}produce$

$Producer''$ ()
ext wr $send$: $Data^*$
  wr $hist$: $Data^*$
  rd $can\text{-}produce$: $\mathbb{B}$
pre $send = [\,] \wedge can\text{-}produce$
post len $send = 1 \wedge$
  $hist = \overleftarrow{hist} \,^\frown send$

Figure 3. Strict priority causing strong termination from weak termination

without priority, the specification is still weakly-terminating. However, if we assert strict priority of *Producer"* over *Producer'*, since *can-produce* can never be falsified, we get a non-terminating specification.

We now consider the second category, namely the case where Op_2 may still be executed. If the introduced priority leads to a specification that is strongly terminating, again Op_1 must in some way remove the non-terminating computations from the specification. For instance suppose we add the operation *Disable'* shown in Figure 4 to the sender-receiver system with the operation *Producer'*. Without priority the specification is non-terminating, as *Disable'* need never be executed. However, if we assert strict priority of *Disable'* over *Producer'*, then after an initial execution of *Producer'*, whenever *Producer'* is enabled so is *Disable'*. However after one execution of *Disable'*, neither *Disable'* nor *Producer'* will be enabled again. Thus with strict priority the specification is strongly terminating. Again, this also holds if we assert non-strict priority rather than strict priority.

The last case to consider is where Op_2 may still be executed and introduction of priority gives a non-terminating specification from a weakly-terminating specification. For such an operation Op_1, we require that $pre\text{-}Op_1$ must differ from $pre\text{-}Op_2$ on the state space Σ, and that $post\text{-}Op_1$ must overcome the partial termination mechanism of $post\text{-}Op_2$. The requisite operation may easily be constructed by considering the previously defined operations *Producer"* and *Disable'*. This gives *Producer"'*.

Without priority this specification is weakly-terminating, as (say) after three executions of *Producer'*, if *can-produce* is falsified then *Producer"'* is not enabled. However, with strict priority of *Producer"'* over *Producer'*, after one execution of *Producer'*, since *Producer"'* is enabled it will always be executed in preference to *Producer'*. Since execution of *Producer"'* cannot falsify its own pre-condition, this ensures that the specification is non-terminating.

The importance of all these examples is that although priority cannot affect conventional logical behaviour, it can be used as a tool to alter the termination behaviour of a system specification.

$Disable'\ ()$
ext wr $can\text{-}produce : \mathbb{B}$
   rd $send : Data^*$
   rd $receive : Data^*$
   rd $chan : Data^*$
pre $\text{len } send + \text{len } receive$
   $+\ \text{len } chan >$
   $\text{len } init\text{-}send$
   $\wedge\ can\text{-}produce$
post $\neg\ can\text{-}produce$

$Producer'''\ ()$
ext wr $send : Data^*$
   rd $receive : Data^*$
   rd $chan : Data^*$
   wr $hist : Data^*$
   wr $can\text{-}produce : \mathbb{B}$
pre $(\text{len } send + \text{len } receive +$
   $\text{len } chan = \text{len } init\text{-}send + 1\ \wedge$
   $\neg\ can\text{-}produce)\ \vee$
   $(\text{len } send + \text{len } receive + \text{len } chan \geq$
   $\text{len } init\text{-}send + 1\ \wedge\ can\text{-}produce)$
post $can\text{-}produce\ \wedge\ \text{tl } send = \overleftarrow{send}\ \wedge$
   $hist = [\text{hd } send] \frown \overleftarrow{hist}$

Figure 4. Strict priority causing strong termination from non-termination

5 Fairness

In our discussion of priority and termination, a number of cases arose where specifications were weakly terminating purely because some operation need never be executed, even if arbitrarily enabled. We refer to such arbitrary non-execution as *operation starvation*. Clearly in many situations operation starvation is undesirable as there is little point in specifying an operation if it is never to be executed. A system specification in which starvation never occurs is called a *fair* specification.

In this section we consider various notions of fairness and how we might go about specifying them in the system specification. We begin by discussing conventional fairness and its limitations in the current framework, and then go on to describe some more novel forms of fairness.

5.1 Traditional fairness

In [10] two notions of fairness are described; weak fairness and strong fairness. Weak fairness of a computation with respect to an operation asserts that at any state during the computation, the operation must eventually be executed or it must become impossible to execute, though perhaps only briefly. Strong fairness of a computation with respect to an operation asserts that at any state during the computation, the operation is eventually executed or it is eventually always impossible to execute. These notions are then formalized using the temporal operators $\Diamond$ and $\Box$ in a logic based on infinite computations.

We now consider how to specify weak and strong fairness in a system specification. First of all, since we work with finite computations rather than infinite ones, we weaken our definitions to exclude the last state in a computation. We take "impossible to execute" to mean falsification of the operation pre-condition. Given operation Op and computation σs, we specify that Op must eventually be executed in σs by asserting the existence of an index j in σs such that $pre\text{-}Op(\sigma s(j))$ and $post\text{-}Op(\sigma s(j), \sigma s(j+1))$. Using the maps $pre\text{-}Ops$ and $post\text{-}Ops$, we get the function $eventually\text{-}executed$:

$$eventually\text{-}executed : \Sigma^+ \times \mathbb{N} \rightarrow \mathbb{B}$$
$$eventually\text{-}executed(\sigma s, o) \underline{\triangle}$$
$$\quad \exists j \in \{1, \ldots, \mathsf{len}\ \sigma s - 1\}\cdot$$
$$\qquad pre\text{-}Ops(o)(\sigma s(j)) \wedge\ post\text{-}Ops(o)(mk\text{-}(\sigma s(j), \sigma s(j+1)))$$
$$\mathsf{pre}\ o \in\ \mathsf{dom}\ pre\text{-}Ops\ \wedge o \in\ \mathsf{dom}\ post\text{-}Ops.$$

Asserting that at any state in σs, Op must eventually be executed amounts to asserting $eventually\text{-}executed(\sigma s', o)$ for every suffix $\sigma s'$ of σs. If it becomes impossible to execute Op in σs, there must be some index j in σs such that $\neg\ pre\text{-}Op(\sigma s(j))$. Asserting this at any state in σs again amounts to the same assertion for any suffix $\sigma s'$ of σs. Thus we specify weak fairness of an operation with respect to a computation by:

$$WF : \Sigma^+ \times \mathbb{N} \rightarrow \mathbb{B}$$
$$WF(\sigma s, o) \underline{\triangle}$$
$$\quad \forall \sigma s' \in\ suffix(\sigma s)\cdot eventually\text{-}executed(\sigma s', o) \vee$$
$$\quad \forall i \in \{1, \ldots, \mathsf{len}\ \sigma s - 1\} \cdot \exists j \in \{i, \ldots, \mathsf{len}\ \sigma s - 1\}\cdot$$
$$\qquad \neg\ pre\text{-}Ops(o)(\sigma s(j))$$
$$\mathsf{pre}\ o \in\ \mathsf{dom}\ pre\text{-}Ops$$

$$suffix : \Sigma^+ \rightarrow \Sigma^+\text{-}\mathsf{set}$$
$$suffix(\sigma s) \underline{\triangle} \{\sigma s(i, \ldots, \mathsf{len}\ \sigma s) | i \in\ \mathsf{inds}\ \sigma s\}.$$

Strong fairness follows similarly. Asserting that Op is eventually always impossible to execute is equivalent to asserting the existence of an index j in σs such that for each index $i \geq j$ in σs, $\neg\ pre\text{-}Op(\sigma s(i))$. Thus we get:

$$SF : \Sigma^+ \times \mathbb{N} \rightarrow \mathbb{B}$$
$$SF(\sigma s, o) \underline{\triangle}$$
$$\quad \forall \sigma s' \in\ suffix(\sigma s)\cdot eventually\text{-}executed(\sigma s', o) \vee$$
$$\quad \exists j \in \{1, \ldots, \mathsf{len}\ \sigma s - 1\} \cdot \forall i \in \{j, \ldots, \mathsf{len}\ \sigma s - 1\}\cdot$$
$$\qquad \neg\ pre\text{-}Ops(o)(\sigma s(i))$$
$$\mathsf{pre}\ o \in\ \mathsf{dom}\ pre\text{-}Ops.$$

Then to assert that a system specification is weakly (or strongly) fair, we assert fairness of each computation in the invariant, that is, if we wish to assert a specification is weakly fair with respect to an operation with pre-condition *pre-Ops(o)* and post-condition *post-Ops(o)*, we include $WF(\sigma s, o)$ as an extra conjunct in the invariant.

5.2 Alternative notions of fairness

Since we are operating in the realm of finite computations, weak and strong fairness essentially amount to non-starvation requirements. Weak fairness states than an operation may starve if it is periodically impossible to execute, and strong fairness asserts that an operation may starve only if it is eventually always impossible to execute. However given a computation σs, for any operation Op, if *pre-Op* is false at $\sigma s(\text{len } \sigma s - 1)$ then σs is both weakly and strongly fair with respect to the operation, even though Op need never be executed! Thus we are forced to consider some alternative notions of fairness.

5.2.1 Finite weak and strong fairness

One way to specify fairness in the system specification is to reframe the traditional notions of fairness in a manner more suited to the system specification. In this context we say a computation is weakly fair with respect to an operation if the operation is executed in the computation or the operation is impossible to execute throughout the computation. This gives the predicate *fin-WF*:

$$fin\text{-}WF : \Sigma^+ \times \mathbb{N} \to \mathbb{B}$$
$$fin\text{-}WF(\sigma s, o) \underline{\triangle}$$
$$\forall i \in \{1, \ldots, \overline{\text{len } \sigma s - 1}\} \cdot \neg \, pre\text{-}Ops(o)(\sigma s(i)) \vee$$
$$\exists j \in \{1, \ldots, \text{len } \sigma s - 1\} \cdot$$
$$pre\text{-}Ops(o)(\sigma s(j)) \wedge post\text{-}Ops(o)(mk\text{-}(\sigma s(j), \sigma s(j+1))).$$

Then we say a computation is strongly fair with respect to an operation if the operation is executed in every maximal contiguous subsequence of the computation in which it is enabled.

$$fin\text{-}SF : \Sigma^+ \times \mathbb{N} \to \mathbb{B}$$
$$fin\text{-}SF(\sigma s, o) \underline{\triangle}$$
$$\forall \sigma s' \in \overline{max\text{-}enabled\text{-}subseq(\sigma s, o)} \cdot$$
$$\exists j \in \{1, \ldots, \text{len } \sigma s' - 1\} \cdot$$
$$pre\text{-}Ops(o)(\sigma s(j)) \wedge post\text{-}Ops(o)(mk\text{-}(\sigma s(j), \sigma s(j+1)))$$

$$max\text{-}enabled\text{-}subseq : \Sigma^+ \times \mathbb{N} \to \Sigma^+\text{-set}$$
$$max\text{-}enabled\text{-}subseq(\sigma s, o) \underline{\triangle}$$
$$\{\sigma s(i, \ldots, j) | i, j \in \text{inds } \overline{\sigma s} \cdot \forall k \in \{i, \ldots, j-1\} \cdot$$
$$pre\text{-}Ops(o)(\sigma s(k)) \wedge (i = 1 \vee \neg \, pre\text{-}Ops(o)(\sigma s(i-1))) \wedge$$
$$(j = \text{len } \sigma s \vee \neg pre\text{-}Ops(o)(\sigma s(j)))\}.$$

5.2.2   Relational fairness

An alternative view of fairness is to consider it as a relation between two operations. This is the opposite to priority in that we wish to assert that a computation is relationally fair with respect to two operations if neither operation receives preference in the computation. We formulate this requirement by saying that given a computation and two operations, the computation is relationally fair with respect to the operations if, when we restrict our interest to those states in the computation in which both operations are enabled, the number of executions of each differs by at most one. This gives us the predicate *rel-fair*:

$$
\begin{aligned}
&rel\text{-}fair : \Sigma^+ \times \mathbb{N} \times \mathbb{N} \to \mathbb{B} \\
&rel\text{-}fair(\sigma s, o_1, o_2)\triangleq \\
&\quad \text{let } both\text{-}enabled = \{i | i \in \{1, \ldots, \text{len } \sigma s - 1\} \cdot \\
&\qquad\qquad\qquad pre\text{-}Ops(o_1)(\sigma s(i)) \wedge \\
&\qquad\qquad\qquad pre\text{-}Ops(o_2)(\sigma s(i))\} \\
&\qquad\quad \text{in} \\
&\quad \text{abs (card } \{i | i \in both\text{-}enabled \cdot \\
&\qquad\qquad post\text{-}Ops(o_1)(mk\text{-}(\sigma s(i), \sigma s(i+1)))\} - \\
&\qquad\quad \text{card}\{i | i \in both\text{-}enabled \cdot \\
&\qquad\qquad post\text{-}Ops(o_2)(mk\text{-}(\sigma s(i), \sigma s(i+1)))\}) \leq 1.
\end{aligned}
$$

There are undoubtedly many more forms of fairness that we could express in our system specification. However the examples we have presented demonstrate that although traditional forms of fairness are inadequate, alternative notions exist which can comfortably capture our intuitive notion of fairness.

6   Discussion

At the beginning of this paper we outlined a shortcoming in the existing VDM-SL literature, namely the absence of dual-level specifications. In this paper we have gone some way towards addressing this shortcoming. In particular, we have demonstrated how a system level model may be systematically constructed from an operation level model. We have used the concepts of termination, priority and fairness to illustrate the usefulness of the system model. By considering operations as atomic transitions we were able to reason at the system level without any extensions or modifications to the VDM-SL semantics. This is pleasing as it shows that we are indeed demonstrating the power of expression in standard VDM-SL, but it is also very useful from a practical point of view as it means that existing VDM-SL tools may be used to analyse such multi-level specifications. Indeed the specifications presented here have been analysed using the IFAD VDM-SL toolbox [5].

Clearly, since the semantic model of VDM-SL is not extended, there are bound to be some limitations to the approach described here compared to formalisms designed specifically for expressing properties such as termination, fairness and priority. In particular, since VDM-SL sequences are finite, only pseudoliveness properties may be expressed – pure liveness properties require infinite sequences to be expressed [10].

A similar approach to that described here is [11], where it is demonstrated that concurrent systems may be specified in Z. However, although the approach is similar insofar as sequences of states are used as a basis for reasoning, the main thrust of this work is the use of a Unity-style logic [12] to reason about concurrent computations.

The approach described here also arises in practice. [13] describes the use of a system-level specification in Z which is used to state security-critical properties of the system. Thus it would appear there is some demand for the current approach.

In the future, we plan to study the refinement of system specifications. Here, we use the term "refinement" in the sense that we would like to specify a property in the system specification then transform the operation-level specification such that this property is guaranteed by the local behaviour of operations. This style of refinement would be useful if we think of operations as distributed processes.

References

1. Dawes, J. (1991). *The VDM-SL Reference Guide*, Pitman.

2. Fields, R. and Elvang-Gøransson, M. (1992). A VDM case study in mural. *IEEE Transactions on Software Engineering*, **18**.

3. Mukherjee, P. and Stavridou, V. (1993). The formal specification of safety requirements for storing explosives. *Formal Aspects of Computing*, **5**, 299–336.

4. Froome, P.K.D. (1990). *SpecBox*, Adelard Software.

5. VDM-SL Tool Group. (1994). *IFAD VDM-SL Toolbox*.

6. Andrews, D. (1993). Information technology programming languages - VDM-SL. *First Committee Draft Standard ISO/IEC JTC1/SC22/WG19 N-20, ISO, Document Reference IN9*.

7. Bicarregui, J.C., Fitzgerald, J.S., Lindsay, P.A., Moore, R. and Ritchie, B. (1994). *Proof in VDM: A Practitioner's Guide*, Springer-Verlag.

8. Keller, R.M. (1976). Formal verification of parallel programs. *Communications of the ACM*, **19**.

9. Hoare, C.A.R. (1985). *Communicating Sequential Processes*, Prentice-Hall International.

10. Lamport, L. (1991). The temporal logic of actions. *Technical Report 79*, Digital Systems Research Center.

11. Evans, A.S. (1994). Specifying and verifying concurrent systems using *Z. FME '94: Industrial Benefit of Formal Methods*, Editors: T. Denvir, M. Naftalin, and M. Bertran, *Formal Methods Europe, Springer Verlag Lecture Notes in Computer Science*, **873**.

12. Chandy, K.M. and Misra, J. (1988). *Parallel Program Design: A Foundation*, Addison-Wesley.

13. Collinson, R. (1994). A critical look at functional specifications. *FME '94: Industrial Benefit of Formal Methods*, Editors: T. Denvir, M. Naftalin and M. Bertran, *Formal Methods Europe, Springer Verlag Lecture Notes in Computer Science*, **873**.

Key Management for Secure Communications

Fred Piper

Department of Mathematics, Royal Holloway, University of London

1 Introduction

One of a network's basic functions is to provide an access path for communications between two users (at remote locations). As network facilities have grown and the volume of data has expanded, there has been an increased dependency on public channels. This has led to an increase in the opportunity for, and ease of, intercepting data. Since there are many areas where users require secrecy or to be assured of the integrity of data, it is now often necessary that a network architecture provides the capability to implement appropriate security measures.

By their very nature, large and/or public networks are vulnerable to attack. If, for instance, a network carries a large volume of traffic which is transported between two remote locations, processed in one place and stored in another then providing physical security for all of its various components is likely to be impossible. These networks frequently rely on the use of cryptographic tools to provide security.

2 Basic cryptography

The idea of a cipher system is to disguise confidential information in such a way that its meaning is unintelligible to an unauthorized person. The information to be concealed is called the **plaintext** (or just the **message**) and the operation of disguising it is known as **enciphering** or **encryption**. The enciphered message is called the **ciphertext** or **cryptogram**. The person who enciphers the message is known as the **encipherer**, while the person to whom he sends the cryptogram is called the **recipient** or **receiver**. The set of rules which the encipherer uses to encipher his plaintext is the **enciphering algorithm**. Normally the operation of this algorithm will depend on an **enciphering key** $k(E)$ which the encipherer inputs to the algorithm together with his message.

In order that the recipient can obtain the message from the cryptogram there has to be a **deciphering algorithm** which, when seeded by the appropriate **deciphering key** $k(D)$ reproduces the plaintext from the ciphertext. This is shown diagrammatically in Figure 1.

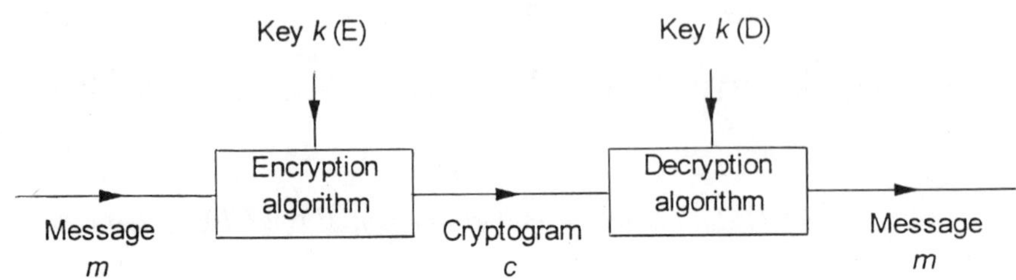

Figure 1. A cipher system

Any person who intercepts a message being transmitted from the encipherer to a recipient is called, not surprisingly, an **interceptor** (other authors use different terms; popular options include "enemy" or "bad guy"). Even if he knows the deciphering algorithm an interceptor will not, in general, know the deciphering key and it is this lack of knowledge which, it is hoped, will prevent him from knowing the plaintext. **Cryptography** is the science of designing cipher systems and **cryptanalysis** is the name given to the process of deducing the plaintext from the ciphertext without knowing the key. **Cryptology** is the collective term for both cryptography and cryptanalysis.

In practice most cryptanalytic attacks involve trying to determine the deciphering key because, if successful, the attacker will then have the same knowledge as the intended recipient and will be able to decipher all other communications until the keys are changed. However there may be instances where an attacker's sole objective is to read a particular message.

One important fact should already be clear from the introduction. That is that knowledge of the enciphering key is not necessary for obtaining the message from the ciphertext. This simple observation has had a dramatic impact on modern cryptology and has led to a natural division into two types of cipher systems.

A cipher system is called **conventional** or **symmetric** if it is easy to deduce the deciphering key $k(D)$ from the enciphering key $k(E)$. However if it is computationally infeasible to deduce $k(D)$ from $k(E)$ then the system is called **asymmetric** or a **public key system**. The reason for distinguishing between these two type of system should be clear. In order to prevent an interceptor with knowledge of the algorithm from obtaining the plaintext from intercepted ciphertext it is essential that $k(D)$ should be secret. Whereas for a symmetric system this necessitates that $k(E)$ should also be secret, if the system is asymmetric then knowledge of $k(E)$ is of no practical use to the attacker. Indeed it can, and often is, be made public.

Although the statements made in the last paragraph may appear to be simple and self-evident, their consequences are far reaching. In Figure 1 the diagram assumes that the sender and recipient have a "matching pair" of keys. It may, in practice, be quite difficult for them to reach this situation. In fact the general problem of key management, which includes key generation, distribution, storage, change and destruction, is one of the most difficult aspects of designing a secure system. The problems associated with key management tend to be different for symmetric and asymmetric systems. If the system is symmetric then there is a need to be able to distribute keys while keeping their values secret. If the system is asymmetric then it is possible to avoid this particular problem. However it is then replaced by the problem of guaranteeing the authenticity of each participant's enciphering key.

It is probably best for the designer of a cipher system to assume that any would-be attacker has as much knowledge and general "intelligence" information as possible. Consequently, in order to assess the security of a system, it is customary to make the following three assumptions, which we refer to as the **worst case conditions**.

- **WC1** The cryptanalyst has a complete knowledge of the cipher system.

- **WC2** The cryptanalyst has obtained a considerable amount of ciphertext.

- **WC3** The cryptanalyst knows the plaintext equivalent of a certain amount of the ciphertext.

Condition **WC1** implies that we believe there is no security in the cipher system itself. Naturally the cryptanalyst's task is considerably harder if he does not know the system used and it is now possible to conceal this information to a certain extent. For instance, with modern electronic systems, the function used for enciphering can be concealed in hardware by the use of microelectronics. By using VLSI or LSI, we can conceal the entire function within a small "chip". To actually "open up" one of these chips is a delicate and time consuming process. Nevertheless it can probably be done, and we should not assume that the cryptanalyst lacks the ability and patience to do it. Similarly, any part of the function which is included as software within the machine can be disguised by a carefully written program. Once again, with patience and skill, this can probably be uncovered. It is even possible that, in some situations, the cryptanalyst will have the precise algorithm available to him. From any manufacturer's or designer's point of view, **WC1** is an essential assumption, since it removes a great deal of the ultimate responsibility involved in keeping a system secret.

It should be clear that **WC2** is a reasonable assumption. If there is no possibility of interception then there is no need to use a cipher system. However if interception is a possibility then, presumably, the communicators will not be able to dictate when the interception takes place and the safest option is to assume that all transmissions will be intercepted.

WC3 is also a realistic condition. The attacker might gain this type of information by observing traffic and making intelligent guesses. He might also even be able to choose the plaintext for which the ciphertext is known. One "classic" historical example of this occurred in the second world war when a lighthouse was subjected to a bombing attack merely to ensure that the distinctive word "leuchtturm" would appear in plaintext messages that were to be enciphered using the Enigma enciphering machine.

One consequence of accepting these worst case conditions is that we have to assume that the only information which distinguishes the genuine recipient from the interceptor is knowledge of $k(D)$. Thus the security of the system is totally dependent on the secrecy of the deciphering key. This reinforces our earlier assertion about the importance of good key management.

If we assume that our deciphering algorithm is known then there is one obvious method of attack available to the interceptor. They could, at least in theory, try each possible deciphering key and "hope" that they identify the correct one. Such an attack is called an **exhaustive key search**. Of course such an attack cannot possibly succeed unless the attacker has some way of recognising the correct key or, as is more common, at least being able to eliminate some obviously incorrect ones. In a known plaintext attack, for instance, it is clear that any choice of $k(D)$ which does not give the correct plaintext for all the corresponding ciphertext cannot possibly be the correct key. However, unless there is sufficient volume of corresponding plaintext/ciphertext pairs, there may be many incorrect choices for $k(D)$ which give the correct answers for all the available data.

3 Network security

The simplest form of security provided in a network is link encryption. This protects data as it is transmitted along a single communications link joining two nodes. For link encryption, a shared key is installed at each end of the link and this is then used to encrypt and decrypt data transmitted between those two ends. Since each node need only share secret keys with its adjoining nodes, the key management problem for link encryption is relatively simple. When a shared key is required for a given link, it may be generated at one end of the link, and "local" arrangements can be introduced to distribute it to the other end of the link. However the security offered by link encryption is limited. Data transmitted between two remote nodes may pass through several intermediary nodes. At each node it needs to be decrypted and then re-encrypted under a different key. This key translation process means that it may be vulnerable.

End-to-end encryption refers to the situation where data transmitted between two nodes is encrypted under a secret key shared by those two nodes. This achieves a logical separation of nodes which do not share keys. Although a node may carry (encrypted) data from one node destined for another, it does not need to process that data.

Clearly two nodes that need to communicate securely must share a common key. Furthermore, greater security is achieved if different keys are used by each pair of communicating nodes. This minimizes the damage caused if a key is compromised and prevents surreptitious or accidental decryption by unintended recipients. However it also increases the complexity of the problems associated with key management. In particular keys must be distributed to remote nodes and there may be the need for every pair of nodes to share a unique secret key.

4 Key management

The first difficulty to note is the sheer volume of key material that may be required. A network of n nodes in which every pair of nodes shares a key requires $\frac{n(n-1)}{2}$ keys. If each node were to store all the keys it needed then each node would need to store $n-1$ keys. A large network may consist of some tens of thousands of nodes. If every pair of nodes in a network of 10,000 nodes were to share a DES key of 56 bits then we might require of the order of 5×10^7 keys or 3 Gbits of key material. Moreover, each node would need to store of the order of 10^4 keys. The problem is compounded by the need to change keys on a regular basis. If, as is often the case, a node needs to store several old keys as well as the current one, then there will be an even heavier storage burden on the nodes.

In order to initialise the security mechanisms, a network is likely to require some facility, in the role of a Key Distribution Centre (KDC), to generate and distribute these keys. This would also keep a register of which nodes own what keys (both current and old versions). As illustrated above, the storage requirement at the KDC could be very large indeed. Further, in order to distribute the keys, the KDC must be able to communicate securely with every node. This requirement necessitates either having a separate secure channel or using the network with the transmissions secured by another key. There are many practical solutions to this problem. For example, the KDC may establish with each node a local key which is used to encrypt only those messages which contain the keys to be distributed. These local keys will then need to be protected by another key, thus creating a key hierarchy. In most situations the top (master) key will be used infrequently and, as a result, a public key cryptosystem such as RSA could be used. When this occurs the authentication of each user's public key is likely to be assured by the use of a Key Certification Centre which issues signed certificates confirming the value of key and the identity of the owner.

5 The need for trust

Whenever a trusted third party is used for key management, a number of important issues are raised. If, for instance, cryptographic keys are generated at a centre, or even appear in clear at a centre, then that centre has the capability to compromise the entire network. Thus the entire system is totally dependent on both the integrity and technical competence of the centre. This immediately transfers many of the security problems from being technical issues into managerial ones. The trusted role of a centre may become even more crucial for key certification centres where, due to the complexity of their generation, the centre may issue secret keys to an individual. In this case the centre may have the (theoretical?) possibility of forging all signatures.

The question of how much trust should be placed in a trusted centre is one of the major issues of modern cryptography.

6   Key escrow

There are many different views on how widely encryption should be used. Many people feel that its availability should be strictly controlled, possibly even forbidden, unless permission is obtained from the appropriate government.

At one "end" of the debate is the argument that the need for law enforcement agencies to control drug trafficking, terrorism etc. suggests that they need to be able to monitor all communications between likely perpetrators. Clearly the difficulty of their task would be dramatically increased if strong encryption devices were easily obtainable. However, there is also no denying that businesses have a legitimate claim that they are entitled to take precautions to prevent company confidential information from being revealed to their competitors and that, since such information may need to be transmitted over public networks, encryption is a valuable tool for achieving their aim. There are many other relevant factors which influence the debate about the control of encryption including, of course, the "basic rights" of the individual to, in this case, privacy.

Despite the fact that it is a fascinating topic, this is probably not the right forum for a general discussion of reconciliation between the rights of the individual and the perceived needs of society. Instead we will concentrate on a potential solution to the encryption problem which could satisfy the requirements of law enforcement agencies, businesses and, possibly, the individual.

We assume that we have a encryption algorithm which is accepted as being strong. This means nothing more than there are sufficiently many keys for a key search to be infeasible and that it is "accepted" that there are no other, feasible attacks. Given current technology, a key length of 80 bits would probably be sufficient to meet the key search requirements. However,the second assumption about the accepted strength is more difficult because, for instance, it poses the obvious question; accepted by whom? For the moment we will ignore that question and explain how the "system" might work.

Use of the encryption algorithm would be "allowed" to anyone who registered as a potential user but whenever they used the algorithm they would have to deposit their key value with a universally accepted trusted third party, for example, a judge. These keys would be stored securely and, under normal circumstances, would not be released to any third parties. If, however, a law enforcement agency could produce evidence to indicate that particular communications might contain information relating to a serious crime or affect national security, then they could request a warrant from the government to authorise the release of the relevant cryptographic key.

If such a system were in use then, at least in theory, users would know that, under normal circumstances, their communications were secure against everyone, but that law enforcement agencies could, if the need arose, apply for a warrant which would enable them to read their traffic.

The situation would be similar to the current situation regarding telephone conversations in the UK. Telephone tapping is illegal and, under normal circumstances, conversations over telephone wires are private. However, the Home Secretary is empowered to authorise a telephone tap if a law enforcement agency can produce a case to justify it. In fact the protection for the individual using our encryption system would probably be better than in the telephone analogy because, whereas illegal telephone tapping is possible, the use of a strong encryption algorithm would mean that the only way an attacker could read a specific communication was by obtaining the relevant cryptographic key.

In 1993 the US White House proposed an Escrowed Encryption Standard for data/voice encryption to be used for both government and civilian applications. It involved the use of a **secret** cipher algorithm, called "Skipjack" which is available only in tamper-resistant hardware, either PCNCIA cards or Clipper chips. At key set-up, the Clipper chips exchange a Law Enforcement Access Field (LEAF) which contains information to help an authorised wiretapper recover the session key.

We will not discuss the technical details. However, we will provide a brief discussion of why the system has been widely criticised and indicate changes that might lead to a future, acceptable replacement.

The first obvious general objection was that the algorithm is secret. Although this does not imply that it is weak, it led to many conjectures that the designers would be able to obtain keys without going through the proposed procedure of obtaining "permission". Clearly, since we have no knowledge of the algorithm, it is not possible to comment on whether these fears are justified. Nevertheless it is equally clear that to accept this type of system without knowledge of the algorithm requires great trust in both the ability and integrity of the designers.

In addition to the "moral" objectives related to the secrecy of the algorithm, there are a number of other technical and/or practical problems. The first is that, in general, without the necessary legislative back-up, key escrow schemes are unenforceable in the sense that no-one will know whether or not the agreed algorithm is being used and, unless there is a penalty for failure to comply, would-be criminals will use other algorithms. Other criticisms relating explicitly to the NIST proposal, include the fact that the proposal can only work if everyone sees the LEAF, and this will only be apparent when "legal taps" are attempted.

Matt Blaze (AT&T Bell Laboratories) published a number of ways in which a system which followed the NIST proposal might be "misused" and illustrated how Skipjack could be used without the user being vulnerable to a government wiretap. In fact he found a number of flaws in the proposal and produced attacks based on the fact that the system used a checksum of only 16 bits and, therefore, allowed trial-and-error searches. Such attacks are not only feasible between two "bad guys" who do not register, but also enable a "bad guy" to communicate with a "good guy" (because sender and receiver share some hardware).

There is now a considerable amount of effort being put into trying to devise a widely acceptable key escrow system. This will probably necessitate the use of a published algorithm, possibly one depending on the type of one-way functions already used for public key systems.

Formal Verification of Fault-Tolerant Processors

G.M. Musyoka* and G. Morgan**

**Institute of Computer Science, University of Nairobi, Kenya and*
***Department of Computer Science, University of York*

Abstract

This paper discusses a general model for fault-tolerant processor design and a structured verification methodology. These two features are central to a formal framework for proving that a fault-tolerant system design meets certain formal correctness properties. The model captures fundamental concepts that form a foundation for understanding the problem independently of which technique for achieving fault tolerance is used. The methodology allows us to identify verification conditions and to discharge proof obligations attending various design instantiations in a transparent manner.

What is novel about this approach is the integration of a general formalised model of a fault-tolerant design and a broadly applicable verification strategy that is evenly matched to the model. This provides a reusable theory that structures both the specification and verification of fault tolerance. Because the theory says precisely what has to be done to obtain correctness results without appealing to the ingenuity of the verifier, it represents an improvement over past approaches to the problem.

1   Introduction

Since the emergence of a general consensus favouring the development of formal verification methods for systems design, these techniques have been applied to a wide variety of designs to verify a diverse set of properties. For example, *software functionality* [1–4], *hardware functionality* [5–11], *communication protocols* [12–14], and *security* [15] have been verified, by demonstrating that a design is free from errors to the extent that its formal descriptions and requirements are related by formal proof. The spectrum of these techniques ranges from pencil-and-paper descriptions and analyses in the style of conventional mathematical discourse, to mechanically checked verification. Because these methods transform the classical design verification problem into the task of theorem proving, challenges associated with general proof procedures have to be met. These include:

1. Limitations of undecidability.

2. Credibility.

3. Complexity management.

Most deficiencies in existing formal verification procedures arise because of difficulties in meeting the above challenges as posed by practical designs. We describe a reusable theory which structures both the specification and the verification of processor fault-tolerance to meet these challenges more effectively.

The failure to prove that a particular behaviour results from a given system implementation may mean many things:

- the axioms used are incorrect or incomplete;

- the representation utilised is not powerful enough;

- the description of the digital system is incorrect;

- the statement of the intended behaviour is incorrect;

- or the conjecture considered is actually undecidable for the implemented proof procedure.

To avoid these pitfalls in processor fault-tolerance verification the paper describes a framework within which:

- the correctness and completeness of axioms is easy to establish;

- all system attributes of interest are expressible;

- the specification of the system is structured to minimise the possibility of errors;

- the statement of the intended behaviour is formally established for precision;

- and finally, the problem of undecidability for useful conjectures is avoided by modelling only decidable properties.

In all formal verification efforts critical assumptions have to be made to prove a conjecture. The extent to which a proof is regarded as evidence of a device's behaviour depends largely on the credibility of the key assumptions. When a digital system is modeled at a high level of abstraction, the underlying assumptions may be questionable or unclear. For one to have confidence in a formal proof, vague or debatable assumptions need to be clarified. To capture the fundamental concepts that form a basis for understanding the problem our framework relies upon a general model for fault-tolerance. This has the desirable effect of basing a general proof procedure firmly on a well defined problem domain, thereby structuring it hierarchically so that assumed or derived conditions become obvious and well understood.

Issues that can limit the effectiveness of a verification methodology include modelling and analysis complexity. Both hierarchical analysis and modelling are required to manage the number and complexity of axioms and the facts that are necessary for the establishing of a proof. The paper describes techniques which allow modeling and verification to proceed hierarchically in order to safeguard problem tractability.

The paper is organised as follows: Section 2 describes some proof fundamentals and how they apply to the verification process. Section 3 discusses the application of abstraction to model and structure the verification of fault-tolerant processor designs. Section 4 applies the fundamentals of fault-tolerance to define fault-tolerance predicates as verification conditions. Section 5 describes the integration of a fault-tolerant processor abstraction and predicates that express the notion of correctness to obtain a structured verification methodology. Section 6 concludes our discussion.

2 Verification proofs

The goal of verification is to establish the correctness of an implementation with respect to its specification, i.e. the existence of a formal relationship between the two which takes into account those aspects which are considered of relevance. In a formal system where design verification is based upon formal theories, specification and proof, great emphasis is placed on syntax. The syntax of the logic is set forth unambiguously and inference rules for manipulating it are clearly defined. Proof takes place syntactically through the application of inference rules in a sequential manner. Their use to transform terms keeps the prover's semantic biases from creeping into the proof.

Within the framework of a suitable formal system, such as *first-order, higher-order, temporal logic*, etc., any verification exercise is characterised by the following four basic steps:

1. Formalisation of a set of assumptions which include possible design and (or) operating environment constraints. This can be represented as a conjunction of assertions

$$A = (A_1, A_2, A_3, \ldots\ldots\ldots, A_n)$$

   where each A_i captures some constraint.

2. The behavioural specification in the attendant formal theory of the properties S that any implementation must satisfy.

3. Formalisation in the theory of an implementation, I. This entails the refinement of the specification into more detailed levels following suitable design hierarchies. Since the design process is typically hierarchical there are a number of implementations each more detailed than its specification (see Figure 1). In practice the bottom level implementation constitutes a structural description of the design, whereas the preceding levels are abstract behavioural descriptions.

4. Finally, proof is required to demonstrate that the implementation I satisfies the specification S under assumptions in A. In formal notation, this corresponds to proof of the following statement, $A \supset (I \supset S)$, where $\supset$ denotes the **satisfied relation**, i.e. given any model of A, then I satisfies the specification S.

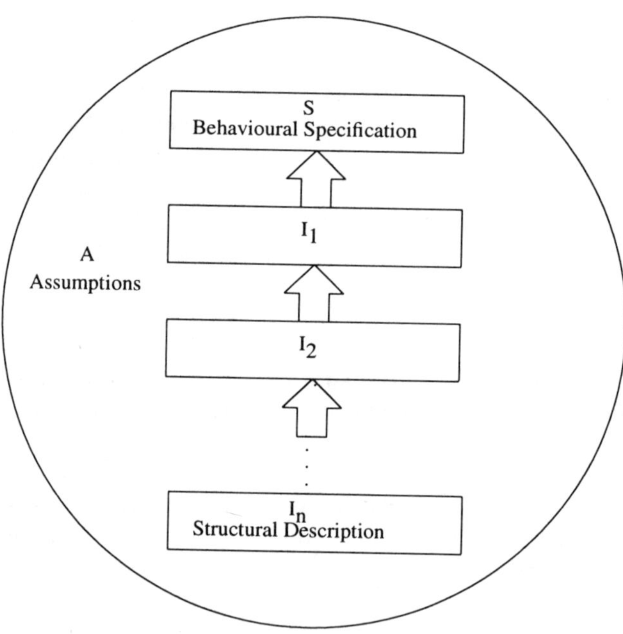

Figure 1. Proof hierarchy

As a whole the verification effort logically entails proof that under assumptions A, if I_1, is shown to implement a specification S, and that I_2 implements I_1, etc., until I_n is shown to implement I_{n-1}, we conclude that I_n inductively implements S. In formal notation:

$$\frac{A \supset (I_n \supset I_{n-1}), A \supset (I_{n-1} \supset I_{n-2}), ..., A \supset (I_1 \supset S)}{A \supset (I_n \supset S)}.$$

Ordinarily, the number of refinements $(n-1)$ required is determined by the level of abstraction one chooses for a design's structural description.

In general, formal proof in a design verification context can be said to be a demonstration within a formal theory of the existence of the satisfies relation between a specification S and an implementation I, or between a property S and a design I. Depending on the theory applied, this relation can be classified as one of:

- Equivalence: $S \equiv I$.

- Logical implication: $I \Rightarrow S$.

- Homomorphism: $M(o(a)) = M(b)$.

The relation I **implies** S captures the idea that an implementation is "more specified" than its specification. However, it has the undesirable property that an inconsistent implementation, i.e. one containing a statement and its negation, satisfies any specification since the logical constant false implies both true and false specifications. Using **logical equivalence** instead of implication as the satisfaction relation would solve the problem given a suitable notion of equivalence, for example observational equivalence for process algebra, trace equivalence for finite state machines, or testing equivalence. But then we could not express the idea of an implementation being more specified than its specification.

For a solution the verifier must prove more properties of an implementation than those pertaining only to the implies relation. Such proofs are called the verification of *reasonableness properties*. The choice of good reasonableness proofs cannot be automated and has in the past relied largely upon the "ingenuity" of the verifier, especially in a poorly structured design abstraction framework. However, in a well structured framework one needs only to prove a minimal set of model validity properties to establish reasonableness. For example, if an implementation were described by a formal programming language semantics then the verifier could prove properties such as variables having one and only one value at any time. When a generic structure is used to model a system then the necessary reasonableness properties may be taken to correspond to the conditions sufficient for instantiating the generic structure in a given formal theory. If an implementation specification does not contain inconsistencies, and it logically implies more abstract specifications, then the higher level specifications can also be deduced to be consistent.

The basic semantic tool for connecting specifications and their implementation is a simulation. An important special case is that of functional simulations, which are easily seen to be homomorphisms. A homomorphism consists of the definition of a homomorphic function "o" and a mapping M that makes possible the comparison between a model "a" of the specification and a model "b" of the implementation. Hoare [16] was one of the first to define refinement formally using homomorphisms and many authors have since followed him. There are two practical reasons for this:

- Functions are in general easier to handle than relations; in particular the existential quantifiers in the definition of a simulation disappear making the approach amenable to support from term-rewriting based verification systems.

- Homomorphisms suffice for most of the verification tasks arising in practice.

The application of generic design abstraction constructs defines homomorphisms corresponding to various design abstraction hierarchies.

The features discussed in the paper structure formal proof by supporting a methodology for obtaining a general correctness result, for fault-tolerant systems, of the form:

$$\text{Behaviour in the presence of faults} \Rightarrow \text{Fault free behaviour}$$

where, although the basic relation investigated is logical implication, the relevant reasonableness properties will be taken to follow from the instantiation requirements of the homomorphic design abstraction structures that our framework supports.

3   Abstraction

Abstraction is the suppression of irrelevant detail or information, and also is a key concept in the domain of design verification by mathematical proof. The use of abstraction makes complex system designs more tractable by providing an important interface between a design and the verification objective as depicted in Figure 2. More specifically, through abstraction a system design is translated into a specification logic and design logic.

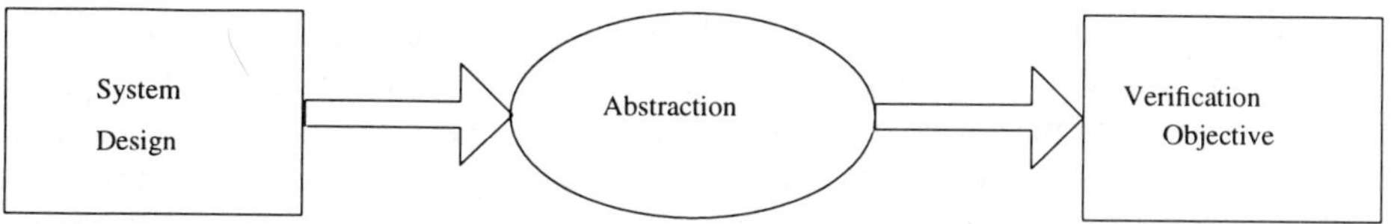

Figure 2. The abstraction interface

Checking for correspondence between the specification logic and the design logic then defines the verification objective. Abstraction also facilitates the characterisation of specific problem domains making possible the development of strategies for solving general problems. This helps to avoid repetition of work by providing reusable structures.

The use of abstraction in hardware verification is well established around the general concepts of structural, behavioural, data, and temporal abstractions. Structural abstraction suppresses detail about the internal structure of a device; behavioural abstraction offers a partial specification of a device; data abstraction suppresses implementation details of a data type so that only its functionality is visible; and temporal abstraction relates different views of time in the specification of a device. We focus on the application of abstraction to model and structure the verification of fault-tolerant processor designs. We define a generic form of behavioural and structural abstraction of fault-tolerant systems that structures the verification of fault tolerance thereby rendering the effort readily tractable. The basic model chosen for this abstraction is the interpreter model.

The interpreter model has four main parts:

1. A representation of the state which depends on the attendant theory.

2. A set of state update functions denoting the I/O behaviour of the processes supported by the component design. Each of these functions takes the state as an argument and returns it updated in some meaningful way.

3. A selection function that selects one of the state update functions according to the current state.

4. A predicate relating the component state at different points in the time continuum by means of the update and selection functions.

The model defines a computing structure with one control point from which one of the state update functions supported by the system design is chosen based on current input and state. The state is then transformed by this function and the cycle begins again.

Different kinds of computation systems can be implemented by a hierarchy of interpretation levels as illustrated in Figure 3. Every one of these levels, except the bottom structural specification of hardware systems, can be modeled as an interpreter. Each level I_i in the hierarchy specifies an abstract view of the system in terms of a set of primitive functions F_i and a predicate Pr_i. In a formal system the specification for the model may be given by a set of axioms, characterising those properties of the model appropriate for a given level of system abstraction.

Showing that one level correctly implements the next higher level is equivalent to showing that the higher level is an abstraction of the lower level. Each operation at a given level in the hierarchy is typically interpreted (directly or indirectly) by one or more operations at the next lower level. Therefore, correspondence between successive levels is demonstrated by expressing each primitive function and predicate of higher level I_i in terms of the functions and predicate of the lower level I_{i+1}. With this mapping one must then prove that each property derivable from the higher level specification can be proved from the lower level specification. For example, in microprocessor verification efforts [10,11], where design abstractions were modeled by interpreter hierarchies,

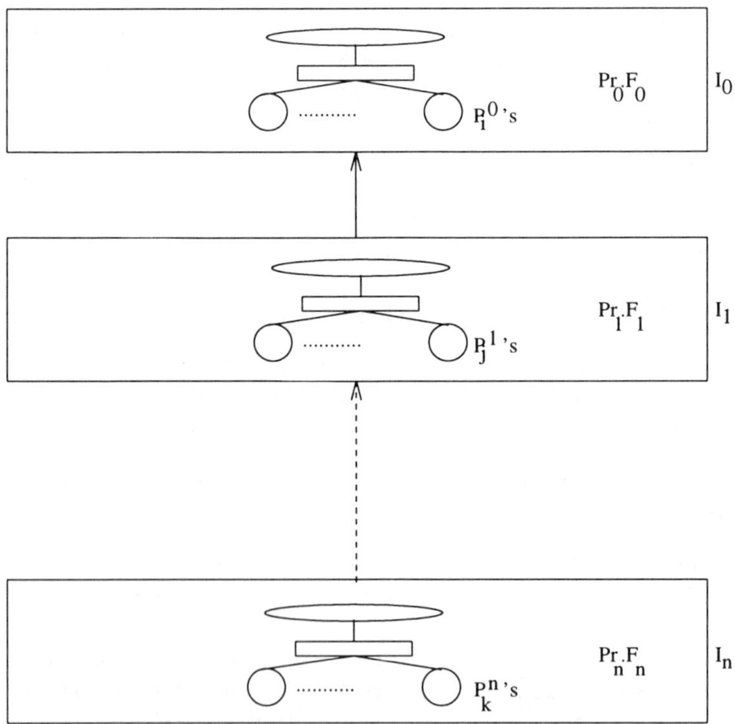

Figure 3. Interpreter hierarchy

correspondence between successive levels was established by symbolic execution[1]. By demonstrating the correspondence between successive levels I_i and I_{i+1}, one can conclude by induction that any property provable from the highest level specification is also provable from the lowest level specification.

4 Fault-tolerance

In order to establish formally the verification objective in the domain of fault-tolerant design, we appeal to the fundamentals of fault tolerance to define criteria which best capture the aspirations of the system designer. We formalise these criteria with general *fault tolerance predicates*. The predicates serve to base verification conditions, arising from the abstraction framework applied, to the problem domain. This has the beneficial effect of providing a clear linkage between the abstraction and the verification objective. The absence of such a linkage often renders the proof steps involved in a verification effort difficult to discern, a fact which inevitably erodes their credibility.

4.1 General criteria for fault-tolerance correctness

In general, given a system design D, let C be a set of fault scenarios under which we desire fault-tolerance and suppose that FTD is a fault-tolerant version of D. Rather than perceive FTD as a homogeneous abstraction of both the functional and the fault-tolerant design, we separate functional and fault-tolerance concerns by adopting the view that any FTD is realised by complementing D with a fault detection and recovery design ftd, for the tolerance of C. Thus, we contend that any FTD can be decomposed effectively into D and ftd, so that $D + ftd = FTD$ holds (where $+$ expresses functional composition). If D is defined as a set $D = \{D_1, D_2, \ldots\ldots, D_n\}$ whose elements are the various designs of a system's components, then it is conceivable that many ftd implementations devoid of a global control structure can be expressed as $ftd = \{ftd_1, ftd_2, \ldots., ftd_n\}$ where each ftd_i corresponds to a component of D, say D_i. Such decomposition enables one to investigate the properties of ftd_i, such as correctness, with minimum intrusion by irrelevant functional concerns of D. Clearly, the correctness of the FTD follows from each ftd_i's meeting certain operational criteria with respect to corresponding D_i's functionality. We assert that the following two general requirements define these criteria:

1. ftd must not adversely modify the functionality of D, the relation $D \leq FTD$ should hold, i.e. FTD be a refinement of D.

2. ftd should mask to D's users occasional disruptions due to C.

---

[1] The term symbolic execution is used here in a descriptive sense for a proof technique which is an aid in demonstrating functional composition by repeatedly unfolding various parts of the specification (or consequences of this specification derived at lower levels).

The functionality implied in the first criterion has to do with the *I/O* specifications of D with respect to its intended use. The term mask in the second criterion is used loosely to mean *ftd*'s ability to contain the effects of C transparently in some cases, or to signal C's presence by executing specified remedial actions in others. Accordingly, *ftd* correctness is determinable by discharging proof obligations pertaining to these two general requirements. The exact nature and number of such obligations is dictated by the character a particular *ftd* instantiation derives from the attendant fault tolerant design paradigm.

The above two general requirements can be stated as follows:

- Allowing for some measure of service degradation, FTD must be shown to implement D in the presence of C under given system failure assumptions.

In the following section we present predicates that formalise the above requirement for FTD correctness. Later, proof of FTD correctness will be shown to be structured by discharging obligations pertaining to these predicates.

4.2   Fault-tolerance predicates

Two features must be present in a system for it to be fault tolerant. First, it must possess some form of redundancy to maintain some system state invariant and ensure that the functions of the system are achievable in diverse but equivalent ways. Second, the system must be able to use this redundancy, in the event of a fault, to ensure that the expected results of the execution of its processes will still be delivered. Therefore, to reason about a system's fault tolerance properties, we should have a formal way of expressing these intuitive attributes of a fault tolerant system. A first step is to notice that these attributes can be expressed in terms of safety and progress properties of the system. The characteristics of being redundant can be expressed as a safety property. On the other hand, the ability to use redundancy in order to ensure the correctness of the final result in the presence of faults can be expressed as a progress property of the system. Three predicates enable us to express formally the properties related to fault tolerance. These predicates are: **correct**, **safe** and **recoverable**.

We define a **correct** predicate as one that is given by the *I/O* specifications of a system and characterises the correctness of the state of a process execution, i.e. a computation.

A **safe** predicate is one that holds in a state such that, as the computation proceeds from that state, and supposing no more faults occur, the component reaches a correct state in a finite number of steps without executing a recovery procedure. Although fault-tolerant architectures offer some degree of immunity from hardware faults, there is a limit to how many simultaneous faults can be tolerated. During system execution, if this limit is not exceeded, the system will mask the occurrence of errors so that it produces no computation errors. If the limit is exceeded, however, the system might produce erroneous results. This requirement can be expressed as a system property by the safe predicate. For example, in an FTD where fault-tolerance is provided by voting distributed redundant processing, proofs associated with the safety predicate can be expressed in a conditional form to account for this limited tolerance. The main results can be abstracted by the following formula:

$$W \Rightarrow u = V([r_1, \ldots\ldots\ldots, r_n])$$

where W is a predicate to define a minimal working hardware subset over time, u is the uniprocessor model's system (i.e. D) results, $r_1, \ldots, r_n$ are the results of the replicated processors, and V is a function that selects the properly voted values at each step. Thus, as long as the system hardware does not experience a flood of component faults, the proof establishes that no erroneous operation will occur at the system level. Individual replicates may produce errors, but they will be out-voted by replicates producing correct results.

If the safe predicate was true at all times, the system would never fail. Unfortunately, real devices are imperfect and this cannot be achieved in practice. The design of any FTD must ensure that this predicate holds with high probability; for instance, $P(\text{safe}) \geq 1 - 10^{-9}$ for a 10 hour mission may be the goal. This provides a vital connection between the system reliability model and the formal correctness proofs. The proofs conditionally establish that system output is not erroneous as long as **safe** holds, and the reliability model predicts that **safe** R will hold with adequately high probability.

A correct state is also safe, but a safe state is not necessarily correct. A fault may cause a component to go from a correct state to a state that is safe, but not correct. A component passing through safe but not correct states will reach a state that would be reached in case of no faults, or to a different one that also meets the system specification.

The **recoverable** predicate expresses the profitable utilisation of redundancy. A recoverable state is one that even when partially contaminated by faults is still healthy enough (due to redundancy) to be restored to a safe or correct state through a recovery procedure. A non-recoverable state is one that is so contaminated that it cannot be restored. A component that reaches a non-recoverable state because of faults will fail because there is insufficient redundancy.

The state traversal represented by the transitions $c_1, c_2, \ldots, c_8, \ldots$ in Figure 4 typifies a computation with no faults. A computation in which a fault causes a safe state to be reached is characterised by the transitions: $c_1, \ldots, c_4, s_1, s_2, s_3, c_6, \ldots, c_9, \ldots$, and $c_1, \ldots\ldots, c_4, s_1, s_2, s_3, s_4, c_8, c_9, \ldots$ The transitions: $c_1, \ldots, c_3, r_1, s_1, \ldots\ldots$, depict a computation in which a fault causes a recoverable, but not safe, state to be reached. An explicit recovery action brings the system back to a safe state. The states, $c_1, \ldots, c_3, r_1, c_4, \ldots$, represent a computation in which a fault causes a recoverable but not safe state to be reached, and where an explicit recovery action brings the system back to a correct state. Finally, a computation

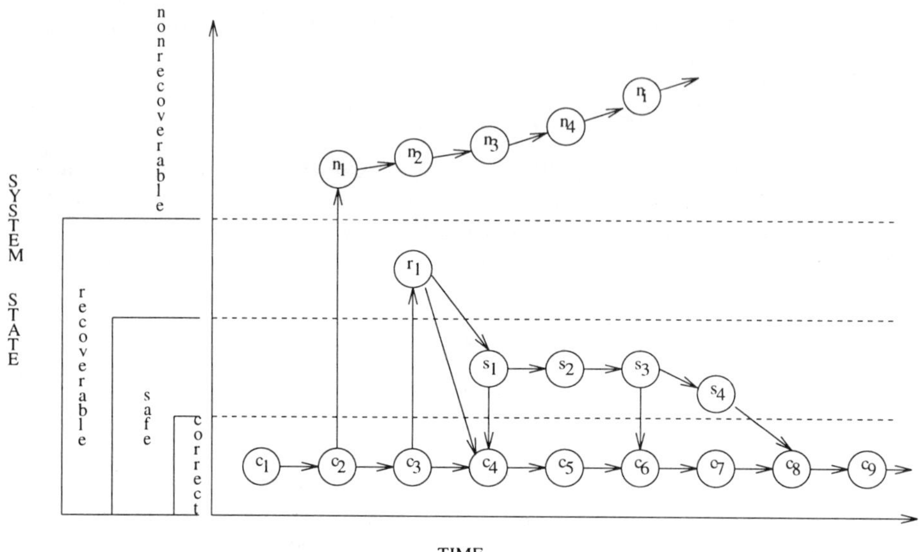

Figure 4. System state transitions in the absence or presence of faults

in which a fault causes a non-recoverable state to be reached is shown by the state traversal: $c_1, c_2, n_1, n_2, n_3, \ldots$ Here the computation does not converge to any one of recoverable, safe or correct state, even if a recovery action is attempted. This corresponds to system failure.

The properties *degrades-to* and *upgrades-to* formally capture the dynamic behaviour of process execution with respect to the predicates we just defined. A transition from recoverable to safe, or from recoverable to correct, is expressed by upgrades-to. A transition from correct to safe, from correct to recoverable, or from safe to recoverable, is expressed by degrades-to.

Assuming that a system initial state is valid, the predicates correct, safe and consequently recoverable hold. It follows, therefore, that correct and safe are invariant in the absence of faults.

Given the predicates correct, safe and recoverable, we assert that a system is fault tolerant with respect to a given set of faults if, when executing elements of its process set (provided that all fault occuring are from the set) the following properties hold:

- Invariant recoverable.

- Recoverable upgrades-to safe.

The first property, *Invariant recoverable*, states that the predicate *recoverable* always holds during the computation assuming it holds in the initial state. If a fault occurs while the computation is in a correct or safe state, the resulting state will be recoverable under the following failure hypothesis: that if a fault occurrence degrades the system to a state where the predicate *Recoverable and not safe* holds, either no additional faults occur until a recovery procedure upgrades the state to safe or correct, or recoverable still holds.

The second property, *Recoverable upgrades-to safe*, states that during the course of computations *safe* eventually holds after a fault degrades the system to a state where *Recoverable and not safe* holds. This property ensures that some recovery procedure is executed to upgrade a recoverable state to a safe or correct one.

Proof that a system satisfies the general FTD correctness criteria is structured by discharging obligations pertaining to these two properties and is achieved by case analysis on fault type.

5 Interpreters and fault-tolerant design

An important property of the interpreter view of a system adopted earlier in our discussion is that it enables one to reason about system processes individually as elements of a set, whereby, interactions can be modelled by some selection function. This is especially useful when formalising the behaviour of systems whose *ftd* is defined for only a subset of its processes, those considered critical. One can safely underspecify system functionality by focusing on only those attributes of a system that are relevant to the *ftd* one wishes to verify. The main advantage of this formalisation is that design abstraction and interfaces between abstraction levels become readily expressible in a wide range of formal systems. This represents a major improvement given that, although hierarchical design abstraction is widely acknowledged as being crucial in any verification effort, choosing appropriate abstractions and selecting convenient interfaces remains more art than science.

The mapping between interpretation levels does not need to be complete; such a mapping may be given as a set of axioms, saying only enough about the correspondence to derive the necessary axioms of the higher levels as theorems from axioms of the lower level. In particular, when an FTD is modelled by an interpreter, it can for verification purposes be characterised by a hierarchy of interpreters, where the mapping axioms between levels need only say enough about the correspondence to derive axioms pertaining to fault tolerance properties as theorems from the axioms of the lower level. In the rest of our discussion we refer to FTD as a fault-tolerant interpreter, i.e. an interpreter whose selection function's choice of some state update functions is predicated on the presence of faults.

We now define two terms, *Fault-free Interpreter* and *Exception Interpreter*, that uniquely characterise a hierarchical interpreter abstraction framework for fault tolerance verification.

1. *Fault-free Interpreter (FfI)* refers to an abstraction that serves as the benchmark model for correct fault-free behaviour against which the efficacy of detection and fault masking in a FTD may be judged. The FfI also represents the highest interpreter in the hierarchy.

2. The term *Exception Interpreter (ExI)* is used to refer to lower level interpreters in the hierarchy that reflect the underlying design to achieve fault tolerance, thereby modelling the fault-prone FTD.

As one moves down the hierarchy, each interpreter below the FfI successively introduces additional features in the design specification to procure fault tolerance and expresses a more detailed operational view of system transformation.

5.1   The correctness concept

Relationships among the various entities for the two interpreters, i.e. FfI and ExI, can be characterised by the commutative diagram in Figure 5. For denotational convenience, we have introduced abbreviated symbols for the sets and mappings involved.

Some additional conventions are elaborated next. We will apply an indexing scheme to the inputs, outputs, and states of FfI and ExI. The initial states have index zero, the interpreters FfI and ExI are defined by initial states u_0 and r_0 respectively. The nth state transition starting from one corresponds to index $n-1$, and produces a state with index n. Inputs and outputs are indexed by state transition number, and transitions in FfI and ExI are indexed identically. The function I_e and o take an additional argument, a fault status vector f_n not shown in Figure 5. Its role is to model hardware integrity and its use will become clear in the subsequent formal development.

Given the above definitions, we assert that ExI correctly implements FfI if they exhibit matching output sequences when applied to matching input sequences and the relevant fault assumptions hold. The approach is based on state machine concepts of behavioural equivalence. What we want to show is that the I/O behaviour of ExI is the same as that of FfI when transformed by the mapping functions k and l.

Sufficient conditions for the correctness property based on the commutative diagram are expressed in the following theorem which shows that Figure 5 commutes. The significance of the theorem is its reduction of proof effort from a formula implicitly quantifying over all transitions to the proof of several conditions that involve only a single state transition.

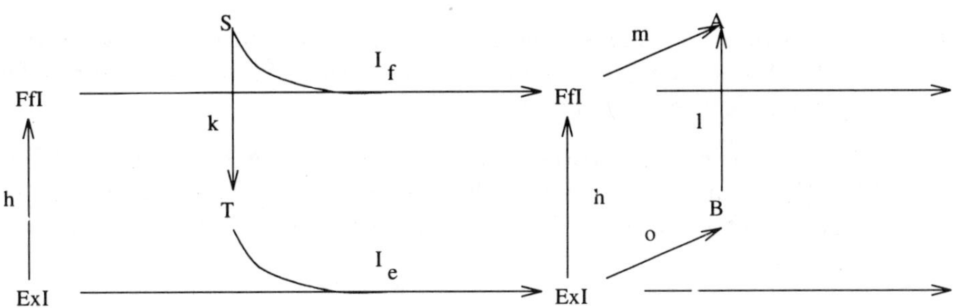

FfI: Fault-free interpreter states

I_f: FfI state transition function

m: FfI output function

A: FfI outputs

S: FfI inputs

k: FfI to ExI input mapping

ExI: Excepetion interpreter states

I_e: ExI state transition function

o: ExI output function

B: ExI outputs

T: ExI inputs

h: ExI to FfI state mapping

l: ExI to FfI output mapping

Figure 5. State transitions commutative diagram

Theorem 1. *Fault tolerance correct theorem*

Let predicate X parameterise the concept of necessary fault assumptions. Then ExI correctly implements FfI if the following conditions hold:

1. $u_0 = h(r_0)$.

2. *for all* $f, X(f) \Rightarrow oppAS, oppAn > 0 : I_f(s_n, h(r_{n-1})) = h(I_e(k(s_n), r_{n-1}, f_n))$.

3. $oppAf, X(f) \Rightarrow oppAS, oppAn > 0 : m(h(r_n)) = l(o(r_n, f_n))$.

The satisfaction of these conditions demonstrates that if an *FTD* gets input similar to that of an ideal fault-free system, then it will deliver equivalent output despite the presence of faults.

- Condition one expresses the state abstraction associated with a given *ftd* technique, by relating the initial states of FfI and ExI.

- The second condition expresses the formal *FTD* property *Invariant recoverable*, by asserting that even in the presence of faults the invariant defined by the FfI is maintained.

- The statement that a correct output is computed in the presence of faults in the third condition expresses the consequence of *Recoverable upgrades-to-safe* property holding. A detailed discussion of Theorem 1 is documented in [17].

This establishes that ExI and FfI have matching I/O behaviour. Although, conditions enumerated in Theorem 1 discretely express the properties which need to be verified about a given *ftd* in general, they follow from some defining properties of a particular *ftd*. After instantiating Theorem 1 with functions used to characterise specific fault-free and exception interpreters, correctness proof can be reduced to demonstrating that these conditions follow from system properties that define the provision for *Invariant recoverable* and *Recoverable upgrades-to safe*.

5.2   Fault-tolerant interpreter verification

Earlier we discussed how a fault-tolerant interpreter can for verification purposes be decomposed into a hierarchy of generic interpreters. Figure 6 depicts such a hypothetical interpreter hierarchy.

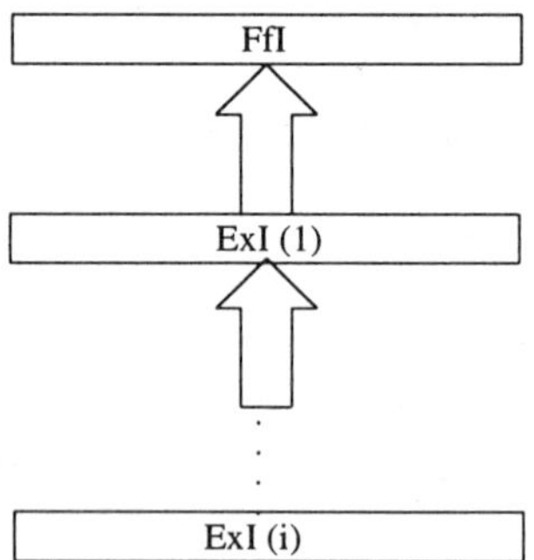

Figure 6. Fault-tolerant interpreter hierarchy

The top level interpreter in the hierarchy, FfI, models the fault-free behaviour that a system user expects some ftd to maintain, and is implemented by $ExI(1)$ which represents the highest level model in an hierarchy of exception interpreters that reflect the underlying ftd. $ExI(1)$ is implemented by the one below it, $ExI(2)$, and so on. Each interpreter in the hierarchy is an abstraction of the one below it. They receive input from the environment, communicate with the interpreters above and below, and use abstraction of the state.

The goal of this formalisation is to prove a correctness relation between interpreters at different levels of system abstraction. In particular, for two interpreters I and I', two state streams, s and s', and two environments, e and e', where $I \leq I'$ (i.e. I is an abstraction of I'), $s \leq s'$ and $e \leq e'$ we wish to show that

$$I'[s'_n, e'_n] \Rightarrow I[s_n, e_n]$$

by discharging proof obligations listed in Theorem 1, so that fault tolerance correctness is established as the following theorem:

$ftd\_correct =$

$ftd\_Abstraction\_correct\ ANDSIGN$

$Invariant\_correct\ ANDSIGN$

$Recoverable\_safe\_correct.$

Where

1. *ftd_Abstraction_correct* requires a demonstration that

$$oppEh.(h(s'_0) = s_0).$$

2. *Invariant_correct*:

$$oppAf_n.faulty(e_n) \text{ is defined}$$

$$oppEk.I(h(s'_{n-1}), e_n) = h(I'k(s'_{n-1}, e_n), faulty(e_n)).$$

Invariant_correct predicate requires a demonstration that ftd supports a function k such that the invariant $I(h(s'_{n-1}), e_n)$ is maintained even in the presence of faults specified by the vector $faulty(e_n)$.

3. *Recoverable_safe_correct*:

$$oppAf_n.faulty(e_n)$$

$$oppEl.Output(h(s'_n)) = l(Output'(s'_n, faulty(e_n))).$$

The *Recoverable_safe_correct* predicate requires a demonstration that the exception interpreter design supports a function which transforms fallible output functions into ones that always compute correct results under suitable assumptions regarding $faulty(e_n)$.

From the description of the interpreter state machine in Section 3.1, it is clear that primitive interpreter instructions implement the redundancy management functions h, k and l by some form of algorithmic composition. In fact, one may argue that the same correctness result may be obtained by reasoning entirely about interpreter correctness without making h, k and l explicit. However, these functions characterise the cumulative properties of primitive interpreter instructions which may not be apparent from the basic model. Furthermore, by making them explicit we realise an important benefit. We are able to focus on only those features of a system which constitute its *ftd* without intrusion from irrelevant functional concerns, and still exploit reasonableness requirements that are well defined for the interpreter model to secure the proof process. The *ftd* correctness result is obtained by a hierarchical proof process. Given N levels of abstraction, and also given that the highest level characterises FfI with subsequent ones representing a hierarchy of $ExIs$, i.e. $ExI(1), ExI(2), ..., ExI(N-1)$. $ExI(1)$ may be shown to implement FfI in a fault-tolerant sense by discharging obligations pertaining to the fault tolerance correctness theorem:

$ftd\_correct =$

$ftd\_Abstraction\_correct\ ANDSIGN$

$Invariant\_correct\ ANDSIGN$

$Recoverable\_safe\_correct\ ANDSIGN.$

From our discussion in Section 5, $ExI(1)$ instantiates the highest design abstraction that reflects the underlying *ftd*. Therefore, given that a *ftd* is defined by elements of the functions h, k and l, it follows that $ExI(1)$ is the highest abstraction in which they are defined.

Proof that $ExI(2)$ implements $ExI(1)$ relies on the demonstration of interpreter correctness, i.e showing that one interpreter implements another. This is done by case analysis on the implemented interpreter's instruction set. Showing that every instruction at the implemented level is implied by the implementing interpreter.

By discharging interpreter correctness obligations the lowest exception interpreter abstraction can be shown to implement the highest, i.e $ExI(1)$, fault tolerance correctness can be shown to follow from the lowest interpreter abstraction. For example, consider a design abstraction characterised by the following hierarchy: programming-level, micro-instruction-level, phase-level and the electronic block model (EBM). In this case if FfI is identified with the programming-level, assuming the underlying *ftd* is not visible to a programmer.

The micro-instruction-level and phase-level would then instantiate $ExI(1)$ and $ExI(2)$ respectively. If the EBM is taken to ground the abstraction hierarchy, the hierarchical proof process should yield a fault tolerance correctness result inferred from the EBM.

The final correctness result obtainable by the above hierarchical proof process is captured in the following *Implementation—_correct* theorem:

$$Implementation\_correct =$$

$$ftd\_correct\ ANDSIGN\ Interpreter\_correct.$$

Recall the expression $FTD = D + ftd$ from Section 4.1, clearly, $ftd\_correct$ expresses the requirements for the correctness of ftd above. $Interpreter\_correct$, on the other hand, shows what requirements must be met for D's correctness. Therefore, in the same spirit $Implementation\_correct$ captures the requirements for the overall FTD correctness.

6 Conclusion

The formal verification of any system presents major challenges regarding the representation of form and meaning. These are especially apparent in the definition of the abstraction interface between the system design and the theorems that express a particular verification objective. Despite this, the literature provides remarkably little methodology to guide meeting these challenges as posed by a range of system designs.

In this paper we have presented a framework within which an abstraction interface between a fault-tolerant design and its verification objective are formalised in a way that uniquely characterises the domain of fault tolerance verification for a class of systems. Predicates which express properties that should hold for fault tolerance correctness have been clearly identified with formal verification conditions. As discussed in Section 3 and depicted in Figure 7, such an abstraction interface serves the crucial role of providing an easily discernible linkage between an FTD and its verification objective.

Within the framework, a general criterion for fault tolerance correctness and a generic abstraction that models a general class of systems have been formalised into a generic theory for fault-tolerance verification. The theory structures the proof process hierarchically so that it becomes easily tractable. We believe that the transparency of the proof process is greatly enhanced specifically for the following reasons:

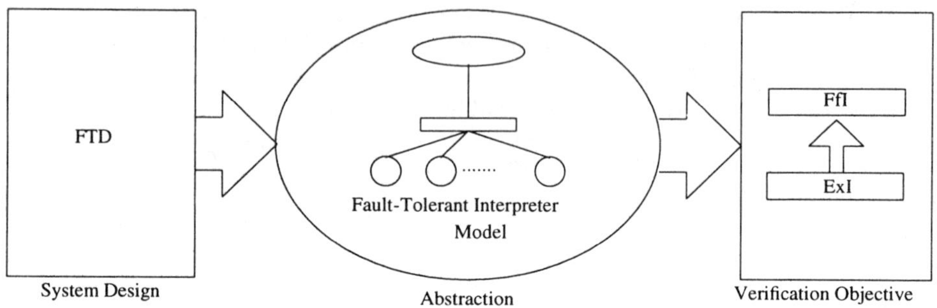

Figure 7. Abstraction interface refinement

1. Formalising well understood fault-tolerance properties to guide the identification of design specific verification conditions as theory obligations. These obligations show exactly what the proof requirements are for system fault-tolerance correctness to be established.

2. Choosing a design abstraction that helps structure the proof process along well established design abstraction views with easily discernible interfaces. This has the profitable property of rendering the proof process readily tractable upto the level below which bivalence logic[2] is no longer viable. Making specification and verification methodical is important to the transformation of what has primarily been a research activity into an engineering one.

References

1. Hoare, C.A.R. (1969). An axiomatic basis for computer programming. *Comm. of the ACM*, **12**, 576–583.

2. Apt, K.R. (1981). Ten years of Hoare logic: a survey - Part I. *Trans. Programming Languages Syst.*, **3**, 431–483.

3. Elspas, B., Levitt, K.N., Waldinger, R.J. and Waksman, A. (1972). An assessment of techniques for proving program correctness. *Comput. Surveys*, **4**, 97–147.

4. King, J.C. (1976). Symbolic execution and program testing. *Comm. of the ACM*, **19**, 385–394.

---

[2] At lower levels of design abstraction where laws of physics reign supreme, multivalence logic systems would be best suited for a faithful representation of behaviour.

5. Gordon, M.J.C. (1989). Mechanising programming logics in higher order logic. *Current Trends in Hardware Verification and Automated Theorem Proving*, Editors: G. Birtwistle and P. Subrahmanyam, Springer-Verlag, 387–439.

6. Camurati, P. (1988). Formal verification of hardware correctness. *IEEE Computer*, 9–19.

7. Gordon, M.J.C. (1986). Why higher-order logic is a good formalism for specifying and verifying hardware. *Formal Aspects of VLSI Design: Proc. 1985 Edinbrugh Conf. VLSI*, Editors: G.J. Milne and P.A. Subrahmanyam, North-Holland Publishing, 153–177.

8. Hunt, W.A. (1987). The mechanical verification of a microprocessor design. *From HDL Descriptions to Guaranteed Correct Circuit Designs*, Editor: D. Borrione, Elsevier Scientific Publishers.

9. Joyce, J.J. (1988). Formal verification and implementation of a microprocessor. *VLSI Specification, verification, and Synthesis*, Editors: G. Birtwhistle and P.A. Subrahmanyam, Kluwer Academic Press.

10. Joyce, J.J. (1989). Multi-level verification of microprocessor-based systems. *PhD Thesis*, Cambridge University.

11. Windley, P.J. (1990). The formal verification of generic interpreters. *PhD Thesis*, University of California.

12. Higashino, T., et al. (1984). An algebraic specification of HDLC procedures and its verification. *IEEE Trans. on Software Eng.*, **SE-10**, 825–836.

13. Kooman, C.J. (1985). Algebraic specification and verification of communication protocols. *Sci. Comput. Programming*, **5**, 1–36.

14. Cardell-Oliver, R. (1990). Formal verification of real-time protocols using higher order logic. *Technical Report No. 206*, University of Cambridge Computer Laboratory.

15. Weber, D.G. and Lubarsky, B. (1987). The SDOS project: verifying hook-up security. *3rd Aerospace Computer Security Conf.*, 7–15.

16. Hoare, C.A.R. (1972). Proof of correctness of data representation. *Acta Informatica*, **1**, 271–281.

17. Musyoka, G.M. (1995). A theory for the formal verification of fault-tolerant processors. *PhD Thesis*, University of York.

Formal Methods for Computer Security[1]

C.T. Sennett

Defence Research Agency, Malvern

Abstract

The use of formal methods within computer security has formed an active field of research for a number of years, but the application of the results of this research in practice has been disappointing. This paper attributes the reasons for this as firstly a failure to formalise security requirements in a way which is operationally satisfactory and secondly an inappropriate use of formal methods for secure system development. As well as discussing these failures, the paper proposes a framework for the effective use of formal methods for the analysis of vulnerabilities and the demonstration of assurance.

1   Historical introduction

This paper is a critique of security policy from the point of view of the mathematical methods and concepts which underlie it. The argument is that mathematical methods are not irrelevant to security but they have been used in inappropriate ways. This has resulted in severe practical difficulties in the form of systems which are costly to procure, difficult to use and questionably secure. It should be emphasised that this is a personal view, and does not necessarily represent that of the department or Her Majesty's Government.

Computer security first began to assume prominence in the 1970s with the introduction of networking. Before this time, computers had been regarded as simply a more sophisticated form of copying machine which could be protected by physical control of access. This approach is still valid for small, dedicated systems, but the use made of computers today inevitably requires inter-connection. The larger the number of users the more effective and useful a computing system is. However the increase in the number of users and in the scope of the functionality has radically transformed the security threat and rendered traditional means of control inappropriate.

Possibly because of its origins in cryptography, the security community naturally turned towards mathematical methods for support. About this time, tools for program verification were becoming sufficiently mature to be capable of being

---

applied to small but real programs. Consequently, program verification was seen as the means to demonstrate that software did not have any security flaws. Formal verification requires a specification to verify against, so adopting this route meant that precise ideas of security would need to be defined. For this it was natural to turn towards the paper world in which documents are labelled with their security level and protected accordingly. The idea of labelling documents to show their sensitivity is extremely widespread and not confined to the military community, so this is obviously a fundamental concept.

The other concept which seemed to be relevant at the time was clearance: that is, a person who had access to classified information would need to be cleared to ensure that they did not misuse the privilege. This concept is also widespread and not confined to the military community: a bank, for example, would not employ a person in a position of trust without some investigation into their background. Thus both these concepts were relevant to security, but the problems started arising when classification and clearance were joined together in an extremely influential report by Bell and LaPadula [1]. This defined the concept of a security model, which in this case used classifications and clearances to form the basis of an access control mechanism for the Multics computer system. Objects in the computer were given classifications, subjects (essentially processes) were given clearances and the access of a subject to an object was only allowed if the clearance was not exceeded by the classification. The report went on to give an interpretation of this model in terms of Multics files in which many other issues relevant to security were also discussed. However, in subsequent years the security model was frequently taken out of this context, in the belief that this was the essence of security, namely a mathematical description of the control of access to objects based on labels.

The thinking behind security models provided the basis for the "Trusted Computer System Evaluation Criteria" [4], a US DoD certification standard, which, because it was originally issued in orange covers, is frequently referred to as the Orange Book. A certification standard is used during the hand-over of a system to operational use and is intended to ensure that systems have the appropriate counter measures to the threats they will be exposed to in operation. The Orange Book defined sets of functional measures which secure systems should have, to meet progressively increasing threats. Associated with these functional measures were sets of assurance criteria aimed at giving increasing amounts of confidence that the functionality was trustworthy. The combinations of functionality and assurance for the various certification classes were seen as meeting typical needs of the day, so that a given certification level could be called up in a procurement specification with the hope that there would be a range of commercial products able to meet it. Formal verification was only required at the topmost level, but this was regarded as a concession in the face of the large amount of effort required to verify a large operating system. Similarly a security model was seen as a necessity which could only be relaxed for the very lowest levels.

This seemed to tie up the security problem rather satisfactorily, but it was not long before some cracks began to appear. The first problem was the realisation that security is not a functional property. What was important to security was not so much the question about the degree of trust needed in the security controls as the degree of trust that the controls were not by-passed. In an attempt to provide a formal approach to this problem, Goguen and Meseguer published a paper [5] defining a non-interference concept which provided a general mechanism for defining lack of information flow. This was a very fruitful idea for the formal methods community because it introduced a way of defining non-functional properties of a system, which turned out to be formalisable within a process algebra such as CSP [6]. Unfortunately, by providing a means to define even more rigid security controls this approach exacerbated the conflict between security and functionality. Much of the work which has been done since then has been concerned with specifying conditional non-interference in an attempt to provide greater flexibility.

Shortly after, McLean [10] published a short paper pointing out that one of the basic theorems in Bell and LaPadula's paper also applied to a system which was manifestly insecure. This is not perhaps as significant as it might appear, but it did indicate that the concept of security was not quite so well defined as had been thought. A further paper by Clark and Wilson [3] pointed out that commercial security policies would actually be quite different from what had been implemented for the military as in this field the integrity of data and the control of privilege were much more important. This lack of relevance was further reinforced by a survey undertaken by Peter Neumann [11] on the basis of entries in the Risks Forum. This is an electronic forum: security or safety incidents experienced by the contributor or reported in the press are sent by electronic mail to the moderator who selects those to be added to the forum. The incidents cover a very wide range but the purpose of the survey was to see how many of the security relevant ones were countered by the security mechanisms proposed in the Orange Book. Important gaps were found. The message was that a certified system could still succumb to the attacks which were commonplace in the real world.

There is therefore quite considerable doubt about whether certified systems are really resistant to the kind of security attacks which are likely to take place, but the problem is compounded by the fact that the security mechanisms which are in place conflict with user functionality and add considerably to costs. The conflict with functionality, and the fact that the mechanisms do not address the threats perceived by the civilian community are reasons behind the lack of success of security products at the higher Orange Book ratings. Originally entered into with some enthusiasm, these systems have had a poor market showing and were extremely costly to produce.

Partly in response to problems encountered with the Orange Book, the European Nations defined their "Information Technology Security Evaluation Criteria" (ITSEC) [2]. This attempted to solve the problem by separating the concepts of functionality and assurance and allowing systems to be certified to functionality criteria combined with separately chosen assurance criteria, rather than the predefined combinations used by the Orange Book. The ITSEC and the Orange Book represent government policy in the European nations and the USA. The ITSEC is a more flexible approach but it is still subject to the criticisms which can be made of the Orange Book, namely that it is too prescriptive about requirements and that the cost of production for certified systems is still very high. In what follows, the ITSEC and the Orange Book will be referred to collectively as "security policy".

The high cost of production has its origins in the assurance requirements which, in effect, mandate a specific development methodology, particularly for the higher levels of assurance. Security evaluation, in which independent evaluators check the software to ensure that the system is trustworthy, was essentially seen as a one-off process. The security requirement would be written down, in the form of a security model for the higher levels of assurance, and the implementation would be demonstrated to comply with this. For the highest levels of assurance the compliance demonstration would involve formal verification, after which the system would be certified and could be transferred into operational use.

This mechanism of assurance, like the formalisation of security, has proved equally flawed. The first problem is that verification on its own cannot establish security. The reasons for this arise from the introduction of vulnerabilities by the particular features of the design and will be discussed later. The second problem is that systems evolve surprisingly rapidly. A commercial product is likely to change within a two year timescale and if each version requires independent evaluation and the evaluation takes a similar length of time, the secure product will always be at least one version behind the standard product. This leads to severe difficulties.

To summarise, the problems with security are:

- It is not clear that the security functionality required by standards like the Orange Book adequately address the threats.

- The security functionality required has unacceptable conflicts with operational use.

- The use of verification for security assurance is inappropriate and costly.

- Evaluation is too costly and long drawn out to keep pace with the rate of change of systems and technology.

The first two problems are a failure in requirements definition while the last two are a failure in the methodology. The cause of these failures will be discussed in the next two sections.

It seems somewhat unjust to blame all of these problems on formal methods when formal specifications and verification are only required for the very highest levels of assurance and are applied to only a few systems in practice. The justification is that although lower levels of assurance are demonstrated with informal methods, the underlying paradigm, namely verification against a specification, is the same. In effect, the lower levels of assurance are cast into the same mould as the higher ones and suffer the same defects as a result. It should be understood also that the practical implementation of secure systems is often subject to compromises which ensure that sensible decisions are taken in spite of what would appear to be required by policy. This is inevitable in any subject as complicated as security, so in practice many of the problems discussed here are avoided. However, where a problem with security policy can be identified, it seems reasonable to change the policy rather than allow operational compromises.

2   The requirements problem

The requirements problem is that the security functionality which was specified conflicts with operational needs and is questionable as a counter to the actual threats. To understand the first aspect, it is necessary to understand two key concepts: mandatory access control (MAC) and discretionary access control (DAC). Both are concerned with controlling access by subjects to objects. To make the discussion concrete it will be assumed that the subjects are processes and the objects are files.

For MAC, it is necessary to have a set of security labels which can be arranged in order. Usually these are based on the national security labels UNCLASSIFIED, RESTRICTED, CONFIDENTIAL, SECRET and TOP SECRET, but enhanced with categories and caveats according to the needs of the project. A security label is placed on each object and this is called the classification of the object. A security label is placed on each process and this is called the clearance. The mandatory aspect arises from the fact that classifications and clearances cannot be changed by the user. A read access to a file is allowed if the clearance of the process dominates (that is, is greater than or equal to, within the order of labels) the classification of the file. The process itself becomes classified as a result of reading files: consequently a write access to a file is only allowed if the classification of the file dominates that of all the files the process has read. The classification of the process is a "high water mark" of the data read, so MAC ensures that once a file has been classified, its contents can only end up in a file of the same classification or higher.

In fact, this is not strictly the case because flows of information can occur as a result of mechanisms other than simply reading or writing files. These other mechanisms, using objects which are not classified, are called covert channels. The more covert channels are controlled, the tighter the flow control becomes, but usually the more unusable the system.

In contrast with MAC, DAC controls access to files on the basis of user identities rather than labels and the access control can be changed by the user and so is called discretionary. DAC has no concept of flow control; if users have read access to a file they can copy it and then set any access control on the copy.

As a result of this flexibility, DAC presents few problems and is usually present in some form or other in all multi-user operating systems.

MAC is the cause of the conflict between security and functionality. Because of MAC, a high security process becomes something of a black hole: information can be sent to it, but it can only send information to processes of its classification or higher. Unfortunately almost every human interaction is a two-way process. You will only send information if you expect something back and you will only be prepared to receive information if you can do something with it. MAC applied rigorously is simply incompatible with any sensible use of a computer.

This fundamental problem is supplemented by a very practical one. Modern applications require an enormous amount of information to be supplied apart from the actual input from the user. For example, a modern word processor requires dictionaries, glossaries, style files and other setting information which is both read and written by the application. For simple control of the display interface alone, megabits of data are written at every interaction. The information flows associated with these sources and sinks far outweigh the information flow associated with the actual classified information and attempting to control it in the same way leads to problems.

A final reason why MAC causes problems is that users accessing a classified system nearly always have the same clearance, which would enable them to see any data stored on the system. The operation of MAC (in particular the high water mark) causes the system to deny users access to data they are cleared to see, which is frustrating and incomprehensible. Clearance applied to processes within computer systems is nearly always meaningless.

MAC thus causes problems with the users, but there are reasons for thinking that it does not cause much trouble to the spies. Neumann [11] classified the problems encountered in computer security under a number of headings as follows.

- **External abuse**

    1. Visual spying: observation of keystrokes or screens.

    2. Misrepresentation: deception of operators and users.

    3. Physical scavenging: dumpster-diving for printout.

- **Hardware abuse**

    4. Logical scavenging: examining discarded or stolen media.

    5. Eavesdropping: electronic or other jamming.

    6. Interference: electronic or other jamming.

    7. Physical attack on or modification of equipment or power.

    8. Physical removal of equipment and storage media.

- Masquerading

  9. Impersonation (false identity external to computer systems).

  10. Piggybacking attacks (on communication lines, workstations).

  11. Playback and spoofing attacks.

  12. Network weaving to mask physical whereabouts or routing.

- "Pest" programs (setting up further abuses)

  13. Trojan-horse attacks (including letter bombs).

  14. Logic bombs (including time bombs), a form of Trojan horse.

  15. Malevolent worm attacks, acquiring distributed resources.

  16. Virus attacks, attaching to programs and replicating.

- Bypassing authentication/authority

  17. Trapdoor attacks (due to any of a variety of sources):
      (a) Improper identification and authentication.
      (b) Improper initialization or allocation.
      (c) Improper termination or deallocation.
      (d) Improper validation.
      (e) Naming flaws, confusions and aliases.
      (f) Improper encapsulation: exposed implementation detail.
      (g) Asynchronous flaws: time-of-check to time-of-use anomalies.
      (h) Other logic errors.

  18. Authorization attacks (for example password cracking, token hacking).

- Active misuse of authority (writing, using, with apparent authorization)

  19. Creation, modification, use (including false data entry).

  20. Incremental attacks (for example salami attacks).

  21. Denials of service (including saturation attacks)

- **Passive misuse of authority** (reading, with apparent authorization)

  22. Browsing randomly or searching for particular characteristics.

  23. Inference and aggregation (especially in databases), traffic analysis.

  24. Covert channel exploitation and other data leakage.

- 25. Misuse through inaction (wilful neglect, errors of omission).

- 26. Use as an indirect aid for subsequent abuse (off-line pre-encryptive matching, factoring large numbers, autodialer scanning).

In the paper Neumann indicates that MAC plays a role in countering many of these attacks, but it is hard to see how. Most of them involve some form of misuse of authorization or masquerading. The whole problem of a Trojan horse is that it has the same clearance as the software in which it is inserted. Nearly all systems with MAC implement a downgrade facility: those which do not have it tend not to be used. Trojan horses can therefore by-pass MAC.

Although some of these forms could conceivably be thwarted by some application of MAC, nevertheless, if the motivation were to counter the threat, MAC would not be the mechanism which would naturally come to mind. In fact most of the misuses are countered by authentication and audit mechanisms, together with special purpose controls to limit capabilities. It is these features which are central to security. The ability to label objects, and to have the system generate labels for output on the basis of the files used in a transaction, are useful user facilities but they do not need to be specially trusted. There are far more important things to control than the labels on files and making the access control mandatory conflicts far too strongly with the operational needs.

It is hard not to reach the conclusion that MAC is simply an incorrect requirement, but this error is made considerably worse by the fact that MAC is treated as the central security property and this is expressed formally, as though proof of compliance with the security model expressed what security was all about. In fact security is not a formalisable concept at all.

There are many reasons for this. The first is that security is a multi-faceted concept. The security of a system involves the people, the organisation in which they operate, the physical security of the computers and communication lines, the logical correctness of cryptographic protocols and many other factors apart from the functional properties of the software. This cannot be captured by one security model.

The second reason why security is not formalisable is that it is a property which can only be established in practice. It is impossible to tell whether a system is secure when it is delivered, only that it has survived so many years in operation. This is rather like the security of castles: none of the medieval castles would have been secure against a nuclear attack, to take an extreme example. But they were never called upon to do so. Some were secure in practice because they had adequate defences to counter the threats which were actually made. The problem with the security of complex systems, a problem which is shared with other concerns such as safety, is that there is always some hypothetical attack which would cause a failure. Consequently security, considered as a property of a system *before* it is used, is only meaningful in terms of a set of identified threats. Formalisation of a counter-measure may be a meaningful activity, but formalisation of security is not.

The final reason why security models fail to capture the essence of the problem is that security cannot be considered in isolation from other concerns such as functionality, cost and risk. The design of a system and the selection of requirements always involves an element of trade-off. It is not the case that security must be provided at any price and if security can only be achieved at the cost of functionality there is no point in the system at all. A practical security policy must allow flexibility in how security requirements are met; the more a policy attempts to be prescriptive about how security is to be achieved, the more risk there is that the system will be unusable and unaffordable.

These are all rather negative comments, but it must surely be true that mathematical methods are of some use. To show how they might apply, it is necessary to consider how methods in general relate to the overall problem of procuring and using a secure system. The approach we have adopted at the DRA [9] involves two concepts called *concerns* and *frames*. *Concerns* represent our attempt to structure the problem space. Each concern is a heading such as functionality, cost, risk, security or safety, representing some aspect of the human problem the system should address. In our experience the requirements for typical information systems can be classified under about twenty of these headings, each of which represents the concern (hence the name) of a particular stakeholder. The art of implementing a system consists in satisfying each of these concerns; the difficulty lies in the fact that they conflict.

A trade-off between two concerns can only be arrived at with a concrete model of the system. Security cannot be traded off against cost in the abstract, it must be done for a particular system, although the system description may be at a high level. Systems are very complicated objects. They include people and the physical environment as well as the software since all these aspects are important to security. Two different mechanisms can be used to structure this solution space. One is to separate out different technical aspects, for example to separate the organisational aspects from the software, and the other is to abstract, that is to leave out detail. *Frames* are used to specify how the solution space is partitioned, thus achieving a separation of technical aspects. Frames correspond to the different engineering views of a system, recognising the fact that for information systems human engineering is as important as software engineering. Typical examples of frames consist of the organisational aspects, the physical configuration, the software structure, the behaviour of the system in time and so on. Figure 1 illustrates how concerns and frames are used. They can be placed in a matrix. If an issue arises as to the conflict between two concerns, security and functionality say, an analyst who was assessing the system would

	Physical layout	Software structure	Human aspects	...
Functionality				
Cost				
Security				
⋮				

Figure 1. Concerns and frames

decide which frames were relevant to this conflict and build a model of the system for each of these frames. For example, the physical layout of the system, in particular the disposition of the secure perimeters is important when balancing security against functionality. Analysis of the model indicates the impact of the concerns for the frame and for the design represented by the model. Building the model clarifies the question "What does security mean?" for a particular engineering point of view. Analysis explores the potential vulnerabilities of the system from this particular point of view.

During requirements definition the models would be simple and at a high level of abstraction. As the implementation proceed they become more concrete and detailed, but each of them is designed to illustrate the impact of the concerns within one particular frame. The frames are usually totally disparate. The frame for organisational aspects for example is a different conceptual space from that for software structure or physical layout. Because of this, it is not possible to make a quantitative judgement on the comparison of the conflict between two frames. This must always be a human judgement. However, modelling within a frame can make the impact of the concern understandable in concrete terms. The advantage of this approach to analysing systems is that it is systematic, it clarifies thought and makes it more likely that the unexpected will be noticed.

The methodology can be summarised as select frames, build models and analyse the models to answer questions relevant to the concerns. Within this framework, formal methods have a role to play in building models and analysing them. However, before discussing what this role should be, it is necessary to discuss the methodological problems associated with the use of formal methods to verify security properties.

3 The methodology problem

3.1 Methods and their roles in the development process

Security policy prescribes a methodology in the form of *evaluation* which is the process whereby the security properties which are claimed for a system are shown to be present, and the assurance, that is the degree of trust which can be placed in them, established. Conceptually evaluation is independent of the actual properties which are being established, although in practice flaws which manifestly breach security in spite of the claims will always be reported. Security evaluation is therefore a combination of *verification* and *validation*, where, for this paper, verification is taken to mean establishing conformity with a requirement or specification, while validation is the open ended question of whether this is a reasonable system to build. Although evaluation is concerned with both verification and validation, the emphasis has always been on verification. The theory has been that security requirements should always be stated and then evaluation consists simply in verifying that they are present. This clearly fits in better with procurement where compliance with a specification can be used for acceptance, but analysis to test whether all security bugs have been found cannot.

Verification and validation are concerned with the system at different levels of abstraction, as illustrated in Figure 2. Verification is always concerned with relating two levels of abstraction. At the topmost level, the design is usually related to the requirement by traceability links (cross-references between documents, possibly maintained in a compliancy matrix). However, in security, a formal security model is seen as being part of the requirement and where formal verification is applied it relates the design to the model. This can be contrasted with safety critical systems, where formal verification usually takes place between the code and the design. Verification between the source code and the system, because the machine code is produced mechanically by the compiler, is usually treated as an issue of compiler validation.

Each of these different levels also requires validation, which, for security, is concerned with the analysis of vulnerabilities. The need for analysis at every level of description is often questioned. Why cannot the requirements be stated initially and then simply verified to be present at each level? The problem this approach presents can be discussed in terms of the Orange Book criteria on trusted path and object re-use, which are attempts to do this. The former is intended to stop attacks in which password swallowing programs masquerade as the system, while the latter is intended to stop programs which read newly allocated but unwritten store in the hope of finding sensitive information. Both these features should properly be expressed at the design level rather than the requirements level because they both refer to aspects of the system design. While many systems do have flaws of this nature not all of them do and there may be many different ways of countering the vulnerability than the particular approach required by the Orange Book. Because the problem can only be stated at the requirement level it has to be interpreted for the design, with considerable scope

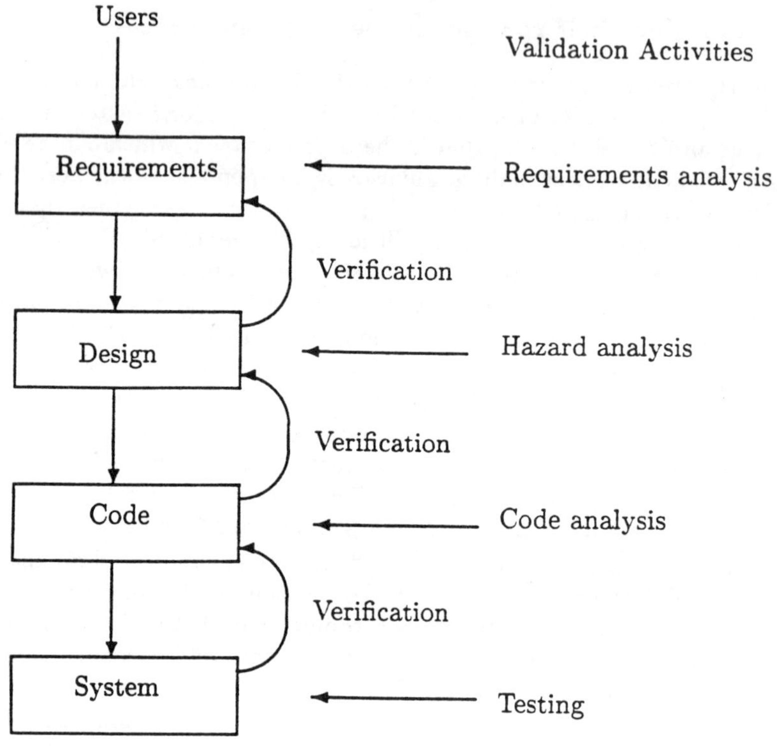

Figure 2. Verification and validation

for confusion and misunderstanding. It is far better to say how the vulnerability arises in a particular design and then how it will be countered in the most cost-effective way. Being prescriptive about designs is always subject to these difficulties, but even worse, attempting to forecast all the vulnerabilities which might be present in a system when the system is not yet designed is likely to lead to gaps.

To summarise, a methodology appropriate for security should contain methods for verification and validation at various design levels from requirements to actual implementations. Each method will be confined to one of a number of frames and they should provide information for other concerns apart from security. This leads to two questions:

1. How does security policy measure up to this categorization?

2. What role do formal and other mathematical methods have to play in it?

3.2 The methodology requirements of security policy

At the requirements level, the emphasis of security policy is not so much on analysis as on the prescriptive specification of what properties should be present and this tends to include the use of MAC. It also requires identification, authentication and audit, but these properties do seem to be universal requirements and cause few problems. This lack of the equivalent of what would be called hazard analysis in safety arises partly from over simplification, but mainly from the fact that the Orange Book and the ITSEC were both seen as being concerned with the certification of products, not the definition of requirements.

Vulnerability analysis is not emphasised at the design or coding levels either, although it does take place within the context of evaluation. This contrasts with safety where analysis at both levels is extremely important. Both safety and security emphasise testing as an important means of vulnerability analysis at the system level. For safety certification formal measures of the degree of test coverage are usually required.

In contrast to safety certification, security is far more concerned with verification than analysis. Formal verification of security is determined by the type of formal model employed. Where the model specifies functional properties (for example, access control models such as the Bell and LaPadula model) the verification method follows that of standard functional refinement. Where a non-functional model (attempting to control by-pass) is employed, the meaning of verification itself has to be specified and the paper by Jones [8] gives one approach to this. For a functional security model, the verification of the non-functional properties is done informally in the form of documentation of the covert channels found in a system. All other aspects of verification (that is, verification of properties other than information flow and verification at levels of description other than design to model) are carried out by traceability, that is informal structure within the documentation enabling one level of description to be related to another. Consequently security certification is very much concerned with specifying documentation.

This methodology can be criticised at a number of points. The most important is that most faults arise at the requirements stage; systems fail because they are used in unexpected ways. Nearly all of these occur as a result of misuse of privilege and should have been countered either by a more selective control of capability or by better audit and monitoring. Because these faults are actually present in the requirement, no amount of verification will ever detect them.

MAC is actually an attempt to prevent misuse; the problem is that it conflicts with functionality and does not adequately address the threats. It is not entirely clear whether this problem should be cured by improved definition of the prescribed security requirements (for example, a more flexible use of labels) or whether the problem is more general than this. In view of the growth in complexity of systems and the novel facilities such as multi-media, telephony services and all the other changes that one can expect to see in IT, it is probably much better to tackle the general problem as security requirements in these systems are difficult to predict and likely to change as the technology changes.

If security requirements cannot be specified prescriptively the policy problem must be solved by focusing on process rather than functionality and raising the prominence of analysis. In the safety world where there is precisely this problem of certification of very diverse systems, the approach taken is to focus on a safety case, a structured document setting out the case for the safety of a given plant or process. The initial input to this should be a hazard analysis of the requirement, repeated at the design and coding stages. Security could be dealt with in a similar fashion. The threats to the system could be related to the vulnerabilities even at the requirements stage, leading to a threat related specification of the requirements. Acceptance of the design should depend on an analysis of the vulnerabilities.

Analysis at the code level does not seem to be quite so important for security as it undoubtedly is for safety. Apart from one or two cases there are very few published incidents which could have been attributed to coding errors. This statement should be treated with some caution as security breaches are difficult to detect and rarely reported and when they are there is usually insufficient information to tell whether the underlying cause was a coding error or not. It should also be pointed out that meeting security vulnerabilities in a more flexible way than has been attempted hitherto (as suggested by this paper) is going to increase the need for analysis at the source code level. A firewall, for example, is a rather more complicated piece of software than the relatively simple coding required to implement an access control mechanism. For such components, coding issues will become more important.

At the system level, testing is used by both safety and security certifiers. Safety certification is much more likely to call for a given level of test coverage, but this would be very difficult to achieve for security because the information systems for which security issues are critical are far more complex than safety critical systems, which tend to be dedicated. Testing plays a very important role in safety critical systems. Its importance in security is much less and it seems to be undervalued. However, to be effective testing must be applied in a systematic manner and methods for doing this have not been developed.

3.3   The role of formal and mathematical methods

From the methodology point of view, the conclusion to be drawn from the previous section is the overriding importance of analysis at various levels of description. At the requirements level, because of the need for readability, formal methods have little to offer. The various initiatives on security models have increased understanding about the specification of properties but have made very little contribution to security. In particular the more comprehensive non-functional models are hard to understand by the specialist, let alone the users and those who are supposed to ensure the security of the system.

Potentially, formal methods have a role to play at design and coding stages when the models are sufficiently well defined to be formalisable and when the description is sufficiently complicated for human analysis to need mechanical support. An example [12] of a very effective use of formal methods is taken from a program of work sponsored by the DRA and concerned with the analysis of cryptographic protocols. In this work, key distribution protocols are specified in CSP, as are the actions of an attacker and the property that the attacker has succeeded. Use of a model checking tool with these specifications enables various protocols to be analysed for vulnerabilities and many have been found, even with quite well established protocols.

The characteristics of this use of formal methods which contribute to its success are as follows:

- The work is in a very well focused part of the overall problem. Although there is a specification of the security property being analysed, it is in no sense intended to be the security of the system as a whole, or even the main contributor.

- As a result of being well focused the interpretation, that is the relation between the abstraction and the real world, does not present any major problem. The significance of the analysis can easily be related to the security of the system as a whole and, in common with most analysis methods, the results in the form of bugs and anomalies found are easily understandable as they can be translated into real world incidents.

- One of the main advantages of formalisation is that the analysis can be mechanised. Protocols are sufficiently complex for human understanding to be unable to probe their weaknesses. One recent bug found involved the interaction between two transactions and the error recovery mechanism to confuse a key server; it is unlikely that this bug could have been found by inspection.

Formal analysis does not figure strongly in the security criteria and instead the main emphasis has been placed on verification. In studying this technique, one of the most interesting topics to emerge has been that verification for security properties is different from standard functional verification. This is discussed in the paper by Jacob [7], but the main essence of the problem is that for normal functional verification, the implementation is allowed to do more than the specification provided it does in fact meet the specification. But for security, doing more is liable to lead to information flows which should not exist. Consequently, standard functional verification is simply not adequate.

But even if it were, the activity as specified in the Orange Book seems pointless. The criteria require verification of the design against the model, both of which involve very high level statements. The functional checks required by security are very simple. Who has ever made a mistake in implementing them? The whole weight of formal methods is being used at what is probably the most reliable part of the development process. It seems that the requirement for formal verification has been driven by the ability of tools to do the verification, rather than whether the verification does in fact offer any improvement to security.

This criticism about the benefit of verification at the design stage can also be levelled at non-functional verification, even though in this case the property being verified can be justified as being relevant to information flow. A flow model has to specify the allowed flows and then show that the system generates only these flows. In order to do this, an interpretation function is necessary to relate the objects in the system to the data in the information flow in the model. The main problem with this is that the validity of the proof rests on the validity of the interpretation function. For any sort of approach to reality, the interpretation function must become immensely complicated and it is not all clear how one could check that the function was an adequate representation. Furthermore, the proof is made very complicated and the difficulties of carrying out the proof obscure the significance of what has been proved. Burying a user under a heap of formalism is no contribution to security.

These difficulties are such that few systems have been formally verified. At lower levels of assurance, the Orange Book criteria specify an informal method, namely covert channel analysis, which is intended to capture the essence of non-functional verification. Covert channels are required to be identified and their operation audited when the bandwidth of the channel exceeds a certain limit. Apart from the difficulty of identifying all the covert channels the counter measure (namely elimination or audit) is not cost effective or threat related. Exploitation of a covert channel requires the introduction of software; surely the best counter measure is configuration control and testing.

The emphasis on verification is also at the root of the problem of maintaining the evaluation rating. Because of the focus on the evaluation of software, there has been a tendency to put more of the security controls into the computer and to regard the certification of the computer as the key element. On this basis, any change to the software can prejudice the security of the system, so evaluation must be repeated whenever the system is changed.

In practice, the security of the system is not solely dependent on the software. It depends on the users, the organisation in which the system operates, its physical surroundings and many other factors. Most of these factors change just as frequently as the software, if not more so. Information systems operate in a highly dynamic world and the context in which a system operates can change quite dramatically thereby affecting the security requirements. This is not a new situation because human systems have always had this fluid nature and security policy is well able to cope. However, it copes by focusing on the rules of operation and by, above all, having a competent person in authority who understands both the operational nature of the system and the threats which might be made to it.

4   Conclusions

The problems with computer security can be attributed to an outbreak of re-
ductionism, a disease to which the formal methods community is rather prone.
The concentration on security models has arisen to some extent from the feeling
that if something cannot be formalised, it cannot be important. There is also a
feeling that formalisation is something which is, in itself, of benefit. Reducing
descriptions to what can be axiomatized is somehow felt to get at the fundamentals of a problem whereas it frequently obscures it and sometimes over simplifies
it.

Security, like safety, is a complex human issue. It is inevitably an issue of
human judgement. The main concern of security policy should be that the human
judgement is properly exercised and on the basis of a thorough understanding of
the problem. Formal specifications can help to clarify, but only when a situation
is complex and needing precision. Formal methods can also help when they
provide the basis for mechanical analysis In this case, formalisation is a route to
mechanisation.

The greatest need is to apply clear thought rigorously. Perhaps what is really
wanted is not more methods, but more mathematicians.

References

1. Bell, D.E. and LaPula, L.J. (1976). Secure computer system: unified expo-
   sition and multics interpretation. *Technical Report ESD-TR-75-306*, Mitre
   Corporation.

2. CEC - DG XIII. (1991). Information technology security evaluation criteria.
   Technical Report, Commission of the European Communities, Brussels.

3. Clark, D.D. and Wilson, D.R. (1987). A comparison of commercial and military computer security policies. *Proc. of the Sym. on Security and Privacy*,
   IEEE Computer Society Press, 184–194.

4. DoD. (1985). *Technical Report DOD 5200.28-STD*, US Department of De-
   fense.

5. Goguen, J.A. and Meseguer, J. (1984). Unwinding and inference control.
   Proc. of the Sym. on Security and Privacy, IEEE Computer Society Press,
   75–86.

6. Hoare, C.A.R. (1985). *Communicating Sequential Processes, Prentice-Hall
   International Series in Computer Science*, Prentice-Hall.

7. Jacob, J. (1989). On the derivation of secure components. *Proc. of the IEEE
   Sym. on Security and Privacy*, IEEE Computer Society Press, 242–247.

8. Jones, R.B. (1992). Methods and tools for the verification of critical properties. *5th Refinement Workshop in Computing*, Editors: R.C. Shaw, C.B. Jones and T. Denvir, Springer-Verlag, 88-118.

9. Rankin, R.M., Hughes, K. and Sennett, C.T. (1994). Taxonomy for requirements analysis. *Proc. of the 1st Int. Conf. on Requirements Engineering*, IEEE Computer Society Press, 176–179.

10. McLean, J. (1985). A comment on the "Basic security theorem" of Bell and LaPadula. *Information Processing Letters*, **20**, 67–70.

11. Neumann, P.G. (1990). Rainbows and arrows: how the security criteria address computer misuse. *Information Systems Security - the Key to the Future, National Computer Security Conf.*, **13**, NIST, 414–422.

12. Roscoe, A.W. (1995). Modelling and verifying key exchange using CSP and FDR. *Proc. of Computer Security Foundation Workshop*, IEEE Computer Society Press, 98–107.

Regular Path Algebra Applied to Non-Functional Properties of Critical Software

Roderick Chapman[*1], **Alan Burns**[**] **and Andy Wellings**[**]

*Praxis Critical Systems, Bath, and **British Aerospace Dependable Computing Systems Centre, Department of Computer Science, University of York*

Abstract

This paper describes a new approach to the static analysis of program worst-case execution time and stack usage. The approach uses path expressions to represesent control-flow in a program, building on an existing formalism that is already used in other types of static analysis. The implementation of the new analysis is discussed in the context of SPATS, a prototype toolset developed at the University of York. The new analysis is finally illustrated with a longer worked example.

Keywords: Path algebra, path expression, regular expression, static analysis, timing analysis, program proof.

1   Introduction

The static analysis of software systems has become increasingly important in recent years, particularly with respect to safety-critical and hard real-time systems [1]. The use of static analysis has grown, but the common techniques remain largely concerned with the purely functional aspects of software. This paper considers the use of a well-understood formalism (regular expressions) to the analysis of non-functional properties, specifically the worst-case execution time (or WCET) and stack usage of programs. These properties are equally important as functionality for critical and real-time systems which often operate in highly constrained environments. A failure to meet required execution time or memory usage in such systems can be as serious as a failure in the functional domain, so static analysis of these properties has been a topic of much recent research [2–4].

Tarjan [5] has shown how regular expressions are a suitable model for the solution of many common problems, such as finding shortest paths in directed graphs, the solution of systems of linear equations, and dataflow analysis problems. In the static analysis of computer software, regular expressions can be used

---

[1] This work was completed while Roderick Chapman was with the British Aerospace Dependable Computing Systems Centre at the University of York

to model program control flow and to solve problems commonly found in opti-
mising compilers, such as data- and information-flow analysis. This paper shows
how regular expressions can be used to solve problems relating to non-functional
properties of software, particularly the execution time and stack usage of such
programs. The regular expressions used to model program timing are built from
a directed graph of a program's basic-paths. This approach offers some level of
integration between the new analyses and classical program proof tools [6,7] .

The remainder of the paper is structured as follows. Section 2 sets out the
definitions and terms used to describe graphs and regular expressions. Section
3 goes on to introduce the SPARK Ada subset in more detail, highlighting its
support for static analysis and program proof. Sections 4 and 5 describe our new
approaches to the static analysis of program timing and stack usage respectively.
Section 6 introduces the SPARK Proof and Timing System (SPATS)—a prototype toolset developed to demonstrate these ideas. Section 6 concludes with a
longer worked example of how the worst-case timing of a simple subprogram is
derived.

2   Definitions

Let $\sum$ be a finite alphabet of symbols disjoint from the symbols $\{\triangle, \emptyset, (,)\}$. A
regular expression over $\sum$ is an expression built according to the following
rules:

Definition 1.

1. *$\triangle$, $\emptyset$ are said to be atomic regular expressions. The symbol "a" such that
   a is a member of $\sum$ is also an atomic regular expression.*

2. *If R_1 and R_2 are regular expressions, then $(R_1 \cup R_2)$, $(R_1 \bullet R_2)$ and $(R_1)^*$
   are* compound *regular expressions.*

   *In regular expressions, $\emptyset$ denotes the empty set, $\triangle$ denotes the empty string,
   $\bullet$ denotes concatenation, $\cup$ denotes set union, and * denotes reflexive, transitive closure under concatenation. Informally, $\bullet$ denotes sequencing of
   regular expressions, $\cup$ denotes alternation, and * denotes zero or more rep-
   etitions of a regular expression. A regular expression R over an alphabet
   $\sum$ defines a set $\sigma(R)$ of strings over $\sum$ according to the following rules:*

3. *$\sigma(\triangle) = \{\triangle\}$; $\sigma(\emptyset) = \emptyset$; $\sigma(a) = \{a\}$ for $a \in \sum$.*

4. *$\sigma(R_1 \cup R_2) = \sigma(R_1) \cup \sigma(R_2) = \{w | w \in \sigma(R_1) \text{ or } w \in \sigma(R_2)\}$*

   $\sigma(R_1 \bullet R_2) = \sigma(R_1) \bullet \sigma(R_2) = \{w_1 w_2 | w_1 \in \sigma(R_1) \text{ and } w_2 \in \sigma(R_2)\}$

   *$\sigma(R_1^*) = \cup_{k=0}^{\infty} \sigma(R_1)^k$ where $\sigma(R_1)^0 = \{\triangle\}$ and $\sigma(R_1)^i = \sigma(R_1)^{i-1} \sigma(R_1)$
   for $i \geq 1$.*

For example, given an alphabet $\sum = \{a,\ b,\ c,\ d\}$, a regular expression R over $\sum$ could be:

$$R = (a \cup b) \bullet d \bullet c^*$$

Members of the set $\sigma(R)$ include the strings: *ad, bd, adc, bdc, adcc, adccc, bdcc, bdccc*, and so on.

Two regular expressions R_1 and R_2 are **equivalent** if $\sigma(R_1) = \sigma(R_2)$. A regular expression R is **simple** if $R = \emptyset$ or R does not contain $\emptyset$ as a subexpression.

Let $G = (N,\ E,\ s,\ t)$ be a directed flow graph where N is a set of nodes, E is a set of directed edges, s is a unique source node in N, and t is a unique terminal node in N. For a directed edge e from a node x to a node y, x is called the **tail** of e, and y is called the **head** of e. A node x in such a graph is said to **dominate** a node y if every path from the source node s to y passes through x. In a **reducible** flow graph, the edges can be partitioned into two disjoint sets called **forward** and **back** edges. The forward edges form an acyclic graph in which every node is reachable from s, and the back edges always have their heads dominating their tails. All paths in G can be seen as a string over E, but not all strings over E are paths in G. A **path expression** P of **type** $(v,\ w)$ is a simple regular expression over E such that every string in $\sigma(P)$ is a path from v to w.

3   The SPARK Ada subset and its analysis

The SPARK Ada subset [8] is a subset of Ada83 [9] designed for programming critical and real-time systems. Its main design goals are logical soundness, formal definition, expressive power, security, verifiability, and bounded space and time requirements. It shares many of the restrictions seen on languages used in program proof systems, such as banning function side-effects, access types, and the aliasing of objects, but maintains many of Ada's strengths such as packages and private types.

To support the static semantic analysis of the language, SPARK includes **annotations** which appear as comments in the source text (and so are ignored by a standard Ada compiler) but are read and processed by the language's supporting static analysis tool [10,11]. Some annotations are mandatory since they are necessary to check the static semantics and security of a program these include annotations to express the import and export of objects from each subprogram and the information flow between them [12]. Other **mandatory** annotations are used to strengthen Ada's visibility rules between packages and so on.

The second, optional class of annotation used in SPARK is the **proof context**. These are annotations that provide formal specifications of program units. In subprogram specifications, for example, the programmer may provide the following:

- A pre-condition regarding the state of input variables or parameters that must hold at the start of the subprogram.

- A post-condition regarding the state of output parameters at the end of the subprogram.

- A proof function which specifies the action of the subprogram.

The expressions allowed in proof contexts are similar to normal Ada expressions extended with logical implication and equivalence operators and the universal and existential quantifiers. These annotations have similar scope and visibility rules to those of Ada but are only visible to other annotations, not to the whole Ada program.

In the body of actual subprograms, the programmer can place other annotations such as loop invariant assertions. Every loop statement must contain at least one assertion. These assertions, in addition to a subprogram's pre- and post-condition form a set of so-called **cutpoints** in a subprogram. The requirement that each loop has at least one assertion means that any program can be decomposed into a finite set of **basic paths**. A subprogram can therefore be modelled as a directed flow graph with the cutpoints forming the nodes, and basic paths as edges. The cutpoint formed by the pre-condition has no predecessors (and so can be treated as the **source** node of the graph.) The post-condition can be similarly treated as the graph's **terminal** node. The execution of a program can be seen as the execution of a sequence of basic paths.

A **program state vector** X is a vector giving the current value of all program variables at any particular point in a program. For program proof, each basic-path P has the attributes shown in Table 1.

Informally the path traversal condition (or PTC) can be thought of as the expression in conditional statements which must be satisfied for a particular path to be executed.

The **weakest pre-condition** of P with respect to R, denoted $wp(P, R)$, is the weakest predicate which holds at the head of P such that R holds at the tail of P. Formally:

$$wp(P, R) = (\text{PTC}(X) \Rightarrow R(A(X)))$$

The **verification condition** (or VC) of P with respect to Q and R is

$$Q(X) \Rightarrow wp(P, R)$$

or

$$(Q(X) \wedge \text{PTC}(X)) \Rightarrow R(A(X))$$

If the VC associated with a basic-path can be shown to be true, then the path is partially correct with respect to its pre- and post-conditions. If all basic paths are partially correct in a program, then the program as a whole is said

Table 1. Basic path attributes

Attribute	Name	Definition
Q	Pre-condition	The assertion at the cutpoint which forms the head of edge P.
R	Post-condition	The assertion at the cutpoint forming the tail of edge P.
$\mathrm{PTC}(X)$	Path traversal condition	A Boolean predicate which guarantees execution of path P with respect to the **program state** X at the head of the path.
$A(X)$	Path action	The effect on the program state X of executing path P.

to be partially correct with respect to its pre- and post-conditions. Another interesting property of this analysis is the **dead-code conjecture** for a path. If a path's PTC is itself contradictory (i.e. is equivalent to false) or the PTC is contradictory with the path's pre-condition, then the path cannot be executed, and so is said to be **dead**. Formally, if

$$(Q(X) \wedge \mathrm{PTC}(X)) = \mathrm{FALSE}$$

then the path P is dead.

Several tools have performed this style of analysis. Q and R for each path are obtained from the program's annotations, while the path actions and traversal conditions can be generated by a variety of methods, such as symbolic execution [7,13], backward substitution [14] or the analysis of fixed-point equations [15,16].

4   Analysis of worst-case execution time

This section describes how the basic-path model of program control flow can be used to model the execution time of SPARK programs. The key problem is to transform a basic-path graph for a subprogram into a path-expression over the path labels. Given such a path-expression, it is possible to map the regular expression operators into the domain of execution time. The use of the basic-path graph also offers some level of integration between the new analyses and the model of program proof supported by SPARK, bringing together these previously disparate techniques.

Analysis of program timing is achieved by adding an attribute to each edge of a basic-path graph which represents the WCET for the execution of that edge. The problem of finding the WCET for a whole graph is then similar to finding the longest path in a weighted digraph. The available literature on longest-path problems [5,17–22] cites many closely related problems, but none of these offered an exact solution, so an entirely new approach was developed. The core algorithm used by our new approach transforms a cyclic basic-path graph (with suitable bounds on loop back edges) into a path-expression that can be evaluated for worst-case execution time. While finding a longest path in a cyclic flow graph is normally insoluble, it is possible given bounds on each loop and a suitably constrained subset of flow graphs such that the nesting of loops can be constructed. The details of this algorithm can be found in a longer report [23]. Timing analysis is then achieved by providing homomorphisms that map the regular expressions representing path sets into the algebras in which the given problems are expressed. We define these mappings by reinterpreting the $\cup$, $\bullet$, and $*$ operations used to construct regular expressions [5].

Tarjan gives a mapping for finding the shortest-path in digraphs. This mapping can be inverted to find longest paths for acyclic digraphs, thus [24]:

Let $G = (N, E, s, t)$ be a acyclic flow graph with a positive-integer valued cost **wcet(e)** for each edge e. A longest path from a node v to a node w is a path $p = e_1, e_2, \cdots, e_k$ from v to w such that $\sum_{i=1}^{k} \text{wcet}(e_i)$ is maximum over all the paths from v to w. The **single-source longest path problem** is to find the cost of a longest path from s to t.

Two mappings are used to solve this problem, as shown below. The *cost* mapping yields the maximum cost (i.e. the cost of the longest path) of the given path-expression. The *lp* mapping yields a sequence of symbols that form a longest path in the given path expression. We first define the mappings for atomic regular expressions:

Definition 2.

$$cost\ (\triangle) = 0,\ lp(\triangle) = \triangle$$

$$cost\ (\emptyset) = -\infty,\ lp(\emptyset) = NOPATH.$$

The cost of a single edge is formed from the sum of the WCET for the machine instructions and the list of subprogram calls executed by that edge. For a basic path e which makes K subprogram calls, its cost and lp mappings are:

$$cost\ (e) = wcet(e) + \sum_{i=1}^{K}\ cost\ (PathExpression\ (CallName_i))$$

$$lp(e) = e$$

assuming that subprograms are identified by some unique, unambiguous identifier CallName and wcet(e) is the worst-case execution time of the machine instruc-

tions of path e. The mappings for the various regular expression operators can now be defined:

$$cost\ (P_1 \cup P_2) = \max\{cost\ (P_1),\ cost\ (P_2)\}$$

$$lp(P_1 \cup P_2) =\ \textit{if cost}\ (P_1) \geq\ cost\ (P_2)\ \textit{then}\ lp(P_1)\ \textit{else}\ lp(P_2)$$

$$cost\ (P_1 \bullet P_2) =\ cost\ (P_1) +\ cost\ (P_2)$$

$$lp(P_1 \bullet P_2) = lp(P_1) \bullet lp(P_2).$$

Instead of the simple repetition operator *, the path expressions built by the new algorithm include a **bounded iteration** operator, denoted #. This operator takes a path expression on its left and a pair of integer-valued expressions on its right. These expressions represent the lower and upper values of an implicit integer counter associated with each program loop. Its mapping into the domain of WCET analysis is as follows:

$$\text{cost}\ (P_1 \# (L, U)) = \sum_{i=L}^{U} \text{cost}\ (P_1)$$

where L and U are the lower and upper bound on the counter variable i respectively. In simple cases, such as a **for** loop over a static range, the compiler can deduce L and U. In other cases, these must be supplied by the programmer. A similar scheme has been proposed by Blieberger [25] using recurrence relations to specify how the loop index variable changes.

4.1   Annotations for loop bounds

In the above model, the bounds on the execution of each loop were applied to the back edges forming each loop in the basic-path graph. For the programmer, though, it is easier to think of the bounds being in terms of the execution of the loop body. SPATS requires programmers to either place loop **exit** statements as the first statement in a loop body or as the last statement. Note that this restriction still allows the use of **while** and **for** loops. In the case of a **while** loop, the bounds on the back edges are the same as the bounds on the loop body. A **for** loop has an upper bound on its back edges which is one less than the upper bound specified for the body. These bounds are supplied by a program annotation that precedes any looping statement:

loopcount_annotation :: =
    −−{ **loopcount** (bound_spec | **infinite**) ;

bound_spec :: = lower_bound , upper_bound | upper_bound

lower_bound :: = expression
upper_bound :: = expression

Such an annotation specifies the lower and upper bound on the counter associated with the loop directly following the annotation. When only the upper bound is given, the lower bound is assumed to be 1. The reserved word **infinite** is used to indicate that the loop does not terminate—such loops are assumed to form the outermost statement in continually executing systems, so the WCET for a single iteration of such loops is normally reported.

Note that the use of nested loops can lead to a nested summation expression for the WCET of inner loops. The question remains of how to automate the transformation and solution of the sum-series produced by such loops. Closely tied to this issue is the question of how general the expressions allowed in loopcount annotations can be. Allowing any integer-valued expression would provide great flexibility, but would lead to many sum-series which cannot be automatically solved. Some tools have been reported that can perform the solution of symbolic sum-series, for example the Mathematica system [26], Maple [27], or the tool described by Pugh [28].

Pugh offers the best advice on which classes of expression can be dealt with in such summations. His approach can deal with a class of formulae within the Presburger subset of integer arithmetic. This implies that the expressions in the bounds of summations may be composed of the following terms: integer constants, free variables (which are assumed to be just symbols representing constants), bound variables (representing the index variables of each loop), the operators $+$, $-$ and multiplication by an integer constant. These restrictions map naturally onto a set of restrictions on the forms of expression that may appear in a loopcount annotation. The types of expression currently allowed in SPATS are:

- Integer constants.

- Names denoting **in** parameters of type NATURAL.

- Names denoting the index variable of an enclosing **for** loop.

- The $+$, $-$ operators.

- Multiplication by an integer constant.

These restrictions guarantee that the expressions appearing in summation operators in WCET expressions always fall within the Presburger subset, and hence will be analysable with the tools mentioned above.

4.2 Subprogram moding, dead paths, markers, and budgets

Other timing annotations include a **budget** annotation (specifies a required or predefined WCET for a subprogram), the **dead-path** annotation (specifies that a basic-path is unexecutable), and the **marker** annotation [3] (specifies that a particular basic-path in a loop is only executable for a subset of the enclosing loop's iterations.) For worst case timing analysis the cost of a dead path is simply $-\infty$. This sentinel value gives the expected behaviour for dead paths when used as a parameter to the $+$ and **max** operators. Loop marker annotations are processed by assigning a **quota** to each path in a loop body. The WCET of such a loop is resolved by repeatedly assigning the remaining number of iterations to the most expensive path in the loop body up to its quota. Unmarked paths have an implicit quota of $+\infty$. A full description of this scheme can be found in reference [23] .

Additionally, all these annotations may be qualified with a **mode name**-an identifier relating to some particular input state under which the annotation applies. This allows different WCETs to be derived for various ranges of the possible input data. Modes may also be formally specified using an extension of SPARK's precondition, assert, and postcondition annotations. A final **call-mapping** optionally supplies a mapping of modes from calling to called subprograms. The combination of moded annotations and call-mappings allows SPATS to analyse programs whose WCET depends on input data, global properties such as a current operating state, or some other assumption such as a failure hypothesis.

If necessary, both dead-path and call-mapping annotations can be formally verified by generation of the appropriate VCs and path traversal conditions.

5 Analysis of worst-case stack usage

An important resource which should be statically analysable in safety critical and real-time systems is the usage of stack space by an application program. This section demonstrates how the basic-path model of analysis can be extended to meet this requirement via another simple mapping of the regular expression operators.

Before considering the mapping of the regular expression operators into the domain of stack usage, a mapping which yields the worst-case stack usage of a single basic path must be developed. Assuming the stack-pointer is known at the head of a basic-path, the SPATS low-level analyser can determine the effect of every instruction on the stack pointer. This is shown in the example in Table 2. The instructions are shown on the left. The value of the stack pointer is shown on the right, relative to its initial value. Note that the **jsr** (jump to subroutine) instruction is assumed to have no **local** effect on the stack pointer. This code is not representative of anything produced by any particular compiler, but has been contrived to illustrate the point. The instruction are for the Motorola

Table 2. Example code sequence for stack usage

Code		SP Offset	Comments
clr.l	-(sp)	-4	These three instructions allocate
clr.l	-(sp)	-8	some space, perhaps for temporary
clr.l	-(sp)	-12	variables to be used later.
pea	-6(a6)	-16	Push a subprogram actual parameter.
jsr	_sub1	-16	Call a subprogram.
addq.l	#4,sp	-12	Deallocate the parameter.

68020 processor [29]. The stack increases in size towards lower addresses in this example.

From this example, a basic path e can be viewed as having the following attributes with respect to its stack usage:

soffset(e)

The offset of the stack pointer at the head of the path relative to the stack pointer at the entry point of the subprogram containing path e. For paths which begin at the pre-condition node, this is defined to be zero. This definition assumes that all paths from the pre-condition to each node cause the same change in stack-pointer to occur. This is normally the case, since it is common for code-generators to "balance" the stack-pointer along a number of alternative paths, especially those which meet at a loop header in the basic path control flow graph.

smaxrel(e)

The value of the **SP offset** column above with the greatest magnitude during the execution of all the instructions in path e. In the example, smaxrel(e) is -16 bytes.

sabs(e)

The worst case stack usage on a path e in the given mode including any stack used by subroutines called in e. In the above example, this is unknown, since the amount of stack used by the subroutine _sub1 is unknown.

Now consider the effect of calling the subprogram _sub1 on the stack. Imagine _sub1 uses an additional 100 bytes of stack. The worst-case stack usage for the above code sequence is therefore 116 bytes (100 for _sub1 and 16 used by the code sequence at the point of the call.) The worst-case stack usage for the i'th subprogram call in a basic path can therefore be defined as:

sabscall (e, i) = sabs (PathExpression (Call Name$_i$)) + scallrel (e, i) + soffset(e)

where scallrel (e, i) is the local stack offset of the i'th call on basic path e. Now consider the code sequence shown in Table 3.

For this instruction sequence, smaxrel(e) is -12 bytes. Now consider what happens if the subroutine _sub1 only uses 6 bytes of stack. The value of sabscall $(e, 1)$ is therefore -10 bytes. In this case, the worst-case stack usage of this instruction sequence is -12 bytes—the value of the smaxrel(e) attribute. This observation leads us to the following definition for sabs(e). A dead path is assumed to consume no stack space, so a special sentinel value **nostack** is returned in these cases.

$$\text{sabs}(e) = \text{if } e \text{ is dead then } \textbf{nostack} \text{ else}$$

$$\min \left[(\text{smaxrel}(e) + \text{soffset}(e)), \min_{i=1}^{N}(\text{sabscall}(e, i)) \right].$$

This expression simply evaluates the worst-case stack usage of each of the N subprogram calls in a basic path and the worst case stack usage of the instructions in the path itself. This equation follows the convention that the stack grows down, so the **min** operator is used to select the worst (i.e. most negative) stack usage.

To evaluate the worst case stack usage of a subprogram, it is tempting to merely evaluate sabs(e) for every basic-path and to take the minimum of these. Unfortunately, this does not correctly respect the semantics of dead paths. In particular, a sequence of basic paths, any one of which is dead, must have a worst case stack usage of **nostack**. The above scheme does not respect this need.

Table 3. Second example code sequence

Code		SP Offset	Comments
pea	-6(a6)	-4	Push a subprogram actual parameter.
jsr	_sub1	-4	Call a subprogram.
addq.l	#4,sp	0	Deallocate the parameter.
clr.l	-(sp)	-4	These three instructions allocate
clr.l	-(sp)	-8	some space, perhaps for temporary
clr.l	-(sp)	-12	variables to be used later.

$$sabs(P_1 \cdot P_2) = \textit{if} \quad sabs(P_1) = \textbf{nostack}$$
$$\textit{or} \quad sabs(P_2) = \textbf{nostack} \quad \textit{then}$$
$$\textbf{nostack}$$
$$\textit{else}$$
$$\min(sabs(P_1), \; sabs(P_2))$$

$$sabs(P_1 \bigcup P_2) = \textit{if} \quad sabs(P_1) = \textbf{nostack} \quad \textit{then} \quad sabs(P_2)$$
$$\textit{elsif} \quad sabs(P_2) = \textbf{nostack} \quad \textit{then} \quad sabs(P_1)$$
$$\textit{else} \quad \min(sabs(P_1), \; sabs(P_2))$$

$$sabs(P_1 \# (L, U)) = sabs(P_1)$$

Figure 1. Operator mappings for worst-case stack usage

Instead, the correct analysis is furnished by another mapping of the path-expression operators, as shown in Figure 1.

A **budget** annotation for worst-case stack usage can also be given for a subprogram, with similar semantics to the timing budget annotation described above.

6   Implementation and case-studies

The analyses presented above have been implemented in a prototype toolset called the SPARK Proof and Timing System (SPATS). The SPATS system consists of three main tools. The SPATS low-level analyser disassembles the object code for Ada units and builds a timing tree for each Ada unit. This is similar to the abstract syntax tree of the unit, but has basic-blocks at the leaves annotated with their worst-case execution time, computed according to the CPU manufacturer's data. The low-level analyser then traverses the timing tree to produce a WCET in machine cycles for each basic-path, along with a list of subprogram calls made by each basic path, and the path's stack usage. This information is written in an intermediate language to the Ada program library.

The high-level analyser is structured as a normal compiler. Its main function is to read and process the source-level timing annotations into an intermediate form suitable for the core timing tool. The high-level analyser also produces functions that yield the verification condition and path-function for each basic path. In SPATS, VC-generation is currently supplied by a modified version of the SESAda symbolic execution system [13,30].

The "core" SPATS tool implements the algorithms needed to produce and evaluate path expressions and supplies a simple command line interface to the user. WCET expressions for a subprogram are evaluated lazily, with the analysis algorithms only being applied as and when required. Useful results, such as the path-expression and simplified WCET for a unit, are saved in memos and re-used as required to improve efficiency.

To test the usefulness and efficiency of the prototype SPATS implementation, it has been applied to several real-world industrial case studies. These are not trivial, small programs, but are real production code from several existing avionics systems. In terms of expressive power, the SPATS timing annotations are at least as expressive as those offered by the MARS project [3], or by Park [4] in the case studies attempted so far. The ability to use moded annotations has proved particularly useful in dealing with programs whose runtime behaviour depends on input data, or global properties such as a system-wide operating mode (as is common in many embedded real-time systems). We know of no other system that also offers analysis of worst-case stack usage. The integration of the program proof and timing analysis systems also offers the ability to verify some classes of timing annotation—a feature not offered by other contemporary WCET analysis tools. The low-level analyser is currently the weakest part of the system. Its predicted WCETs are some 25–30% over the actual execution times for typical instruction sequences, since it does not attempt any analysis of the CPU pipeline or cache. A more capable low-level analyser, such as that described by Harmon, Baker, and Whalley [31], may be added to SPATS in future.

In terms of efficiency of implementation, the SPATS core tool, even in its prototype form, is able to analyse large programs with ease. The low-level analyser adds approximately 25% to the compilation time for any unit and the high-level analyser is at least an order of magnitude faster than the compiler. On a program consisting of some 35000 source lines, comprising some 1050 unit bodies in 270 compilation units, SPATS requires 18 seconds of elapsed time to compute the WCET of every unit running of a Sun SPARCclassic workstation. SPATS also saves useful intermediate results for later reuse (such as a unit's path expression), so subsequent queries are significantly faster.

6.1   Example analysis

The example subprogram, shown in Figure 2, includes a nested **for** loop, typically found, for example, in mathematical applications. The function TRI_MATSUM computes the sum of the upper triangular portion of a two-dimensional array. This example illustrates the use of a symbolic loop bound on the inner loop. For the purposes of this example, the loop-invariant assertions are not of great interest, and so have been simply left as "TRUE" for simplicity. The two loops

```
type INDEX is range 1..10;
type MATRIX is array(INDEX,INDEX) of NATURAL;

function TRI_MATSUM(A : in MATRIX) return NATURAL is
    TOTAL : NATURAL;
begin
    TOTAL := 0;
    --{ loopcount(1,10);
LI: for I in INDEX loop
       --# assert TRUE;
       --{ loopcount(1,I);
LJ:    for J in INDEX range 1..I loop
          --# assert TRUE;
          TOTAL := TOTAL + A(I,J);
       end loop;
    end loop;
    return TOTAL;
end TRI_MATSUM;
```

Figure 2. TRI_MATSUM example subprogram

have been labelled LI and LJ for reference. For the generation of basic-paths, the function body is analysed as shown in Figure 3.

The basic path graph for this subprogram is shown in Figure 4. The nodes forming the loop cutpoints have been labelled LI and LJ as above. The edges have been given labels a to e for convenience.

The algorithm described in Section 4 yields a path expression PE for this subprogram, as shown below.

$$PE = a \cdot (b \cdot (d\#(1, I-1)) \cdot e)\#(1,9) \cdot b \cdot (d\#(1,9)) \cdot c.$$

Interpreted as a WCET and simplified, this is:

$$\text{cost}(PE) = \text{cost}(a) + \sum_{i=1}^{9} \text{cost}(b) + \text{cost}(b) + \text{cost}(c) +$$

$$\sum_{i=1}^{9}\sum_{j=1}^{i-1} \text{cost}(d) + \sum_{i=1}^{9} \text{cost}(d) + \sum_{i=1}^{9} \text{cost}(e).$$

Assuming none of the basic paths make any subprogram calls, then the WCET for this path expression is:

$$\text{WCET}(PE) = \text{wcet}(a) + 10\text{wcet}(b) + \text{wcet}(c) + 45\text{wcet}(d) + 9\text{wcet}(e).$$

```
    TOTAL := 0;
    I := 1;
    --{ loopcount(1,10);
LI: loop
        --# assert TRUE;
        J := 1;
        --{ loopcount(1,I);
LJ:     loop
            --# assert TRUE;
            TOTAL := TOTAL + A(I,J);
            exit when J = I;
            J := J + 1;
        end loop;
        exit when I = 10;
        I := I + 1;
    end loop;
    return TOTAL;
```

Figure 3. TRI_MATSUM function body with loops expanded

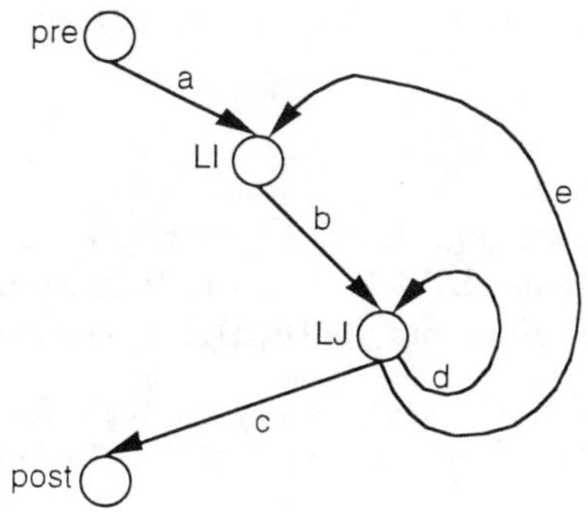

Figure 4. BPG for MATSUM function

Table 4. Edge attributes for TRI_MATSUM

Edge	wcet(cycles)	soffset	smaxrel
a	322	0	-32
b	29	-32	0
c	378	-32	0
d	288	-32	0
e	322	-32	0

Table 4 shows the various attributes for each basic-path produced by the SPATS low-level analyser.

This data yields a WCET of 16848 cycles and a worst-case stack usage of 32 bytes. Further examples of the use of SPATS, the proof of timing annotations, and its application to several industrial case-studies can be found in reference [23].

7   Conclusions

This paper has presented a new approach to the analysis of program timing and stack usage in terms of an existing, well-understood formalism. The use of basic-path graphs offers integration of the new techniques with classical program proof tools and allows some classes of timing annotation to be formally verified. The analyses described in this paper have been implemented in a prototype toolset for a realistic language and applied to several large, real-world case studies with encouraging results. The analysis algorithms and annotation language have been shown to scale well, both in terms of efficiency and expressive power, to problems of this size.

References

1. Wichmann, B.A., Canning, A.A., Clutterbuck, D.L., Winsborrow, L.A., Ward, N.J. and Marsh, D.W.R. (1995). Industrial perspective on static analysis. *Software Engineering J.*, **10**, IEE Press, 69.

2. Stoyenko, A.D. (1987). A schedulability analyzer for real-time Euclid. *Proc. of the IEEE Real-Time Systems Sym.*, IEEE Computer Society Press, Los Alamitos, 218–227.

3. Puschner, P. and Koza, C. (1989). Calculating the maximum execution time of real-time programs. *J. Real Time Systems*, **1**, Kluwer Academic Publishers, 159–176.

4. Park, C.Y. (1993). Predicting program execution times by analyzing static and dynamic program paths. *J. of Real Time Systems*, **5**, Kluwer Academic Publishers, 31–62.

5. Tarjan, R.E. (1981). A unified approach to path problems. *J. ACM*, **28**, 577–593.

6. Hantler, S.L. and King, J.C. (1976). An introduction to proving the correctness of programs. *ACM Computing Surveys*, **8**, 331–353.

7. Kemmerer, R.A. and Eckmann, S.T. (1985). UNISEX: A UNIx-based symbolic EXecutor for Pascal. *Software - Practice and Experience*, **15**, John Wiley, 439–458.

8. Carré, B.A., Jennings, T.J., Maclennan, F.J., Farrow, P.F. and Garnsworthy, J.R. (1992). SPARK: the SPADE Ada Kernel (edition 3.1). Program Validation Limited.

9. DoD. (1983). *Reference Manual for the Ada Programming Language ANSI/MIL-STD 1815A*.

10. Praxis Critical Systems (1995). *SPARK Examiner with Verification Condition Generator User Manual Release*, **2.0**.

11. Carré, B. and Garnsworthy, J. (1990). Experiences with SPARK and its support tool, the SPARK examiner. *Ada User*, **11**, Ada Language UK Limited. (Supplement.)

12. Carré, B.A. and Bergeretti, J.F. (1985). Information-flow and data-flow analysis of while-programs. *ACM Transactions on Programming Languages and Systems*, **7**, 37–61.

13. Coen-Porisini, A. and DePaoli, F. (1990). SYMBAD - A symbolic executor of sequential Ada programs. *Safety of Computer Control Systems (SAFE-COMP '90), IFAC Symposia Series ISS.17*, 105–111.

14. Manna, Z. (1974). Mathematical theory of computation. McGraw Hill.

15. Carré, B.A. (1990). Validation techniques II. *Software Engineering for Electronic System Designers*, Editor: D.G. Jenkins, Peter Peregrinus Limited, 248–255.

16. Praxis Critical Systems (1995). *SPARK Examiner with Verification Condition Generator, Generation of Verification Conditions for SPARK Programs-Release*, **2.0**.

17. Tarjan, R.E. (1981). Fast algorithms for solving path problems. *J. ACM*, **28**, 594–614.

18. Ihm, H.S. and Ntafos, S.C. (1984). On legal path problems in digraphs. *Information Processing Letters*, **18**, Elsevier Science, 93–98.

19. Gutin, G. (1993). Finding a longest path in a complete multipartite graph. *SIAM J. Discrete Maths.*, 6, 270–273.

20. Ausiello, G., Italiano, G.F., Spaccamela, A.M. and Nanni, U. (1992). On-line computation of minimal and maximal length paths. *Theoretical Computer Science*, 95, Elsevier Science, 245–261.

21. Ajtai, M., Komlos, J. and Szemeredi, E. (1981). The longest path in a random graph. *Combinatorica*, 1, 1–12.

22. DeFraysseix, H. and Imsi, H. (1989). Notes on oriented depth-first search and longest paths. *Information Processing Letters*, 31, Elsevier Science, 53–56.

23. Chapman, R. (1995). Static timing analysis and program proof. *DPhil Thesis*, University of York.

24. Carré, B.A. (1979). Graphs and networks. *Oxford Applied Maths. and Computing Science Series*, Clarendon Press, Oxford.

25. Blieberger, J. (1994). Discrete loops and worst case performance. *Computer Languages*, 20, 193–212.

26. Wolfram, S. (1988). Mathematica: a system for doing mathematics by computer. Addison-Wesley, Redwood City.

27. Char, B.W., Geddes, K.O., Gonnet, G.H., Leong, B.L., Monagan, M.B. and Watt, S.M. (1992). First leaves: A tutorial introduction to Maple V. Springer-Verlag.

28. Pugh, W. (1994). Counting solutions to Presburger formulas: How and why. *ACM SIGPLAN 94' Conf. Programming Language Design and Implementation*, ACM Press, 121–134.

29. Motorola. (1985). *MC68020 32-Bit Microprocessor User's Manual (2nd Edition)*, Prentice Hall Inc.

30. Coen-Porisini, A. and DePaoli, F. (1991). SESAda, an environment supporting software specialization. *3rd European Software Engineering Conf. - ESEC 91'*, Springer-Verlag, Berlin, 226–289.

31. Harmon, M.G., Baker, T.P. and Whalley, D.B. (1994). A retargetable technique for predicting the execution time of code segments. *J. Real Time Systems*, 7, Kluwer Academic Publishers, 159–182.

Safety Specification in Deontic Logic

N. Nissanke

Department of Computer Science, University of Reading

Abstract

This paper concerns the formal specification of safety requirements of critical systems. Its primary concern is the means of guaranteeing safe behaviour in the event of failures and not the enhancement of safety by elimination of design errors affecting the functional behaviour. However, it advocates the treatment of safety issues with the same level of rigour and formality as that applied in the functional design of high integrity systems. The safety issues concerned encompass, in general, a range of activities: such as understanding hazards and their possible consequences, stating what is meant by safety in terms of unsafe patterns of behaviour and safety criteria, and developing safety mechanisms that guarantee safe behaviour. In this respect, the paper presents a formal approach based on deontic logic for identifying hazardous system states and for specifying the actions required for safe management of such states. It relies on features built-in in deontic logic for dealing with compulsion, permission, prohibition, states, actions and agents. The approach is illustrated using railway signalling as a case study, which involves a diverse set of safety requirements, namely, fail-soft and fail-safe safety mechanisms and transitions between low risk and high risk states. The static aspects of the controlled system are captured effectively in Z, while safety requirements and dynamic behaviour are captured in deontic logic. Although the specification includes the notions of a controller, a safety executive and an operator as agents, the paper does not attempt their formal descriptions fully, and instead, concentrates on a precise definition of their role in safe delivery of the required service.

Keywords: Safety, Deontic Logic, Railway Signalling, Formal Specification.

1   Introduction

There is a growing need to establish the role of formal methods in safety critical systems as formal methods are seen as crucial for their development. A general discussion of related issues may be found in [1,2]. An earlier paper [3] by us investigated the applicability of formal methods in the safety critical area, with emphasis on safety issues as compared to the traditional role played by formal methods in functional design as exemplified in works such as [4–6]. Our work [3] relied on time history functions for specifying safe patterns of behaviour and suggested several high level linguistic constructs such as,

⟨global_state⟩ **prohibits** (⟨low_risk_local_state⟩
         leading_to ⟨high_risk_local_state⟩)

⟨global_state⟩ **requires** (⟨low_risk_local_state⟩
         within ⟨time_value⟩)

with precise meanings in predicate logic. However, the notions *"prohibits"* and *"requires"* used there bear only a declarative character and the relevant constructs simply characterise the time histories of the equipment and abstract attributes of the system. This is a limitation when dealing with dynamic aspects of certain important safety mechanisms. Maibaum [7] attributes limitations of this nature to confusion between descriptions of change and descriptions of behaviours.

Undeniably, the notions *prohibits* and *requires* are deontic concepts, and therefore, deontic logic [8] appears to be a more natural framework for specification of safety requirements. The formulation of deontic logic given in [7] is designed to capture the dynamic aspects such as actions, agents and participants involved in actions. The most important features of deontic logic are the notions of obligation, permission and prohibition. These make it possible to demand from different agents varying degrees of commitment to actions.

An important contribution of [3] is a classification of safety related timing requirements, enabling a systematic approach to their formalisation. These include the following safety related timing constraints. Function related admissible risks (*"calculated risks"* or *operational risks*), function related prohibitive risks (*operational failure prevention* in transitions from a low risk state to a high risk state), failure averting timing requirements (for averting *imminent failures* through transitions from a high risk state to a low risk state), and failure handling timing requirements (*amid failures or hazards*). In any safety critical application, the responsibility for the above different safety functions must be clearly delegated to its various subsystems, namely the controlling system providing the required service, the environment involving sensors and actuators, and the safety executive responsible for the overall safety. A clear advantage of deontic logic is that these responsibilities may be made explicit and identified with specific equipment and subsystems.

This paper uses as a case study a popular choice in safety related research, namely railway signalling. One of its objectives is to establish the applicability of deontic logic and its advantages. Among the previous studies involving railways, the work [9] originating from the FOREST project is especially relevant since it uses practically the same framework, that is modal action logic [10]. Our work differs from the latter by its emphasis on the approach instead of the method. The distinction made here between *approach* and *method* is that the former is problem-oriented while the latter is tool-oriented. Our concern is the development of a systematic approach to the analysis and specification of safety requirements. Furthermore, it illustrates how a specialised system of logic such as deontic logic may be used in conjunction with more familiar notations such as *Z* and VDM. An advantage of this is the resulting layered approach to specification, facilitating the separation of concerns and the possibility of staged and flexible deployment of expertise. These are strategies of practical importance for dealing with complexities of large real-life systems. The functional requirements may be developed first as in [4,5]. This may then be augmented with a separate safety specification as advocated in this paper. Our work has greatly benefited from the seminal work by Leveson [11]. The latter work and the work in [12] use Petri nets and deal with safety issues relevant to railway (rail-road and rail-rail) crossings. Relying similarly on railways as an illustration, the work in [13] introduces a synchronous data-flow language LUSTRE for dealing with safety issues, again with greater emphasis on the method. The work in [14] also concerns railway signalling and discusses an efficient form of local reasoning about safety issues based on Formal Concept Analysis.

2 Deontic logic and extensions

This section provides a brief outline of the deontic concepts used in this paper. The reader is referred to [8] for a more detailed account.

Deontic logic allows reasoning within a single framework about three kinds of information: static information as it is dealt with in the prevalent specification languages such as Z and VDM, action descriptions as it is done, for example, in [15,16] and action prescriptions unique to deontic logic. Safety critical systems involve all three, and hence, deontic logic offers considerable versatility for dealing with different aspects of a system in a uniform manner or in isolation depending on the need.

Although there are different variants of deontic logic, we rely exclusively on that due to Maibaum et al. as documented in [7]. It consists of the following objects and conceptual categories:

AGT	A type. Its values correspond to the agents bringing about the occurrence of actions, events or transitions.
ACT	A type. Its values correspond to actions, events and transitions.
$[\cdots, \cdots]\cdots$	A logical connective involving an agent, an action and a state. Informally, $[a, e]\varphi$ means that "the action e brought about by the agent a results in the state described by the predicate φ".
PER$(\cdots, \cdots)$	A predicate symbol. PER(a, e) means informally that "bringing about the action e by the agent a is permitted".

OBL($\cdots$, $\cdots$)   A predicate symbol. OBL(a, e) means informally that "the agent a is obliged to bring about the action e".

Per($\cdots$, $\cdots$)   A predicate symbol. Per(a, φ) means informally that "bringing about the state φ by the agent a is permitted".

Obl($\cdots$, $\cdots$)   A predicate symbol. Obl(a, φ) means informally that "the agent a is obliged to bring about the state φ".

Maibaum suggests two different frameworks for normative specification of systems, that is Deontic Action Logic (DAL) and an improved first-order modal logic for DAL (MDAL - an acronym used in this paper). In addition to the formal semantics given in [7], MDAL has a number of interesting features useful for purposes of system specification, and in particular, the notions of reference and transition events and separation of reasoning about the system state and about the consequences of specification. The reference events typically represent initialisation states of components, but in safety critical applications, they may be used additionally for referring to failure states requiring the launch of recovery measures.

This work deviates from Maibaum [7] with respect to the style of presentation of *static information* about the system and *action descriptions* by making limited use of the Z notation [17]. Our style of presentation may be related easily to that of Maibaum [7], but it is not done here for brevity.

In order to deal with failure on the part of any agent to honour its obligations within a specified time limit as well as to impose such time limits, we extend the logic with two additional predicate symbols. Our approach is based on a simple treatment of time based on its clock representations and differs from that given in [10,18] based on a continuous metric for time. Using an appropriate function (a function that conforms with monotonicity and uniformity of clock times) from "true" real time (say, in real number representation) to its clock representations, we avoid the complexities associated with states applicable to particular instances in real time. Such an approach is especially relevant to distributed systems incorporating autonomous clocks. The first predicate we introduce, $Persist\_min(e, t)$, has the informal meaning that the obligation for transition or action e persists continuously at least as long as t time units from the time when the obligation first ocurred. The second predicate is $Persist\_max(e, t)$, having the informal meaning that the obligation for transition or action e persists continuously at most for t time units since it first ocurred. One may attempt a formal definition of these predicates in the following manner relying on the semantic notions in Maibaum [7]. Maibaum introduces Kripke style semantics using, among others, a pair ($\mathcal{W}$, $\mathcal{M}$) and two relations $\mathcal{O}$ and $\mathcal{P}$. In the case of transition events, $\mathcal{M}$ is a function which takes an event and a state and returns another (successor) state. Thus, for any transition event e, $\mathcal{M}(e)$ is the successor function on the system state space $\mathcal{W}$. In the case of reference events (for example initialisation), $\mathcal{M}$ is a function which takes such an event and returns a state. $\mathcal{O}$ and $\mathcal{P}$ are each a relation from the set of state transitions or events to $\mathcal{W}$, denoting respectively the obligatory and permissive transitions in each state. For example, given an event e and a state w, $(e, w) \in \mathcal{P}$ if and only if the occurrence of e is permitted in the state w.

We adopt the above framework by extending it with a distinguished regular repetitive transition called *tick*, which is a special (central) clock event having no effect on its own on the system state. Letting Δ be the clock granularity between successive occurrences of *tick*, we define $Persist\_min(e,t)$ and $Persist\_max(e,t)$ as:

$Persist\_min(e,t)$ iff $e \neq tick$ and there exists a natural number n: $\mathbb{N}$ such that $(n-1) \times \Delta < t \leq n \times \Delta, (e, w') \notin \mathcal{O}$ for all predecessor states w' of the given state w and $(e, \mathcal{M}^i(tick)(w)) \in \mathcal{O}$ for every $i \in \{0, \cdots, n-1\}$.

$Persist\_max(e,t)$ iff $e \neq tick$ and there exist two natural numbers m, n : $\mathbb{N}$ such that $m \leq n$ and $(n-1) \times \Delta < t \leq n \times \Delta, (e, w') \notin \mathcal{O}$ for all predecessor states w' of w, $(e, \mathcal{M}^i(tick)(w)) \in \mathcal{O}$ for every $i \in \{0, \cdots, m\}$ and $(e, \mathcal{M}^{n+1}(tick)(w)) \notin \mathcal{P}$.

where $\mathcal{M}^i(e)$ is i-th iteration of $\mathcal{M}(e)$.

3   A high level system view

Many safety critical systems delegate specific safety functions to different subsystems or equipment. Provision of safety therefore depends on how and whether these responsibilities are discharged by the agents concerned. Safety specification in systems of deontic logic such as DAL can account for the role of agents in addition to the normative aspects of system behaviour.

We view any safety critical system as consisting of a controlled system that comprises sensors and actuators and a "safety critical controller" that comprises a conventional controlling system and a "safety executive". The safety executive may be seen as that component of the system with the ultimate responsibility for overseeing and ensuring the safety of the overall system. In this connection, we introduce three constants of type AGT to our specification. Namely,

> contlr   representing the controlling system,
> exec   representing the safety executive and
> optr   representing the operator.

These are just identifiers and the definition of their internal structure is not absolutely necessary here.

We refer to inputs and outputs of the controlling system respectively as *sensor data* and *control signals*. Although the majority of states of the equipment may be associated with the values of appropriate sensor data and control signals, there are states associated with other indirect attributes of equipment which do not relate directly to sensor data and control signals. In relation to our case study, these concern the notions of *subroutes* and *routes*.

Since the safety critical system incorporates a number of agents responsible for different safety functions and because of the vulnerability of agents as well as equipment to failure, we allow these agents to have potentially different views about any given item at a given instance in time. These views may be factually inconsistent with one another at the times of component or system failure, but the intention is to ensure that the information held within each agent is consistent with the overall safety objectives. With different views of the state of any equipment or the complete system in mind, we use the notation s_a to represent a's view of the object or the system s, a being an appropriate agent. In the absence of failures, these views must be factually consistent with one another, perhaps, to a permitted tolerance to account for different communication delays.

4   Description of system state and behaviour

The remainder of the paper illustrates the approach using the case study on railway signalling. This involves a detailed description of the system states, which is carried out in the Z notation [17]. The use of Z is limited to the introduction of state variables and specification of state invariants. The rest is conducted in deontic logic.

The signalling system detects the presence of trains on the track and facilitates the correct movement of trains. It consists of two major components. The *permanent way* comprises the tracks, the points and the signals on the ground as shown in Figure 1. The second component is the *interlocking*, which is a safety mechanism designed to prevent system operation resulting in hazardous circumstances or danger. It also monitors the permanent way in order to ensure a safe state.

4.1   Tracks

Our abstraction of track sections (or *track circuits*) incorporates only some means of their identification using the elements of a type Trk_Id and a flag indicating whether a given track is *occupied* or *clear*. Train movements activate the relays located on each track circuit, and thereby, enable the relays to detect the state of tracks. This information is accessible to the controlling system.

```
┌─ Track ────────────────────────────────────────────────
│   id          : Trk_Id
│   occupancy   : clear | occupied
└────────────────────────────────────────────────────────
```

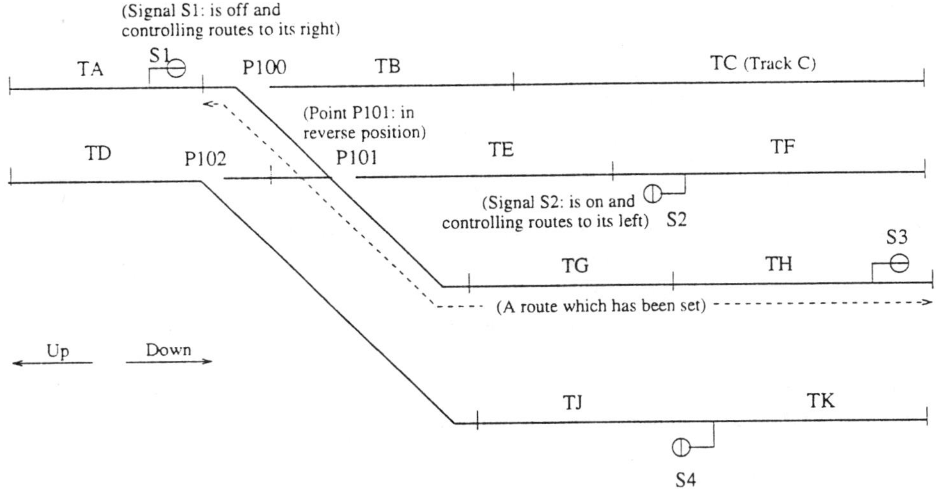

Figure 1. Sketch of a permanent way

Since this paper does not cover the full specification, we need a general statement
as the one below on the uniqueness of tracks:

$$\forall t_1, t_2 : Track \bullet t_1 \cdot id = t_2 \cdot id \Rightarrow t_1 \cdot occupancy = t_2 \cdot occupancy$$

where, for example, $t \cdot occupancy$ denotes the value of the state variable *occupancy*
of the track t.

4.2   Signals

This section deals with the structural description of railway signals. Signals
are the standard means for giving instructions to drivers on train movements. A
signal displays typically three possible aspects with the obvious meanings. Thus,
the general state of signals may be specified as,

```
┌─ Signal ─────────────────────────────────────────────
│   aspect           : red | green | amber | unlit
│   lamp             : in | out
│   location         : Track × Track
│   berth, overlap   : Track
├───────────────────────────────────────────────────────
│   location = (berth, overlap)
│   lamp = out ⇒ aspect = unlit
└───────────────────────────────────────────────────────
```

Using the above as a type for all possible signals, the following introduces certain predicates about the states of interest of any given signal $s : Signal$,

$$\forall s : Signal \bullet$$
$$signalOn(s) \overset{def}{\Leftrightarrow} s.aspect = \mathsf{red}$$
$$signalOff(s) \overset{def}{\Leftrightarrow} s.aspect \in \{\mathsf{green}, \mathsf{amber}\}$$
$$failedSig(s) \overset{def}{\Leftrightarrow} s.lamp = \mathsf{out}.$$

In strict interpretation of the specification, the predicate $failedSig(s)$ above can be true if and only if the signal s has been turned off. In this particular case, however, its intended meaning is such that the predicate can also be true as a consequence of the failure of the sensor monitoring the signal s. This is because we have chosen not to account for the signal sensor explicitly in the specification.

Having defined the system states of interest, we turn our attention to actions and transitions. These may now be specified in DAL as,

$$\forall s : Signal; x : sfAGT \bullet$$
$$[x : turnOn(s)] \quad signalOn(s)$$
$$[x : turnOff(s)] \quad signalOff(s)$$
$$failedSig(s) \Rightarrow [x, light(s)] \quad \neg failedSig(s)$$
$$[x, fail(s)] \quad failedSig(s)$$

where, for example, $turnOn(s)$ is a parameterized event designator. For convenience, we also assume that each transition discharges the minimum obligation expected of it. In other words, it does not alter the values of system attributes (state variables) unless stated so in the specification.

4.3   Points

Points provide the physical means for directing trains at junctions with multiple directions for forward movement. This is achieved by remote control of points into one of the two positions *normal* and *reverse*. These two values are denoted by **normalPos** and **reversePos** respectively. A third possible state is *undetected*, which is an intermediate state when a given point is in transition between *normal* and *reverse*. If this does not take place within a prescribed time interval after issuing the control signal, the point is to be regarded as *broken*. Once the points are moved to the desired position, they may be *locked* to prevent any change in position. The points are also equipped with sensors for enabling the controlling system to know about the current positions of points. The state of any point, again with no notion of the attached sensor, may be characterised as in the following specification.

```
┌─ Point ──────────────────────────────────────────────────────────────
│   trkSet              : 𝔽 Track
│   normal, reverse     : 𝔽(Track × Track)
│   setting             : normalPos | reversePos | undetected | broken
│   pointFixity         : locked | free
│ ─────────────────────────────────────────────────────────────────────
│   trkSet ≠ ∅
│   trkSet = dom normal = dom reverse
│   ran normal ∩ ran reverse = ∅
└───────────────────────────────────────────────────────────────────────
```

The following predicates describe the possible states of any particular point p : *Point*,

$$isFreeNormalPt(p) \overset{def}{\Leftrightarrow} p.pointFixity = \text{free} \land p.setting = \text{normalPos}$$
$$isFreeReversePt(p) \overset{def}{\Leftrightarrow} p.pointFixity = \text{free} \land p.setting = \text{reversePos}$$
$$isLockedNormalPt(p) \overset{def}{\Leftrightarrow} p.pointFixity = \text{locked} \land p.setting = \text{normalPos}$$
$$isLockedReversePt(p) \overset{def}{\Leftrightarrow} p.pointFixity = \text{locked} \land p.setting = \text{reversePos}$$
$$brokenPt(p) \overset{def}{\Leftrightarrow} p.setting = \text{broken}.$$

One may envisage the following actions for bringing about the above:

$$[\text{contlr}, FreeNormal(p)]isFreeNormalPt(p)$$
$$[\text{contlr}, FreeReverse(p)]isFreeReversePt(p)$$
$$[\text{contlr}, LockNormal(p)]isLockedNormalPt(p)$$
$$[\text{contlr}, LockReverse(p)]isLockedReversePt(p)$$
$$\forall a : \text{AGT}; x(p) : \text{ACT}[Point] \bullet a \neq \text{contlr} \Rightarrow [a, x(p)]p.$$

The last assertion ensures that points are insensitive to any action by all agents other than the controlling system.

4.4   Subroutes and routes

Subroutes and routes are abstract (logical) entities founded on components of the permanent way supporting the management of safe movement of trains on tracks. Safety is ensured by keeping track of the states of subroutes and routes in one of the two distinct lock states: *locked* and *free*.

$$LockState ::= \text{locked} \mid \text{free}.$$

The adjacent track sections on the ground are linked so that they form two continuous tracks for train movements in two primary directions running opposite to each other. In British Rail practice, these are referred to as *up* and *down* directions (see Figure 1). We assume all tracks to be in one of these two directions. Subroutes are pairs of track sections reachable in a given direction via a third intermediate track section. The component *subRouteFixity* contains the information on the lock state of each subroute. This is formalised in the schema *Tracks*.

A route is a section of a track in a given direction lying between two adjacent signals. It also includes all other ground equipment lying within its boundary, namely the signals and points, as well as the subroutes. Let us deal with these three aspects first. The signals at the extremities of the route are referred to as *entry* and *exit*, while the track connections along the route as *routeCons*; see schema *RouteSignals*.

$$
\begin{array}{|l}
\underline{\text{Tracks}} \\[4pt]
\begin{array}{ll}
tracks & : \ \mathbb{F}\ Track \\
up, down, bothDir & : \ Track \leftrightarrow Track \\
subRoutes & : \ Track \leftrightarrow Track \\
subRouteFixity & : \ Track \times Track \to LockState
\end{array} \\[4pt]
\hline
up = down^{-1} \\
bothDir = down \cup up \\
\text{id}\ tracks \cap down = \varnothing \\
subRoutes = up^2 \cup down^2 \\
\text{fld}\ bothDir = tracks \\
\text{dom}\ subRouteFixity = subRoutes
\end{array}
$$

$$
\begin{array}{|l}
\underline{\text{RouteSignals}} \\[4pt]
\begin{array}{ll}
entry, exit & : \ Signal \\
routeCons & : \ Track \leftrightarrow Track
\end{array} \\[4pt]
\hline
entry \neq exit \\
\{entry.location,\ exit.location\} \subseteq routeCons \\
routeCons^{\#routeCons} = \{(entry.berth,\ exit.overlap)\}
\end{array}
$$

The components *normalPts* and *reversePts* in the schema below denote the sets of points along the route in *normal* and *reverse* positions.

```
┌─ RoutePoints ─────────────────────────────────────────────────
│   normalPts, reversePts   :  F Point
│   routeCons               :  Track ↔ Track
├───────────────────────────────────────────────────────────────
│   normalPts   =   {p : Point  |  p.normal ∩ routeCons ≠ ∅}
│   reversePts  =   {p : Point  |  p.reverse ∩ routeCons ≠ ∅}
└───────────────────────────────────────────────────────────────
```

The information on the subroutes within a route includes the actual subroutes *routeSubs* forming the route, the first subroute *firstSub* on the route and an injective function *prevSub* on the set *routeSubs* giving the subroute immediately preceding a given subroute.

```
┌─ RouteSubroutes ──────────────────────────────────────────────
│   routeSubs, routeCons   :  Track ↔ Track
│   firstSub               :  Track × Track
│   prevSub                :  Track² ↣ Track²
│   routeTrks              :  F Track
├───────────────────────────────────────────────────────────────
│   routeSubs = routeCons²
│   routeTrks = {t : Track  |  trkSubs(t) ⊆ routeSubs}
│   firstSub ∈ trkSubs(entry.overlap))
│   firstSub ∈ dom prevSub
│   ran prevSub = routeSubs − {firstSub}
│        where
│        trkSubs      : Track → F(Track × Track)
│        trkSubs(t)   = {(t₁, t₂)  |  (t₁, t₂) ∈ routeSubs ∧ {(t₁, t), (t, t₂)} ⊆ routeCons}
└───────────────────────────────────────────────────────────────
```

We may define *prevSub* introduced in the above in the following manner:

$$prevSub : Track^2 \to Track^2$$
$$prevSub(t_1, t_2) = s$$

such that

$$t_1 = midTrk(s) \land s \in subRoutes \land \exists t_3 \bullet s = (t_3, midTrk(t_1, t_2))$$

where

$$midTrk(s) : Track^2 \to Track$$
$$midTrk(s) = y$$

such that

$$\exists x, z : Track \bullet s = (x, z) \land \{(x, y), (y, z)\} \subseteq routeCons.$$

The above three may be incorporated in a single specification giving the state of routes, but with an additional component recording the lock state of the route.

$$\begin{array}{|l}
\hline
\;Route \\
\hline
\quad Tracks \\
\quad RouteSignals \\
\quad RoutePoints \\
\quad RouteSubroutes \\
\quad routeFixity \qquad : LockState \\
\hline
\end{array}$$

$$\begin{array}{|l}
\hline
\;Routes \\
\hline
\quad routes \qquad : \mathbb{F}\,Route \\
\quad Tracks \\
\hline
\quad \bigcup_{r\,\in\,routes}\{r.entry, r.exit\} = signals \\
\quad \forall\,s : Signal;\; r : Route \;\bullet\; r \in routes \wedge s \in signals \Rightarrow \\
\qquad (s.location \in r.routeCons \Rightarrow s = r.entry \vee s = r.exit) \\
\quad \forall\,r : Route \;\bullet\; r \in routes \Rightarrow (r.routeCons \subseteq up \vee r.routeCons \subseteq down) \\
\hline
\end{array}$$

Within the context of a given route r, one may make the following observations as to whether a given subroute is locked or free.

$$\forall r : Route;\, s : Track^2;\, Routes \bullet$$
$$isFreeSub(r, s) \quad \overset{def}{\Leftrightarrow} \quad subRouteFixity(s) = \mathsf{free}\ \wedge s \in r.routeSubs \wedge$$
$$r.routeFixity = \mathsf{free}$$
$$isLockedSub(r, s) \overset{def}{\Leftrightarrow} \quad subRouteFixity(s) = \mathsf{locked}\ \wedge s \in r.routeSubs.$$

We may now define two specific actions on subroutes.

$$[\mathsf{contlr}, FreeSub(r, s)] \quad isFreeSub(r, s)$$
$$[\mathsf{contlr}, LockSub(r, s)] \quad isLockedSub(r, s).$$

Similar definitions are introduced for route states:

$$\forall r : Route;\, s : Track^2 \bullet$$
$$isFreeRoute(r) \quad \overset{def}{\Leftrightarrow} \quad r.routeFixity = \mathsf{free}$$
$$isLockedRoute(r) \overset{def}{\Leftrightarrow} \quad r.routeFixity = \mathsf{locked}$$
$$isLockedRoute(r) \;\Rightarrow\; \forall s \bullet s \in r.routeSubs \Rightarrow isLockedSub(r, s) \wedge$$
$$\forall p \bullet p \in r.normalPts \Rightarrow isLockedNormalPt(p) \wedge$$
$$\forall p \bullet p \in r.reversePts \Rightarrow isLockedReversePt(p)$$

and actions bringing about such states,

$$[\text{contlr}, FreeRoute(r)] \quad isFreeRoute(r)$$
$$[\text{contlr}, LockRoute(r)] \quad isLockedRoute(r)$$

Note that sub-routes remain locked while routes remain locked.

5 Prescription of system actions in the event of failures

This section presents a normative specification of the system behaviour in DAL. The specification consists of five sub-specifications dealing respectively with fail-soft mechanisms, fail-safe mechanisms, safe initialisation of equipment, transitions from low to high risk states and transitions from high to low risk states. These are related to different categories of safety requirements which are discussed in the relevant sections.

5.1 Specification of fail-soft behaviour

Let us first consider measures to be undertaken in the event of failure of a signal. All signals are normally at red unless they are explicitly set otherwise. It is therefore essential that, following the failure of a signal, or since putting it out, it is restored to this normal operational mode as soon as possible by the controller or the operator.

$$\forall s : Signal \bullet failedSig(s) \Rightarrow \mathsf{OBL}(\text{contlr}, turnOn(s)) \wedge \mathsf{OBL}(\text{optr}, turnOn(s)).$$

The controlling system receives information from the sensor at each signal about the state of the signal lamp. The failure to restore the signal within the permitted time limit t_{light} by either party, namely the controller or the operator, obliges the safety executive to take corrective actions in order to ensure ground safety. If the lamp in a signal has failed, or the signal sensor malfunctions, the overall system needs to be returned to such a state that prevents the operational use of the faulty signal. Therefore, we must consider a statement such as the following as a safety requirement:

$$Persist\_min(turnOn(s), t_{light}) \Rightarrow \mathsf{Obl}(\text{exec}, \mathsf{Obl}(\text{contlr}, signalOut(s_{\text{contlr}})))$$

where s_{contlr} represents the controller's view of the state of the signal s (see Section 3). In the event of transition $turnOn(s)$ not being successful, or in the event of failure of the sensor to confirm the outcome, the above places the responsibility with the safety executive to ensure that the controller assumes the signal to be in the out state. However, subsequent restoration of the signal must also restore controller's view so that it is consistent with the actual state of the signal. That is,

$$\neg failedSig(s) \wedge \neg failed(\text{contlr}) \Rightarrow \mathsf{Obl}(\text{contlr}, s_{\text{contlr}} = s).$$

In the case of the points, any risk may be associated only with the broken state of a point. Having only one state of risk (see Section 5.4), the points introduce an important distinction in requirements as compared with signals, namely, that a single state is to be viewed as both a low risk and a high risk state.

$$Persist\_min(\alpha(p), t_{point}) \wedge$$

$$\alpha(p) \in \{FreeNormal(p), FreeReverse(p), LockNormal(p),$$

$$LockReverse(p)\} \Rightarrow \mathsf{Obl}(\mathsf{exec}, \mathsf{Obl}(\mathsf{contlr}, brokenPt(p_{\mathsf{contlr}}))).$$

According to the above, the failure to move a point to the desired position, or the failure to lock it, within t_{point} time units results in the controller having to assume the relevant point to be in a broken state. Otherwise, the point is to be regarded as in an undetected state.

Although safe passage of trains depends on subroutes and routes, these do not require directly associated fail-soft safety requirements since subroutes and routes are not physical equipments. However, since the task of route setting depends indirectly on the fail-soft states of signals and points lying on the route, both subroutes and routes are affected by fail-soft states of other equipment.

5.2   Specification of fail-safe behaviour

Consider now the failure of the controlling system. In this case, every signal in the system must be returned to its safest state. This is so, because in the eyes of train drivers, each signal is deemed to always function correctly since there is no other information available to them during train operation about the state of the controlling system.

$$failed(\mathsf{contlr}) \Rightarrow (\forall s : Signal \bullet s \in signals \wedge \neg failedSig(s) \Rightarrow$$

$$\mathsf{Obl}(\mathsf{exec}, \mathsf{Obl}(s, signalOn(s))).$$

This requirement again makes the safety executive responsible for ensuring that every signal is instructed to return to its safest state.

A similar condition applies to points, but unlike in the case of the signals, the relevant safety requirement does not mean that the points are forced physically into their safest state, that is, to the broken state, but that no control signals are to be issued to points by the controller.

$$failed(\mathsf{contlr}) \Rightarrow (\forall p : Point \bullet p \in points \wedge \neg brokenPt(p) \Rightarrow$$

$$\mathsf{Obl}(\mathsf{exec}, brokenPt(p_{\mathsf{exec}})) \wedge \mathsf{Obl}(\mathsf{contlr}, brokenPt(p_{\mathsf{contlr}}))).$$

The above places the responsibility with the safety executive for ensuring that the controller assumes every point to be in its broken state. Here we have an apparent contradiction between two consequences from the above statement. On one hand, we are being led to assume that the controller has failed, while on the other, we require the controller to assume that the points are broken. This situation is not a drawback of the logic but of the absence of a detailed model of the controller within our specification.

As far as the subroutes and routes are concerned, the argument made in the last sub section remains applicable.

5.3 Specification of safe initialisation

Following a total or partial system shutdown, all equipment and abstract entities must be initialised to safe states before resumption of service. Thus, signals must be returned to service in a state displaying the aspect **red** using a transition such as $light(s)$, points in a locked state, subroutes in a locked state to prevent interference with any points lying on them and routes in a free state. These initialisation requirements are stated below.

$$\forall s : Signal, p : Point; subr : Track^2; r : Route \mid$$
$$s \in signals \land p \in points \land subr \in subRoutes \land r \in routes \bullet$$
$$restoredSig(s) \;\Rightarrow\; \mathsf{OBL}(\mathsf{contlr}, turnOn(s)) \land$$
$$restoredPt(p) \;\Rightarrow\; \mathsf{Obl}(\mathsf{contlr}, p.pointFixity = \mathsf{locked}) \land$$
$$restored(\mathsf{contlr}) \;\Rightarrow\; \mathsf{Obl}(\mathsf{contlr}, subRouteFixity(subr) = \mathsf{locked}) \land$$
$$restored(\mathsf{contlr}) \;\Rightarrow\; \mathsf{Obl}(\mathsf{contlr}, r.routeFixity = \mathsf{locked})$$

where $restoredSig(s)$, $restoredPt(p)$ and $restored(\mathsf{contlr})$ mean respectively that the signal s, the point p and the controller have been restored to service. For brevity, these predicates are not defined here. We have made the above initialisation actions obligatory actions. Alternatively, these could have been listed under recommended practice by the use operators PER and Per instead of OBL and Obl.

5.4 State transitions for preventing and averting failures

Safety must address not only how to deal with on-going failures but also how to prevent failures and how to avert imminent failures. A more detailed discussion of this classification is given in [3].

The failure prevention measures considered here concern the circumstances that forbid a move from a low risk state to a high risk state. On the other hand, measures directed at averting imminent failures deal with bringing the system down swiftly from a high risk state to a low risk state. These risk states are not unique and may be identified in relation to every equipment (and abstract entity). More accurately, the risk posed by different states of any equipment should not be assessed in isolation but in the context of the global system state. Thus, the risk should be examined in relation to the overall system state, and the local states of equipment giving rise to extreme risks. The former either sanctions or forbids the transition while the latter determines local states posing different levels of risks. An implicit assumption in this is that all equipments are in perfect working order, as otherwise, the safety has to be addressed as a

Table 1. Risk levels associated with component states

Equipment (Attribute)	Low Risk Value	High Risk Value
Signal (aspect)	red	amber,green
Point (setting)	normalPos,reversePos	normalPos,reversePos
Point (fixity)	locked	free
Subroute (fixity)	locked	free
Route (fixity)	free,locked	free,locked

fail-safe or as a fail-soft option. Risk states associated with equipments (strictly, their attributes) as shown in Table 1.

5.5   Low to high risk state transitions

Let us consider first the change of signals from red to either amber or green. Obviously, such a transition is sought in order to respond to a route request, which may be granted only after ensuring overall safety. The requirements on overall safety may not be obvious from those written in natural language and the following is an interpretation of such a statement.

$$RouteClear(r) \stackrel{def}{\Leftrightarrow} isLockedRoute(r) \wedge$$
$$r.exit.lamp = \mathsf{in} \wedge$$
$$\forall t : Track \bullet t \in r.routeTrks \Rightarrow t.occupancy = \mathsf{clear} \wedge$$
$$\forall p : Point \bullet p \in r.normalPts \Rightarrow p.setting = \mathsf{normalPos} \wedge$$
$$\forall p : Point \bullet p \in r.reversePts \Rightarrow p.setting = \mathsf{reversePos}.$$

According to the above, a route is considered clear if and only if the route has been set by locking it, the signal at route exit is in working order, all tracks are clear and the points have been moved to their correct positions. Note that the predicate $\neg RouteClear(r)$ describes precisely the circumstances of a hazardous state. With this we may state the requirements on a safety action for setting the signal off to either green or amber from other possible values.

$$\neg RouteClear(r) \Rightarrow \neg \mathsf{PER}(contlr, TurnOff(r.entry)).$$

The safety requirements on movements of points are more complex. The points are to be maintained locked in their correct positions during the passage of trains over any given route. Therefore, points are neither to be moved nor set free while subroutes passing over them remain locked or track sections where the points are located are occupied by a (stationary) train, resulting in what is called *dead locking*. Let us formalize these circumstances separately.

The subroutes crossing over points and aligned with either the normal or the reverse point positions may be identified by the following predicates.

$$\forall Tracks; s : Track^2; p : Point\bullet$$

$$normalRunningSub(s,p) \overset{def}{\Leftrightarrow} s \in subRoutes \wedge p.setting = \mathsf{normalPos} \wedge$$
$$midTrk(s) \in p.trkSet$$

$$reverseRunningSub(s,p) \overset{def}{\Leftrightarrow} s \in subRoutes \wedge p.setting = \mathsf{reversePos} \wedge$$
$$midTrk(s) \in p.trkSet$$

where *midTrk* is as defined in Section 4.4. The following predicate states whether a given point is, or is not, under the dead locked condition because of the presence of a train above it.

$$DeadLocked(p) \overset{def}{\Leftrightarrow} \exists t : Track \bullet t \in p.trkSet \wedge t.occupancy = \mathsf{occupied}.$$

The following two predicates establish whether any point is in a locked state by virtue of the fact that a subroute crossing the point is in a locked state.

$$\forall Routes; p : Point \bullet$$

$$NormalLockedSub(p) \overset{def}{\Leftrightarrow} \exists s : Track^2 \bullet \forall r : Routee \bullet r \in routes \wedge$$
$$normalRunningSub(s,p) \wedge isLockedSub(s)$$

$$ReverseLockedSub(p) \overset{def}{\Leftrightarrow} \exists s : Track^2 \bullet \forall r : Routee \bullet r \in routes \wedge$$
$$reverseRunningSub(s,p) \wedge isLockedSub(s).$$

Using the above predicates, it is possible to state formally the conditions under which the safety requirements on freeing points are violated either because of dead locking of points or locking imposed by route setting. Thus, it is forbidden to free points if the following condition prevails:

$$Deadlocked(p) \wedge NormalLockedSub(p) \Rightarrow \neg \mathsf{PER}(\mathsf{contlr}, FreeNormal(p))$$
$$Deadlocked(p) \wedge ReverseLockedSub(p) \Rightarrow \neg \mathsf{PER}(\mathsf{contlr}, FreeReverse(p)).$$

Let us turn our attention now to subroutes. Changing subroute fixity from locked to free carries some risk since, as a consequence of any unwarranted freeing of subroutes, the points may be moved, potentially endangering any moving train, or damaging the points if the points are dead locked by the presence of a train. Subroutes may be freed only if the route on which they lie and all predecessor subroutes along the route are freed first.

$$\forall Routes; r : Route; s : Track^2\bullet$$

$$clearRoute(r) \overset{def}{\Leftrightarrow} \forall t\bullet \in routeTrks \Rightarrow t.occupancy = \mathsf{clear}$$

$$safeToFreeFirstSub(r,s) \overset{def}{\Leftrightarrow} isFreeRoute(r) \wedge clearRoute(r) \wedge$$
$$s = r.firstSub$$

$$safeToFreeOtherSub(r,s) \overset{def}{\Leftrightarrow} isFreeRoute(r) \wedge clearRoute(r) \wedge$$
$$s \in r.routeSubs \wedge isFreeSub(prevSub(s)).$$

The safety requirement on freeing subroutes is therefore,

$$\forall r : Route; s : Track^2 \bullet \neg(safeToFreeFirstSub(r, s) \vee$$
$$safeToFreeOtherSubs(r, s)) \Rightarrow$$
$$\neg\text{PER}(\text{contlr}, FreeSub(s)).$$

Let us now examine safety issues to be checked prior to locking a route. Firstly, none of the subroutes on the route must be locked for a route in the opposite direction. Secondly, the points along the route should not be locked.

$$\forall Routes; r : Route \bullet$$
$$safeRoute(r) \overset{def}{\Leftrightarrow} (\neg \exists x : Route; s : Track^2 \bullet s \in r.routeSubs\text{\textasciitilde} \wedge$$
$$s \in x.routeSubs \wedge isLockedSub(x, s)) \wedge$$
$$\forall p \bullet p \in r.normalPts \Rightarrow isFreeNormalPt(p) \wedge$$
$$\forall p \bullet p \in r.reversePts \Rightarrow isFreeReversePt(p)$$

If the above condition does not prevail, it is unsafe to lock a route. That is,

$$\forall r : Route \bullet \neg safeRoute(r) \Rightarrow \neg\text{PER}(\text{contlr}, isLockedRoute(r)).$$

5.6   High to low risk state transitions

Transitions from high to low risk states may be motivated either by general strategic considerations to minimise risks or for being prepared for averting failures in the event of unforeseen hazards. More critical is the latter kind of scenario, which invariably requires swift action on the part of safety monitoring agents. This means that such safety requirements necessarily involve timing constraints, usually in the form of deadlines. Let us examine first the change of signals, but from either **amber** or **green** to **red**.

$$\neg RouteClear(r) \Rightarrow \text{Obl}(\text{contlr}, signalOn(r.entry)) \wedge$$
$$Persist\_max(turnOn(r.entry), t_{turn\_}red)$$

where t_{turn_red} is the time limit for turning the signal at the entry to route r to the aspect **red**. An analogous safety assertion may be made with respect to points, obliging the controller to lock the points within a specified time limit if any of the points is found free while either a subroute over it remains locked or the point is effectively under dead locked condition. Thus,

$$(Deadlocked(p) \vee NormalLockedSub(p)) \wedge$$
$$isFreeNormalPt(p) \Rightarrow \text{OBL}(\text{contlr}, LockNormal(p)) \wedge$$
$$Persist\_max(LockNormal(p), t_{lock\_pts})$$
$$(Deadlocked(p) \vee ReverseLockedSub(p)) \wedge$$
$$isFreeNormalPt(p) \Rightarrow \text{OBL}(\text{contlr}, LockReverse(p)) \wedge$$
$$Persist\_max(LockReverse(p), t_{lock\_pts})$$

where t_{lock_pts} is the time limit for locking the point p.

6   Conclusions

We have demonstrated that deontic logic can be used effectively for the specification of a large class of safety requirements characteristic to many realistic safety critical systems. These requirements concern fail-soft and fail-safe safety mechanisms and transitions between low risk and high risk system states. Naturally, fail-soft and fail-safe safety mechanisms tend to rely more on the notions of obligation and permission. In contrast, safe transitions between states of extreme risks rely exclusively on the notions of prohibition and obligation. However, these deontic notions alone are not sufficient for safety specification. This is because the safety provisions must be discharged in a timely manner and this introduces an important dimension to the logic, namely, real time. In this regard, the paper suggests a simple augmentation to the logic for dealing with real time.

However, this requires further scrutiny, especially from the view point of the logic of time. The complexity of large systems requires a more powerful framework for system specification than that provided by the common variants of Deontic Logic. In this respect, we found it effective to rely on established state based specification languages such as Z and VDM for capturing the system structure and its hierarchical organisation. Deontic logic may then be brought in for dealing with actions and their normative specification. Advantages of such an approach include separate treatment of functional and safety requirements and rational deployment of professionals with different expertise.

Research in progress concentrates on how to reason about safety issues. This includes verification of safety features (mechanisms) with respect to safety requirements. For example, a safety feature in the given case study concerns the circumstances under which a railway *route* is presumed unsafe for the controller to lock it, that is, to *set* the route. An instance where a route is regarded unsafe is the existence of another opposing route along some length of the given route. A safety requirement within the scope of this safety feature is that no collision of trains could possibly take place.

Acknowledgement

This work is partially funded by Rockwell International. The author is grateful to Rockwell for this support and to anonymous reviewers of the paper for their suggestions on improvements.

References

1. Barroca, L.M. and McDermid, J.A. (1992). Formal methods: Use and relevance for the development of safety-critical systems. *The Computer J.*, **35**, British Computer Society, 579–599.

2. Place, P.R.H. and Kang, K.C. (1993). Safety-critical software: Status report and annotated bibliography. *Technical Report CMU/SEI-92-TR-5, ESC-TR-93-182*, Carnegie Mellon University, Pittsburgh.

3. Nissanke, N. and Robinson, R. (1994). Formal methods in safety analysis. *SAFECOMP'94, Int. Conf. on Computer Safety, Reliability and Security*, Editor: V.J. Maggioli, Instrument Society of America, 239–248.

4. S&T Systems and Standards Engineer (compiled by T. King,). (1994). Logical elements of interlocking systems. *Technical Report S.P0339.41.1*, Railtrack PLC, London.

5. Hansen, K.M. (1994). Formalising railway interlocking systems. *Technical Report ID/DTH KMH3/1, ProCos II*, Technical University of Denmark.

6. Cullyer, J. and Wong, W. (1993). Application of formal methods to railway signalling - a case study. *Computing and Control Engineering J.*, 15–22.

7. Maibaum, T. (1993). Temporal reasoning over deontic specifications. *Deontic Logic in Computer Science*, Editors: J.-J.Ch. Meyer and R.J. Wieringa, John Wiley, 141–202.

8. Meyer, J.-J.Ch. and Wieringa, R.J. (Editors). (1993). *Deontic Logic in Computer Science*, John Wiley.

9. Cunningham, J. and Atkinson, W. (1991). Proving properties of a safety-critical system. *Software Engineering J.*, 41–50.

10. Potts, C. et al. (1986). Structured common sense - a requirements elicitation and formalization method for modal action logic. *Technical Report*, Imperial College of Science and Technology, University of London.

11. Leveson, N.G. and Stolzy, J.L. (1987). Safety analysis using Petri nets. *IEEE Trans. on Software Engineering*, **13**, 92–103.

12. de Lemos, R., Saeed, A. and Anderson, T. (1992). A train set as a case study for requirements analysis of safety-critical systems. *The Computer J.*, **35**, 30–40.

13. Halbwachs, N., Lagnier, F. and Ratel, C. (1992). Programming and verifying real-time systems by means of the synchronous data-flow language LUSTRE. *IEEE Trans. on Software Engineering*, **18**, 785–793.

14. Ingleby, M. (1993). A Galois theory of local reasoning in control systems with compositionality. *IMA Conf. Proc. on The Mathematics of Dependable Systems*.

15. Harel, D. (1979). First-order dynamic logic. *LNCS*, **68**, Springer-Verlag.

16. Rescher, N. (1966). *The Logic of Commands*, Routledge and Kegan Paul Ltd..

17. Spivey, M. (1992). *The Z Notation*, Prentice Hall.

18. Maibaum, T. (1987). A logic for formal requirements specification of real-time embedded systems. *Technical Report*, Imperial College of Science and Technology, University of London.

Algebraic Models of Microprocessors: The Correctness and Verification of a Simple Computer

N.A. Harman and J.V. Tucker

Department of Computer Science, University of Wales Swansea

Abstract

We show a general algebraic method for modelling microprocessors at different levels of abstraction in a modular way. We formalise the relationships between each level, and show how correctness can be established by equational reasoning. We consider Gordon's Computer — a simple, commonly-studied example — giving algebraic descriptions at two levels of abstraction, corresponding to the architecture and abstract implementation. We formulate the correctness conditions for these two levels. The algebraic methods and tools described extend existing algebraic tools, and are not linked to specific languages and software tools but are generally applicable.

1   Introduction

This paper presents a general algebraic method for modeling microprocessors at different levels of abstraction in a modular fashion, for expressing algebraically the relationships between each level, and verifying the correctness of those relationships by means of equational reasoning. Our algebraic tools are demonstrated by their application to a simple, commonly-studied, example. We give algebraic descriptions at two levels of abstraction: the *programmer's level* specification, and the *abstract circuit design* representation.

We describe a general method of verifying the correctness of one level of abstraction with respect to another, and outline the process of verifying the correctness of the abstract circuit design with respect to the programmer's model. The algebraic methods and tools described in this paper extend the algebraic tools developed in [16,18]. The mathematical models of machines are not linked to specific specification languages or input languages to theorem provers and proof checkers; rather they are representable in, and can be processed by, most machine-oriented reasoning systems.

The example considered is commonly studied because it is simple enough to enable a substantial account of its specification, design and verification to be given in a single paper. The techniques developed here are not restricted to small examples, and have been applied to substantial case studies, including:

135

DEC Alpha, Motorola 68000, and Berkeley RISC II. In addition, the techniques are easy to learn, and are successfully employed in undergraduate project work and teaching at Swansea.

We employ a model of time based on counting events by means of a *clock*. A clock is a means of dividing time into segments defined by events, which need not be equal in length. We model a computer (at several levels of abstraction) by means of the iterated map

$$F : T \times A \times [T \to In] \to A \times Out,$$

over discrete time $T = \{0, 1, 2, \ldots\}$, described by the following equations:

$$
\begin{aligned}
F_1(0, a, i) &= a, \\
F_1(t + 1, a, i) &= f(F_1(t, a, i), i(t)), \\
F_2(t, a, i) &= out(F_1(t, a, i)),
\end{aligned}
$$

for $t \in T$, $a \in A$, $i \in In$, where $f : A \times In \to A$ represents the *next-state function* of the computer, and $out : A \to Out$ represents the *output function*.

The set A models the state of the computer, the set In models input to the computer and the function f is the next-state map; thus $F_1(t, a, i)$ is the state of the computer at time $t \in T$ starting from initial state $a \in A$, with input *stream* $i \in [T \to In]$, and $F_2(t, a, i)$ is the output of the computer at time $t \in T$, starting from initial state $a \in A$, with input stream $i \in [T \to In]$. The nature of the set of states A, In, Out and clock T is determined by the level of abstraction of the computer. A typical clock would be the *system clock*. However, we can consider *instruction clocks*, where each cycle represents the execution of an instruction. We characterise a computer at two levels of abstraction by two functions F and G, and express correctness by equations involving F and G.

We illustrate our algebraic tools by specifying a simple computer, characterised by the following features:

- 16-bit word; 13-bit memory address; 8192 16-bit word memory;

- single accumulator Acc; program counter PC; and link bit L;

- basic input-output mechanisms (dial, switches, button, and lights);

- eight basic instructions; and

- a basic, microprogrammed, implementation.

The example was first developed and used in [10], where it was formally specified, described and verified in LCF-LSM [9]. We consider a specification at the programmer's level, and an implementation at the microcode level. We formulate correctness conditions between the two levels of abstraction, and outline the process of verification. The example we consider has been examined in a number of works: [23] describes and verifies the computer using HOL; [11,28] performs a partial verification using OBJ3 [8]. In addition, Joyce's version has been proposed as a standard case study by IFIP WG 10.2 [27]. Related work on the formal specification and verification of microprocessors includes the following.

- [16,18] discuss the algebraic specification and representation of a PDP-8-based processor. [18] further discusses the process of verifying the correctness of the representation with respect to the specification.

- [4–6] discuss *Viper* and its partial verification in HOL.

- [2,12,13] discuss an implementation of Landin's SECD machine [24].

- [19–22] discuss a PDP-11-based processor, the FM8501, and its more advanced successor the FM9001 (see also [3]).

- [1,26] discuss parts of the Inmos T800 and T9000 Transputers, using an Occam-based transformation system.

- [7] discusses the Intel 8085 processor.

This work forms part of a project on *synchronous concurrent algorithms* (SCAs). An SCA is an algebraic model of parallel deterministic computation with discrete space and time. For further information see [29,30]. For work on case studies on hardware, see [14,15,16,18]. In particular, [14,16,18] are concerned with the specification, design and verification of computers. The algebraic tools in this paper, and in the SCA project in general, form part of the theoretical basis of a new hardware description language for microprocessors (and other hardware systems), being developed by Esprit Working Group NADA (No. 00 85 33).

2 Algebraic tools

In this section, we introduce the formal tools we need for writing algebraic specifications of computers, based on the theory of modeling *abstract data types* by *many-sorted algebras* (see, for example, [25,32]).

2.1 Clocks and streams

A clock is an algebra $(T \mid 0, t+1)$ where $T = \{0, 1, \ldots\}$ identifies *clock cycles*, 0 denotes the first clock cycle, and $t+1$ allows us to count clock cycles.

A *stream* $\alpha : T \to A$ is a map from time to data, representing a sequence of time-separated data items, where $a(t)$ is the data item on stream a at time t. Let $[T \to A]$ be the set of all streams.

2.2   Algebraic notation

To systematically represent the algebras employed in this paper, we introduce the following notation, which we illustrate with the clock algebra from Section 2.1.

> **Algebra T**
> **Sets** T
> **Constants**
> $\qquad 0 : T$
> **Operations**
> $\qquad t + 1 : T \to T$
> **End Algebra.**

We permit any number of sets, constants and operations. Observe that we use T to stand for both the clock algebra, and the carrier set of the clock algebra.

2.3   Iterated maps and primitive recursion

Let A, In and Out be non-empty sets, let T be a clock and consider the function,

$$F : T \times A \times [T \to In] \to A \times Out$$

defining the state and output of a computer at time $t \in T$, given starting state $a \in A$, and input stream $in \in [T \to In]$. We define the *state algebra* of the computer as follows.

> **Algebra State**
> **Sets** $T, A, In, Out, [T \to In]$
> **Operations**
> $\qquad F : T \times A \times [T \to In] \to A \times Out$
> **End Algebra.**

Let $f : A \times In \to A$ and $out : A \to Out$ be maps respectively representing the next-state and output functions of the computer, defined in terms of f and out by the following set E_F of equations. For $t \in T$, $a \in A$, $i \in In$, let

$$F_1(0, a, i) = a,$$
$$F_1(t + 1, a, i) = f(F_1(t, a, i), i(t)),$$

represent the evolution of the state $a' \in A$ of the computer, from initial state $a \in A$, and input stream $i \in In$. The state evolves by repeated application of *next-state function* f to the current state, and the current input, $i(t)$.

For $t \in T$, $a \in A$, $i \in In$, let

$$F_2(t, a, i) = out(F_1(t, a, i))$$

represent the output of the computer, at time t. The output at time t is a function of the state of the computer at time t. Observe that $F = (F_1, F_2)$ is a simultaneous primitive recursive function over the *next-state algebra*

Algebra Next-State
Sets $\quad T, A, In, Out, [T \to In]$
Constants
$\qquad 0 : T$
Operations
$\qquad t + 1 : T \to T,$
$\qquad f : A \times In \to A,$
$\qquad out : A \to Out,$
$\qquad eval : T \times [T \to In] \to In$
End Algebra,

representing the state and output of a computer in time, starting from an initial state a and input stream i (see [18,30,31]).

The algebra used to construct the next-state algebra is called the *machine algebra*. Typically, the machine algebra will be made up of carriers consisting of bit vectors, together with functions and constants representing the basic operations of the machine, and the algebras of the Booleans and natural numbers.

The hierarchy of algebras structures and modularises the computer's representation. The *state algebra* reveals the state, input, output and clock of the computer, and the existence of a function transforming state, and generating output. The state algebra is represented by primitive recursive equations over the *next-state algebra*, which makes explicit the iterated map structure of the computer's state evolution and output functions. The next-state algebra is represented by primitive recursive (or polynomial) equations over the *machine algebra*, which makes explicit the next-state and output mechanisms, and the level of temporal abstraction, in terms of bit vectors, and operations on bit vectors. We can consider a further level, the *fundamental algebra*, which explicitly, and formally, represents the bit-level operations of the machine algebra by means of primitive recursive equations.

2.4 A decomposition

Let $A = A_1 \times \cdots \times A_k$, where each A_i, $i = 1, \ldots, k$ is a non-empty set, $I = I_1 \times \cdots \times I_n$, where each I_i, $i = 1, \ldots, n$ is a non-empty set, and $Out = Out_1 \times \cdots \times Out_m$, where each Out_i, $i = 1, \ldots, m$ is a non-empty set. Consider the function $F : T \times A \times [T \to I] \to A \times Out$ as defined in Section 2.3. The function F can be rewritten

$$
\begin{aligned}
F(t, a_1, \ldots, a_k, i_1, \ldots, i_n) \;=\; & (F_1(t, a_1, \ldots, a_k, i_1, \ldots, i_n), \ldots \\
& F_k(t, a_1, \ldots, a_k, i_1, \ldots, i_n), \\
& F_{k+1}(t, a_1, \ldots, a_k, i_1, \ldots, i_n), \ldots \\
& F_{k+m}(t, a_1, \ldots, a_k, i_1, \ldots, i_n))
\end{aligned}
$$

for $t \in T$, $a_i \in A_i$, $1 \leq i \leq k$, and $i_j \in [T \to I_j]$, $1 \leq j \leq n$, and where

$$F_i : T \times A_1 \times \cdots \times A_k \times I_1 \times \cdots \times I_n \to A_i$$

is the ith component function for F, $1 \leq i \leq k$, describing the next state, and $F_j : T \times A_1 \times \cdots \times A_k \times I_1 \times \cdots \times I_n \to Out_j$ is the jth component function for F, $k+1 \leq j \leq k+m$, describing the output.

Furthermore, the functions $f : A \times I \to A$ and $out : A \to Out$ can be rewritten

$$f(a_1, \ldots, a_k, i_1, \ldots, i_n) = (f_1(a_1, \ldots, a_k, i_1, \ldots, i_n), \ldots f_k(a_1, \ldots, a_k, i_1, \ldots, i_n)),$$

for $a_i \in A_i$, $1 \leq i \leq k$, $i_j \in I_j$, $1 \leq j \leq n$, and where $f_i : A_1 \times \cdots \times A_k \times I_1 \times \cdots \times I_n \to A_i$ is the ith component function for f, $1 \leq i \leq n$, and

$$out(a_1, \ldots, a_k) = (out_1(a_1, \ldots, a_k), \ldots out_m(a_1, \ldots, a_k)),$$

where $out_j : A_1 \times \cdots \times A_k \to Out_j$ is the jth component function for out, $1 \leq j \leq m$.

Substituting these component functions for F, f and out we may rewrite the equations E_F in Section 2.3 as follows:

$$F_1(0, a_1, \ldots, a_k, i_1, \ldots, i_n) = a_1,$$

$$\vdots$$

$$F_k(0, a_1, \ldots, a_k, i_1, \ldots, i_n) = a_k,$$

$$F_1(t+1, a_1, \ldots, a_k, i_1, \ldots, i_n) = f_1(F_1(t, a_1, \ldots, a_k, i_1, \ldots, i_n), \ldots$$
$$F_k(t, a_1, \ldots, a_k, i_1, \ldots, i_n), i_1(t), \ldots, i_n(t)),$$

$$\vdots$$

$$F_k(t+1, a_1, \ldots, a_k, i_1, \ldots, i_n) = f_k(F_1(t, a_1, \ldots, a_k, i_1, \ldots, i_n), \ldots$$
$$F_k(t, a_1, \ldots, a_k, i_1, \ldots, i_n), i_1(t), \ldots, i_n(t)),$$

$$F_{k+1}(t, a_1, \ldots, a_k, i_1, \ldots, i_n) = out_1(F_1(t, a_1, \ldots, a_k, i_1, \ldots, i_n), \ldots$$
$$F_k(t, a_1, \ldots, a_k, i_1, \ldots, i_n)),$$

$$\vdots$$

$$F_{k+m}(t, a_1, \ldots, a_k, i_1, \ldots, i_n) = out_m(F_1(t, a_1, \ldots, a_k, i_1, \ldots, i_n), \ldots$$
$$F_k(t, a_1, \ldots, a_k, i_1, \ldots, i_n)).$$

Functions $F_1, \ldots, F_k$ are called the *state functions*, and functions $F_{k+1}, \ldots, F_{k+m}$ are called the *output functions*.

2.5 Retimings

Specifications may contain multiple clocks, running at different speeds. Furthermore, different cycles of a clock T need not all be the same length: that is, clocks can be irregular.

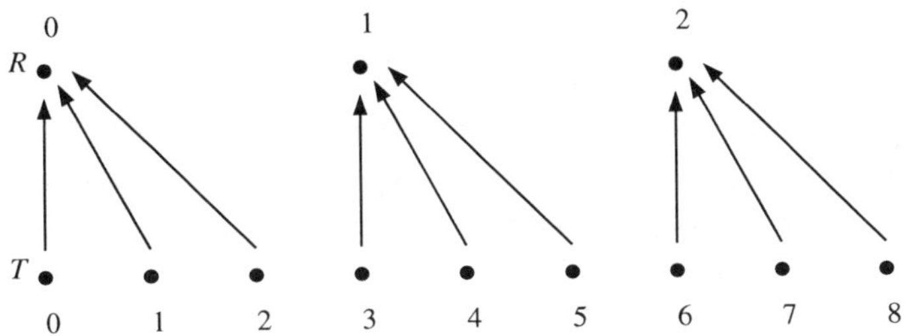

Figure 1. A retiming between clocks T and R

We introduce *retimings* to relate times on multiple clocks. Let T and R be two clocks. A retiming $\lambda : T \to R$ is a surjective, monotonic map, and the set of retimings from clock T to clock R is denoted by $Ret(T, R)$. A typical retiming is illustrated in Figure 1.

For each retiming λ there is a corresponding *immersion* $\overline{\lambda} : R \to T$,

$$\overline{\lambda}(r) = (least \ t \in T)[\lambda(t) = r].$$

2.5.1 State-dependent retimings

Retimings may be *state-dependent*: given some non-empty set A, for each state $\sigma \in A$, we may define a retiming $\lambda(\sigma) \in Ret(S, T)$. An example of such a retiming would be that between the instruction clock T and system clock S of a microprocessor, where the number of cycles of S corresponding to a cycle of T depends on the instruction being executed, and hence on the state of the machine (and perhaps on any input streams). Precisely such a case is illustrated in Section 2.6.2.

2.5.2 Further tools for retimings, clocks and streams

We introduce some formal tools that will be used in the formal representation of the correctness condition between microprocessor representations, at different levels of abstraction (see Section 2.6). Further formal tools can be developed for retimings, clocks and streams: see [14–16].

When considering representations of microprocessors, each clock cycle $r \in R$, will typically represent the number of cycles of a system clock T required for the completion of the machine instruction executed at time $r \in R$, where clock R is an instruction clock (see Section 2.6.2). Given a stream $x : R \to \mathbf{N}^+$ of positive integers, the function $L : [R \to \mathbf{N}^+] \to Ret(T, R)$ defines a retiming in which each clock cycle $L(x)(r)$ lasts $x(r)$ cycles of clock T.

$$L(a)(t) = \begin{cases} 0, & \text{if } t = 0; \\ (\mu \ r \in R)[a(0) + a(1) + \cdots + a(r) > t], & \text{if } t > 0. \end{cases}$$

The function $sch : Ret(S,T) \times [T \to A] \to [S \to A]$ *schedules* a stream $a \in [T \to A]$ by retiming λ, and is defined by

$$sch(\lambda, a)(s) = a\lambda(s).$$

The function $trans : [A \to B] \times [T \to A] \to [T \to B]$ *translates* a stream $a \in [T \to A]$ to a stream $b \in [T \to B]$ by applying some function $f : A \to B$ to each element of A. We define $trans$ as follows:

$$trans(f, a)(t) = f(a(t)).$$

We commonly wish to both translate and schedule a stream at the same time. We define the function $transch : Ret(S,T) \times [A \to B] \times [T \to A] \to [S \to B]$:

$$transch(\lambda, f, a) = sch(\lambda, trans(f, a)).$$

Although not strictly necessary, $transch$ is a convenient abbreviation.

The function $tail : T \times [T \to A] \to [T \to A]$ skips over an initial segment of a stream a, and is defined by

$$tail(t', a)(t) = a(t + t').$$

2.6   Comparing iterated maps

Given two systems described by iterated maps $F : T \times A \times [T \to W] \to A \times X$, defined by

$$\begin{aligned}
F_1(0, a, w) &= a, \\
F_1(t + 1, a, w) &= f(F_1(t, a, w), w(t)), \\
F_2(t, a, w) &= out_X(F_1(t, a, w)),
\end{aligned}$$

and $G : S \times B \times [S \to Y] \to B \times Z$, defined by

$$\begin{aligned}
G_1(0, b, y) &= b, \\
G_1(s + 1, b, y) &= g(G_1(s, b, y), y(s)), \\
G_2(s, b, y) &= out_Z(G_1(s, b, y)),
\end{aligned}$$

how may we formally compare F and G? We wish to establish that the lower level system representation G *correctly implements* system F. Observe, that as is usual in formal treatments of the correctness of hardware and software, the word *correct* is used in a precise formal sense, defined in Sections 2.6.1 and 2.6.2. This formal definition refers to a specific mathematical relationship between representations F and G. It makes no statement about the correctness of any physical realisation of F and G. While it is likely that formal representations improve the likelihood of error-free implementations of hardware and software, this cannot be guaranteed in the presence of real-world constraints.

2.6.1 A general case

We say G *simulates* F if there are maps $\alpha : T \times A \times [T \to W] \to S \times B \times [S \to Y]$ and $\beta : B \times Z \to A \times X$. such that the following diagram commutes.

$$
\begin{array}{ccc}
T \times A \times [T \to W] & \xrightarrow{F} & A \times X \\
\Big\downarrow{\alpha} & & \Big\uparrow{\beta} \\
S \times B \times [S \to Y] & \xrightarrow{G} & B \times Z
\end{array}
$$

Hence for $t \in T$, $a \in A$, $w \in [T \to W]$,

$$
F(t, a, w) = \beta(G(\alpha_1(t, a, w), \alpha_2(t, a, w), \alpha_3(t, a, w))),
$$

where α_1, α_2 and α_3 are coordinate functions of the map α.

2.6.2 Time-independent state comparison

The form of comparison of interest in the case of microprocessors is different. Time is state-dependent and input-dependent, and hence the timing of any input streams is also state and input-dependent. However, state is not time-dependent. We derive the map α, with coordinate functions α_1, α_2, α_3, from the following functions:

$$
\overline{\lambda} : A \times [T \to W] \to [T \to S], \ \phi : A \to B,
$$
$$
transch : Ret(S, T) \times [W \to Y] \times [T \to W] \to [S \to Y].
$$

We denote α_1 by $\overline{\lambda}$ because α_1 is the immersion (Section 2.5) of a retiming $\lambda(a, w)$: see Section 6. In addition, we require some map $h : W \to Y$ to map input elements of F to the corresponding input elements of G. The map β has coordinate functions β_1 and β_2 respectively:

$$
\psi : B \to A, \ \chi : Z \to X.
$$

Furthermore we require that $\psi(\phi(a)) = a$. We say G simulates F with respect to $(\overline{\lambda}, \phi)$ and ψ if the following diagram commutes.

$$
\begin{array}{ccc}
T \times A \times [T \to W] & \xrightarrow{F} & A \times X \\
\Big\downarrow{(\overline{\lambda}, \phi, transch)} & & \Big\uparrow{(\psi, \chi)} \\
S \times B \times [S \to Y] & \xrightarrow{G} & B \times Z
\end{array}
$$

Hence for all $t \in T$, $a \in A$, $w \in [T \to W]$, and appropriate $h : W \to Y$

$$
F(t, a, w) = (\psi, \chi)[G(\overline{\lambda}(a, w)(t), \phi(a), transch(\lambda(a, w), h, w))].
$$

2.6.3 Canonical state sets

Given state sets A and B of the systems, and representation maps $\psi : B \to A$ and $\phi : A \to B$, what may we say about the relationship between A and B? Typically, since ϕ is an injection, we see that B extends A with elements representing components of implementation G, not visible in the higher-level representation F. Map ψ will typically be a projection function, discarding those parts of $b \in B$ not in A. Map ϕ must "pad" $a \in A$ with appropriate values to construct $\phi(a) \in B$, where $\phi(a)$ represents the state of G at the start of an instruction execution cycle. Elements of B not in A can be characterised as follows:

1. *canonical* elements, whose values at time $t \in T$ (the start of the instruction cycle) affects the value of elements of B also in the state A of F at time $t+1$ (the end of the instruction cycle); and

2. *non-canonical* elements, whose values at time $t \in T$ will not affect the value of elements of B also in A at time $t+1$.

Non-canonical elements can be padded with arbitrary constants of the appropriate sort. They typically represent components of the datapath: for example, memory address register, ALU buffer register etc. The starting values of such elements clearly should not affect the outcome of instruction execution if G is to be a correct implementation of F, and the padding constants can be regarded as *don't care* values.

Canonical elements must be padded with appropriate values. They typically represent components of the controller: for example, the microprogram counter. The padding values will be specific constants (for example, a microprogram memory) or computed from the current state $a \in A$ of F.

We can consider a set $C \subset B$ of *canonical states* of G. An element $c \in C$ is constructed from $b \in B$ by replacing all non-canonical elements in b by the same *don't care* constants inserted by padding function ϕ. Consider $b_1, b_2 \in B$, and suppose both reduce to the same canonical state $c \in C$. Evaluating G for some sequence of instructions will give finishing states $\sigma_1, \sigma_2 \in B$ such that

$$\psi(\sigma_1) = \psi(\sigma_2).$$

For each F, G, A and B we can define a set $C \subset B$ of canonical states, and a function $can : B \to C$ that maps elements of B to their canonical forms in C, by replacing non-canonical elements with the *don't care* values inserted by ϕ.

Function *can* allows us to formalise an important correctness condition for G with respect to F. Omitting input streams, suppose $\rho \in A$ represents the state of F at some time $t \in T$, starting from state $a \in A$, and that $\sigma \in B$, represents the state of G at the equivalent time $\overline{\lambda}(a)(t)$, starting from state $\phi(a) \in B$. For G to be a correct implementation of F for all times $t \in T$, we require $\psi(\sigma) = \rho$: that is, the lower-level implementation G produces the same result as the higher-level representation F. However, in addition, to be assured that G will *continue* producing correct results at times $t' > t$, we must ensure that the canonical elements of B are consistent with correct future execution: that is, we require

$$\phi(\psi(\sigma)) = can(\sigma).$$

Function ψ strips away elements of B not in A, both canonical and non-canonical, and function ϕ pads out $\psi(\sigma)$ with the required values in the case of canonical elements, and *don't care* in the case of non-canonical elements. Function *can* just replace the non-canonical elements of σ with the same *don't care* values inserted by ϕ. Hence, if the canonical elements of σ do not match the expected values, then $\phi(\psi(\sigma)) \neq can(\sigma)$, and G does not correctly implement F.

2.7 Correctness of iterated maps

Given representations F and G, and maps $\overline{\lambda}$, ϕ, *transch*, h, ψ and χ as in Section 2.6.2, how may we establish correctness? Given that F and G are iterated maps, and hence have a restricted form, we may considerably simplify proofs. First we introduce the concepts of *time-consistent* iterated maps and *uniform* retimings. Then we show how correctness proofs may be simplified in Section 2.7.3. Finally we show how output functions may be verified in Section 2.7.4. All proofs omitted from Section 2.7 can be found in [17].

2.7.1 Time-consistent iterated maps

A function $F : T \times A \times [T \to W] \to A$ is said to be *time-consistent* if and only if

$$F(t_1 + t_2, a, w) = F(t_1, F(t_2, a, w), tail(t_2, w)).$$

Lemma 1. *It is sufficient that F be of the form*

$$
\begin{aligned}
F(0, a, w) &= a, \\
F(t + 1, a, w) &= f(F(t, a, w), w(t))
\end{aligned}
\tag{2.1}
$$

for F to be a time-consistent function.

2.7.2 Uniform retimings

Let $F : T \times A \times [T \to W] \to A$ be a time-consistent function. A state-dependent retiming $\lambda : A \times [T \to W] \to Ret(S, T)$, with immersion $\overline{\lambda} : A \times [T \to W] \to [T \to S]$ is said to be *uniform* if and only if $\overline{\lambda}$ is of the form

$$
\begin{aligned}
\overline{\lambda}(a, w)(0) &= 0, \\
\overline{\lambda}(a, w)(t + 1) &= h(F(t, a, w)) + \overline{\lambda}(a, w)(t).
\end{aligned}
$$

Informally, the number of cycles of clock S corresponding with any cycle $t \in T$ is independent of the actual value of t, and is solely a function of the state of F at time t, given starting state a and input stream w.

Lemma 2. *Given $F : T \times A \times [T \to W] \to A$ a time-consistent function, and $\lambda : A \times [T \to W] \to Ret(S, T)$ a uniform retimings, then*

$$F(\overline{\lambda}(a, w)(t_1 + t_2), a, w) \;\;=\;\; F(\overline{\lambda}(\sigma, \omega)(t_1), \sigma, \omega), \tag{2.2}$$

where $\sigma = F(\overline{\lambda}(a, w)(t_2), a, w)$ represents the state of F after t_2 cycles of clock T, and $\omega = tail(t_2, w)$ represents input stream w with the first t_2 elements removed.

2.7.3   Verification process

Recall the commutative diagram from Section 2.6.2. For all $t \in T$, $a \in A$, $w \in [T \to W]$, and appropriate $h : W \to Y$, we require

$$F_1(t, a, w) = \psi(G_1(\overline{\lambda}(a, w)(t), \phi(a), transch(\lambda(a, w), h, w))), \tag{2.3}$$

$$F_2(t, a, w) = \chi(G_2(\overline{\lambda}(a, w)(t), \phi(a), transch(\lambda(a, w), h, w))). \tag{2.4}$$

The verification strategy will be induction on time. We will first consider the next-state functions Equation 2.3, and then the output functions Equation 2.4 in Section 2.7.4.

The base case is

$$F_1(0, a, w) = \psi(G_1(0, \phi(a), transch(\lambda(a, w), h, w))). \tag{2.5}$$

The correctness of Equation 2.5 should follow straightforwardly from the definitions of F and G.

The induction hypothesis is as follows: for all $t \in T$,

$$F_1(t, a, w) = \psi(G_1(\overline{\lambda}(a, w)(t), \phi(a), transch(\lambda(a, w), h, w))). \tag{2.6}$$

The induction step is then to prove that:

$$F_1(t + 1, a, w) = \psi(G_1(\overline{\lambda}(a, w)(t + 1), \phi(a), transch(\lambda(a, w), h, w))). \tag{2.7}$$

In addition, we have the following two identities from Sections 2.7.1 and 2.7.2 respectively.

1. Given that F_1 is an iterated map, then from Section 2.7.1 F is *time-consistent*, and hence from Equation 2.2, for all $a \in A$, $w \in [T \to W]$, $t_1, t_2 \in T$:

$$F_1(t_1 + t_2, a, w) = F_1(t_1, F_1(t_2, a, w), tail(t_2, w)). \tag{2.8}$$

2. Given that $F : T \times B \times [T \to W] \to B$ is an iterated map (and hence from Section 2.7.1 time-consistent), λ is a *uniform* retiming (Section 2.7.2), and $can : B \to C$ maps elements of B to the appropriate canonical states $C \subset B$ (see Section 2.6.3), then from Equation 2.2, for all $b \in B$, $w \in [T \to W]$, and $t_1, t_2 \in T$:

$$\overline{\lambda}(b, w)(t_1 + t_2) = \overline{\lambda}(F(t_2, b, w), tail(t_2, w))(t_1) + \overline{\lambda}(b, w)(t_2), \tag{2.9}$$

given that $\phi(\psi(F(t_2, b, w))) = can(F(t_2, b, w))$.

We require that $\phi(\psi(\sigma)) = can(\sigma)$ to ensure that the state σ of G is consistent with correct future execution (see Section 2.6.3).

Lemma 3. *Given iterated maps F and G, and uniform retiming λ, then the following are equivalent.*

1. *For all $t \in T$, $a \in A$, $w \in [T \to W]$, and appropriate $h : W \to Y$*

$$F_1(t, a, w) = \psi(G_1(\overline{\lambda}(a, w)(t), \phi(a), transch(\lambda(a, w), h, w))).$$

2. *For all $a \in A$, $w \in [T \to W]$, and appropriate $h : W \to Y$*

$$F_1(0, a, w) = \psi(G_1(0, \phi(a), transch(\lambda(a, w), h, w))).$$

   and

$$F_1(1, a, w) = \psi(G_1(\overline{\lambda}(a, w)(1), \phi(a), transch(\lambda(a, w), h, w))). \qquad (2.10)$$

It is a corollary of Section 2.7.3 that given iterated map representations F_1 and G_1 of the next-state function of a microprocessor at different levels of abstraction, with clocks T and S respectively, to verify that G_1 simulates F_1 it is sufficient to show that:

- F_1 and G_1 are equivalent at time $t = s = 0$;

- that F_1 and G_1 are equivalent at time $t = 1$, $s = \lambda(a, w)(1)$; and

- that $\phi(\psi(\sigma)) = can(\sigma)$, where σ is the state of G at time $s = \lambda(a, w)(1)$.

2.7.4 Output functions

We now consider the case of the output functions.

Lemma 4. *Given output functions F_2 and G_2 defined by:*

$$F_2(t, a, w) = out_W(F_1(t, a, w)),$$
$$G_2(s, b, y) = out_Y(G_1(s, b, y)),$$

where $F_1 : T \times A \times [T \to W] \to A$ and $G_1 : S \times B \times [S \to Y] \to B$ are appropriate next-state functions, it is sufficient for

$$\chi(out_Y(\phi(a))) = out_W(\psi(\phi(a)))$$

for

$$F_2(t, a, w) = \chi(G_2(\overline{\lambda}(a, w)(t), \phi(a), transch(\lambda(a, w), h, w))),$$

where $a \in A$ and $\overline{\lambda}$, ϕ, ψ and χ are as defined in Section 2.6.2.

3   Gordon's computer—informal specification

We will now consider Gordon's computer as a simple example. We choose this example solely because of its simplicity, and because it has been widely-studied. The tools introduced in this paper have also been applied to more substantial examples (Section 1). Gordon's computer has 2^{13} 16-bit words of memory, a 16-bit accumulator ACC, a 13-bit program counter PC, and a one-bit idle flag. A full informal description can be found in [10], which we summarise below.

The computer has three input mechanisms: a four-position dial; a bank of 16 two-position toggle switches; and a push button. There are four outputs: a bank of 13 lights that display the contents of PC; a bank of 16 lights that display the contents of ACC; a *ready* light; and an *idle* light that displays the contents of the idle flag. The four positions of the dial are labelled as follows.

Table 1. Instruction set of Gordon's computer

Operation	Code	Meaning
HALT	000	Stops execution.
JMP L	001	Jumps to memory location L.
JZRO L	010	Jumps to memory location L if ACC is zero.
ADD L	011	Add contents of memory location L to ACC.
SUB L	100	Subtract contents of location L from ACC.
LD L	101	Load contents of memory location L into ACC.
ST L	110	Store contents of ACC in memory location L.
SKIP	111	Skip to next instruction.

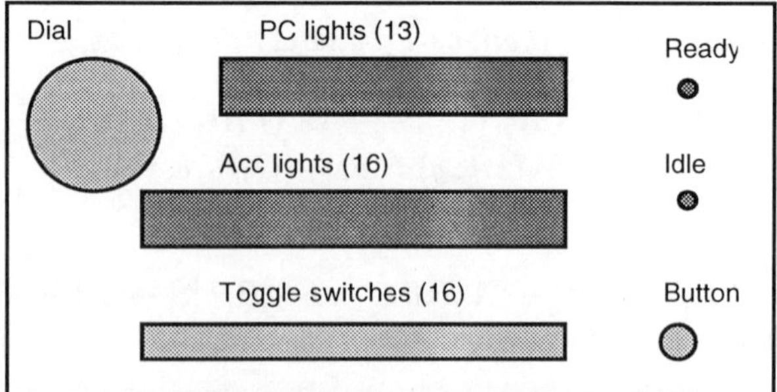

Figure 2. Gordon's simple computer

- *Load PC*, where pressing the push-button replaces the contents of PC by the binary value represented by the 13 right-most toggle switches.

- *Load ACC*, where pressing the push-button replaces the contents of ACC by the binary value represented by all 16 toggle switches.

- *Store*, where pressing the push-button replaces the contents of the memory location specified by PC, with the contents of ACC.

- *Run*, where pressing the push-button starts program execution at the memory location specified by PC.

The *idle* light is illuminated whenever a program is not running. The *ready* light is illuminated whenever the computer is not running, and also when the computer is interruptible (between instructions). Pressing the button when the *ready* light is on interrupts program execution.

The computer has eight instructions, all one word long. The first three bits specify the operation, and the remaining 13 bits specify a memory address (not always used). The operations, together with their opcodes, is shown in Table 1.

Figure 2 illustrates the conceptual front panel of the computer.

4 Programmer's level specification

We will construct a formal specification, at the programmer's model level of abstraction, of the machine described informally in Section 3, in the form outlined in Section 2.3. We choose a clock T such that each clock cycle $t \in T$ lasts for exactly one machine instruction. Typically, this will mean that cycles of clock T are irregular in length, when measured with respect to a typical system clock S. However, from the point of view of a programmer, such a clock is obvious and natural. First, we construct the state of the machine, and describe all inputs and outputs. Next we describe the state algebra functions. Then we construct the machine algebra. Finally, we construct the next-state function and output function.

4.1 The state and next-state algebras

Let $W_n = \{0,1\}^n$. The processor state consists of 16-bit accumulator ACC, 13-bit program counter PC and a single *idle* bit. Hence the state of the machine Gc is defined as follows:

$$Gc = A \times PC \times Bit \times Mem,$$

where $A = W_{16}$, $PC = W_{13}$ and $Mem = [PC \to A]$.

There are three inputs: a control dial with four positions, **load ACC**, **load PC**, **store** and **run**; a bank of 16 two-position switches; and a button. The state of the control dial is represented by

$$D = \{loadACC, loadPC, store, run\}.$$

Formally, input to the machine at time $t \in T$ will consist of a dial-position, a switch position, and a button press:

$$In = D \times A \times \mathbf{B}.$$

There are four outputs consisting of banks of lights representing ACC and PC, and the ready and idle lights:

$$Out = A \times PC \times \mathbf{B} \times \mathbf{B}.$$

The idle light comes on when the processor is not running. At such times, appropriate combinations of dial position and button presses can load switch values into ACC, PC or memory, and can start the processor running. The ready light comes on whenever the processor is *interruptible*, which is at the end of each instruction. Since our top level specification will be over instruction clock T, we only observe the machine at times $t \in T$ corresponding to the intervals between each machine instruction. Consequently, at the programmer's level of abstraction, the ready light is always on. However, when we construct the abstract circuit representation in Section 5, where each clock cycle represents a shorter time interval than at the programmer's model, the behaviour of this output becomes more interesting.

The state algebra function will be

$$GC : T \times Gc \times [T \to In] \to Gc \times Out,$$

and hence the state algebra is

> **Algebra** Gordon State
> **Sets** $T, Gc, In, Out, [T \to In]$
> **Operations**
> $GC : T \times Gc \times [T \to In] \to Gc \times Out$
> **End Algebra.**

We define GC below:

$$GC_1(0, g, i) = g,$$
$$GC_1(t + 1, g, i) = gc(GC_1(t, g, i), i(t)),$$
$$GC_2(t, g, i) = out(GC_1(t, g, i)),$$

where $gc : Gc \times In \to Gc$ is the next-state function, and $out : Gc \to Out$ is the output function. Hence, the next-state algebra is as follows.

Algebra Gordon Next-State
Sets $\quad T, Gc, In, Out, [T \to In]$
Constants
$\qquad 0 : T$
Operations
$\qquad t + 1 : T \to T,$
$\qquad gc : Gc \times In \to Gc,$
$\qquad out : Gc \to Out,$
$\qquad eval : T \times [T \to In] \to In$
End Algebra,

where the *stream evaluation function* $eval : T \times [T \to In] \to In$ is abbreviated by $eval(t, i)$ to $i(t)$. We define GC by primitive recursive equations over the next-state algebra.

4.2 The machine algebra

We define the carriers and operations of the machine algebra for Gordon's computer. Let $A = W_{16}$, $PC = W_{13}$ and $Mem = [PC \to A]$. In addition, we will require Bit, the Booleans **B**, the natural numbers **N**, together with appropriate operations on the Booleans and natural numbers. We require addition and subtraction operations, and equality, on W_{16}, and addition on W_{13} to represent arithmetic operations.

As well as functions to represent ALU operations, and the usual Boolean and natural number operations, we add functions for manipulating bit vectors, converting bit vectors to **N**, performing memory substitution, and extracting useful sub-fields from W_{16}.

The *trimming functions* $trim_Y^X : W_Y \to W_X$, $X, Y \in \mathbf{N}^+$ are defined by

$$trim_Y^X(a_1, \ldots, a_Y) = (a_{Y-X+1}, \ldots, a_Y).$$

We will write $trim_{16}^{13}$ as $trim_A^{PC}$.

The function $pn : A \to \mathbf{N}$ interprets a bit vector $(a_1, \ldots, a_{16}) \in W_{16}$ as a natural number, using the usual interpretation of binary vectors as positive integers.

The function $sub : Mem \times A \times PC \to Mem$ is the *memory substitution function*, defined by

$$sub(m, a, l)(i) = \begin{cases} m(i), & \text{if } l \neq i; \\ a, & \text{if } l = i. \end{cases}$$

We will use $m[a/l]$ as a shorthand notation for $sub(m, a, l)$.

The function $op : A \to \mathbf{N}$ is the *opcode extraction function* defined by $op(a_1, \ldots, a_{16}) = pn(0, \ldots, 0, a_1, a_2, a_3)$.

The function $maddr : A \to PC$ is the *memory address extraction function* defined by $maddr(a_1, \ldots, a_{16}) = (0, 0, 0, a_4, \ldots, a_{16})$.

Summarizing, the machine algebra for Gordon's computer will be as follows.

Algebra Gordon Machine
Sets $\quad Bit, A, PC, Mem, \mathbf{B}, \mathbf{N}, D$
Constants
$\qquad 0 : \mathbf{N}, 0 : A$
Operations
$$+ : PC \times PC \to PC,$$
$$+ : A \times A \to A, - : A \times A \to A,$$
$$=: A \times A \to \mathbf{B},$$
$$=: \mathbf{N} \times \mathbf{N} \to \mathbf{B},$$
$$=: D \times D \to \mathbf{B},$$
$$and : \mathbf{B} \times \mathbf{B} \to \mathbf{B}, or : \mathbf{B} \times \mathbf{B} \to \mathbf{B},$$
$$not : \mathbf{B} \to \mathbf{B},$$
$$trim_A^{PC} : A \to PC,$$
$$pn : A \to \mathbf{N},$$
$$sub : Mem \times A \times PC \to Mem,$$
$$maddr : A \to PC$$
End Algebra.

4.3 Next-state and output functions

We can now define the next-state function of Gordon's computer. Recall from Section 4.1 that $Gc = A \times PC \times Bit \times Mem$ and $In = D \times A \times \mathbf{B}$. We define the next-state function $gc : Gc \times In$ as follows.

$$gc(a, pc, idle, m, d, sw, b) =$$
$$\begin{cases} (a, trim_A^{PC}(sw), tt, m), & \text{if } idle \text{ and } (b \text{ and } d = loadPC); \\ (sw, pc, tt, m), & \text{if } idle \text{ and } (b \text{ and } d = loadACC); \\ (a, pc, tt, m[a/pc]), & \text{if } idle \text{ and } (b \text{ and } d = store); \\ (a, pc, tt, m), & \text{if } (idle \text{ and } \neg b) \text{ or } (\neg idle \text{ and } b); \\ execute(a, pc, ff, m), & \text{if } (\neg idle \text{ and } \neg b) \text{ or } (idle \text{ and } b \text{ and } d = run). \end{cases}$$

The first three cases capture the loading of values into program counter, accumulator, and memory. The fourth case captures the behaviour of the machine both when no activity is occurring (*idle* and $\neg b$), and when the machine is executing a program and is interrupted by a button press ($\neg idle$ and b). The fifth case captures the behaviour of the machine when a program is being executed ($\neg idle$ and $\neg b$), and when a program starts execution (*idle* and b and $d = run$).

We define a sub-function $execute : Gc \to Gc$ to specify the behaviour of each machine instruction.

$$execute(a, pc, idle, m) =$$

$$\begin{cases}
(a, pc, tt, m), & \text{if } op(m(pc)) = 0; \\
(a, maddr(m(pc)), f\!f, m), & \text{if } op(m(pc)) = 1; \\
(a, jzero(m, pc, a), f\!f, m), & \text{if } op(m(pc)) = 2; \\
(a + mval(m, pc), pc + 1, f\!f, m), & \text{if } op(m(pc)) = 3; \\
(a - mval(m, pc), pc + 1, f\!f, m), & \text{if } op(m(pc)) = 4; \\
(mval(m, pc), pc + 1, f\!f, m), & \text{if } op(m(pc)) = 5; \\
(a, pc + 1, f\!f, m[a/maddr(m(pc))]), & \text{if } op(m(pc)) = 6; \\
(a, pc + 1, f\!f, m), & \text{if } op(m(pc)) = 7.
\end{cases}$$

Each case captures the behaviour of the machine instruction whose operation code corresponds with the value of $op(m(pc))$: see Table 1.

It remains to define the subfunctions $mval : Mem \times PC \rightarrow A$ and $jzero : Mem \times PC \times A \rightarrow PC$, used in the definition of execute:

$$mval(m, pc) = m(maddr(m(pc))).$$

$$jzero(m, pc, a) = \begin{cases} maddr(m(pc)), & \text{if } a = 0; \\ pc + 1, & \text{otherwise.} \end{cases}$$

The status of *execute*, *mval* and *jzero* with respect to the algebraic structure of the programmer's model specification of Gordon's computer deserve some discussion. They are part of neither the next-state algebra, nor the machine algebra, but are *auxiliary functions*, forming part of a *hidden function specification*.

Finally, we define the output function. In the case of Gordon's computer, the output function simply projects out parts of the state, except for the ready light which is always on. In most cases, we would expect the output function to be a relatively simple function of the state of the machine, though this need not be the case.

$$out : Gc \times Mem \rightarrow Out,$$
$$out(a, pc, idle, mem) = (a, pc, tt, idle).$$

5 Abstract circuit design

We now consider the abstract circuit representation of Gordon's Computer. A diagram of the basic implementation is shown in Figure 3.

From the implementation representation in Figure 3 we can see that the following elements have been added to the datapath, in order for it to function: A memory address register (MAR) of 13 bits, an instruction register (IR), an argument register (ARG), and a buffer register (BUF), all of 16 bits. All components of the datapath, and the memory, are connected by a 16-bit bus, though this is not properly part of the state of the datapath. The controller is seen to consist of a microprogram counter (MPC), and a microprogram memory (ROM) consisting of 32 words of 30 bits each, together with a decoder.

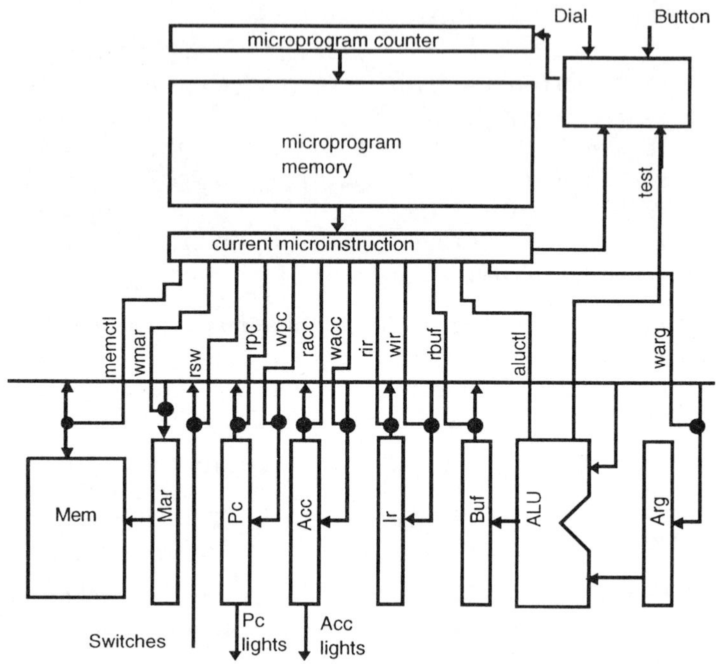

Figure 3. Abstract circuit design of Gordon's computer

5.1   Controller: informal description

Each 30-bit microprogram word consists of four fields: a three-bit *test* field; two five-bit *next address* fields, A and B; and a 17-bit *control* field. The control field is used to direct the operation of datapath and memory, with each individual bit (or, in some cases bit-pair) controlling a single datapath or memory component. The other three fields, together with inputs from the datapath, dial and button, control the decoder, which in turn determines the address of the next microinstruction to be executed. If the *test* field is 1, and the button is pressed, or if the *test* field is 2, and ACC is zero, the controller jumps to B. If the *test* field is 3, the controller jumps to A+*dial*, where *dial* is the numerical value of the dial position, with *loadPC* = 1, *loadACC* = 2, *store* = 3 and *run* = 4. If the *test* field is 4, the controller jumps to A+*opcode*, where *opcode* is the numerical value of the current instruction's operation code. In all other cases, the controller jumps to A.

One suitable microprogram for Gordon's computer, originally given in [10], consists of 26 microinstructions. A symbolic representation of the microprogram, in a format similar to that in [10], is given in Table 2. The format of each microinstruction is

$$control; next\ address,$$

where *control* is a list of zero or more control signals to be activated, and address is the next microinstruction to execute. The notation

$$condition \rightarrow a, b$$

means branch to address a if *condition* is true, and address b otherwise.

Table 2. The microcode for Gordon's computer

Address		Microinstruction	Comment
0	ready,idle	;button$\rightarrow 1, 0$	Idling loop
1		;dial+1	Decode dial
2	rsw,wpc	;0	Load switches in PC
3	rsw,wacc	;0	Load switches in ACC
4	rpc,wmar	;7	Write ACC to Memory
5	ready	;button$\rightarrow 0, 6$	Begin execution cycle
6	rpc,wmar	;8	PC to MAR
7	racc,write	;0	ACC to Memory
8	read,wir	;9	Instruction to IR
9		;opcode+10	Decode instruction
10		;0	Halt
11	rir,wpc	;5	JMP
12		;$acc = 0 \rightarrow 11, 17$	JZRO
13	racc,warg	;19	ADD
14	racc,warg	;22	SUB
15	rir,wmar	;24	LOAD
16	rir,wmar	;25	STORE
17	rpc,inc	;18	Increment...
18	rbuf,wpc	;5	... program counter
19	rir,wmar	;20	IR to MAR
20	read,add	;21	Addition operation
21	rbuf,wacc	;17	Buffer to ACC
22	rir,wmar	;23	IR to MAR
23	read,sub	;21	Subtraction operation
24	read,wacc	;17	Load operation
25	racc,write	;17	Store operation

Microinstruction 0 represents the idle state, continually looping until the button is pressed; microinstructions 1–4 decode the dial position; microinstructions 5–8 fetch the current machine instruction; microinstruction 9 decodes the current instruction; and microinstructions 10–25 are responsible for instruction execution, with 17 and 18 incrementing the program counter.

5.2 Datapath and controller states

We define the states of the datapath and controller:

$$
\begin{aligned}
Gdp &= A \times PC \times Bit \times PC \times A \times A \times A, \\
Gct &= \mu PC \times \mu M,
\end{aligned}
$$

where $\mu PC = W_5$, and $\mu M \subset [\mu PC \to \mu IR]$, where $\mu IR = W_{30}$. The memory state is just $Mem = [PC \to A]$ as in Section 4. Observe that μM is a subset of all possible microprogram memories $[\mu PC \to \mu IR]$. This is because not all possible combinations are allowed; for example, it is not meaningful to write two different values to the data bus at the same time (see Section 5.4). The input GIn is similar to that of the programmer's model level. We replace D of the programmer's level with GD:

$$
GD = \{1, 2, 3, 4\}.
$$

The intention is that the symbolic values of D at the programmer's level are replaced by numeric values at the abstract circuit level. The other components of GIn are the same as the corresponding elements of In:

$$
GIn = GD \times A \times \mathbf{B}.
$$

The output of the abstract circuit level representation remains the same as that of the programmer's level. Hence, we employ the same set Out of outputs.

The state algebra functions will be

$$
\begin{aligned}
GDP &: S \times Gct \times Gdp \times Mem \times [S \to GIn] \to Gdp, \\
GCT &: S \times Gct \times Gdp \times Mem \times [S \to GIn] \to Gct, \\
GMEM &: S \times Gct \times Gdp \times Mem \times [S \to GIn] \to Mem, \\
GOUT &: S \times Gct \times Gdp \times Mem \times [S \to GIn] \to Out,
\end{aligned}
$$

and hence the state algebra is as follows:

Algebra Abstract Circuit State
Sets $S, Gdp, Gct, Mem, GIn, [S \rightarrow GIn], Out$
Operations
$$GDP : S \times Gct \times Gdp \times Mem \times [S \rightarrow GIn] \rightarrow Gdp,$$
$$GCT : S \times Gct \times Gdp \times Mem \times [S \rightarrow GIn] \rightarrow Gct,$$
$$GMEM : S \times Gct \times Gdp \times Mem \times [S \rightarrow GIn] \rightarrow Mem,$$
$$GOUT : S \times Gct \times Gdp \times Mem \times [S \rightarrow GIn] \rightarrow Out$$
End Algebra.

We define GDP, GCT, $GMEM$ and $GOUT$ below:

$$GDP(0, gc, gd, m, i) = gd,$$
$$GCT(0, gc, gd, m, i) = gc,$$
$$GMEM(0, gc, gd, m, i) = m,$$
$$GDP(s + 1, gc, gd, m, i) = gdp(GCT(s, gc, gd, m, i), GDP(s, gc, gd, m, i),$$
$$GMEM(s, gc, gd, m, i), i(s)),$$
$$GCT(s + 1, gc, gd, m, i) = gct(GCT(s, gc, gd, m, i), GDP(s, gc, gd, m, i),$$
$$GMEM(s, gc, gd, m, i), i(s)),$$
$$GMEM(s + 1, gc, gd, m, i) = gmem(GCT(s, gc, gd, m, i),$$
$$GDP(s, gc, gd, m, i), GMEM(s, gc, gd, m, i), i(s)),$$
$$GOUT(s, gc, gd, m, i) = gout(GCT(s, gc, gd, m, i), GDP(s, gc, gd, m, i),$$
$$GMEM(s, gc, gd, m, i), i(s)).$$

Observe that we define the state of the controller GCT at time $s = 0$ to be the initial state. In practice, it may be more appropriate to explicitly initialise GCT to some default, initialisation value, in this case:

$$GCT(0, gc, gd, m, i) = (0, \mu m).$$

An initial value of $\mu pc = 0$ would initialise the computer to *idle* and *ready* status, waiting for input (see the informal description of a suitable microprogram in Section 5.1).

The next-state algebra is as follows:

Algebra Abstract Circuit Next-State
Sets $S, Gdp, Gct, Mem, GIn, [S \rightarrow GIn], Out$
Constants
$$0 : T$$
Operations
$$gdp : Gct \times Gdp \times Mem \times GIn \rightarrow Gdp,$$
$$gct : Gct \times Gdp \times Mem \times GIn \rightarrow Gct,$$
$$gmem : Gct \times Gdp \times Mem \times GIn \rightarrow Mem,$$
$$gout : Gct \times Gdp \times Mem \times GIn \rightarrow Out$$
End Algebra.

It remains to define the next-state and output functions, and μM. We will closely follows the method described in [18]. First we construct the machine algebra; then we define the set of allowable microprogram memories; then we define the next-state functions for datapath and controller; and finally we define the output function.

5.3   The machine algebra

As in Section 4.2, the machine algebra for the abstract circuit model consist of vectors of bits, the Booleans **B**, the natural numbers **N**, and appropriate operations.

Let

$$rsw, rpc, racc, rir, rbuf, wacc, wpc, wmar, wir, warg : \mu IR \rightarrow \mathbf{B}$$

be functions that project out single bits of the current microinstruction, and

$$memctl, aluctl : \mu IR \rightarrow \{0, \ldots, 3\}$$

be functions that project out bit-pairs. We omit the definitions of $rsw, \ldots, warg$, *memctl* and *aluctl*. Let

$$test : \mu IR \rightarrow \{0, \ldots, 7\}$$

be a function that projects out the 3-bit field of the current microinstruction that determines the next microinstruction to be executed, and

$$aaddr, baddr : \mu IR \rightarrow \mu PC$$

be functions that project out the 5-bit next address fields of the current microinstruction. Again, we omit the definitions of *test*, *aaddr* and *baddr*.

Let $np : \{0, \ldots, 8191\} \rightarrow PC$ be a function that maps natural numbers in the range 0 to 8191 to the usual binary notation, extended with zeros if required to 13 bits.

Let the *padding* functions $pad_i^j : W_j \rightarrow W_i$, $j \leq i$ be defined as follows:

$$pad_i^j(a_1, \ldots, a_j) = (0, \ldots, 0, a_1, \ldots, a_j).$$

We will write pad_{16}^{13} as pad_A^{PC}.

We can now define the machine algebra as follows:

Algebra Abstract Circuit Machine
Sets $\quad A, PC, Bit, \mathbf{B}, \mathbf{N}, \mu IR, \mu PC, [\mu PC \to \mu IR], [PC \to A]$
Constants
$\qquad 0, 1, 2, 3, 4 : \mathbf{N},$
$\qquad 0 : A$
$\qquad tt, ff : \mathbf{B}$
Operations
$\qquad rsw, rpc, racc, rir, rbuf, wacc, wpc, wmar, wir, warg : \mu IR \to \mathbf{B},$
$\qquad memctl, aluctl : \mu IR \to \{0, \ldots, 3\},$
$\qquad aaddr, baddr : \mu IR \to \mu PC,$
$\qquad test : \mu IR \to \{0, \ldots, 7\},$
$\qquad =: \mathbf{N} \times \mathbf{N} \to \mathbf{B},$
$\qquad =: D \times D \to \mathbf{B},$
$\qquad + : PC \times PC \to PC,$
$\qquad + : A \times A \to A,$
$\qquad + : \mathbf{N} \times \mathbf{N} \to \mathbf{N},$
$\qquad - : A \times A \to A,$
$\qquad and : \mathbf{B} \times \mathbf{B} \to \mathbf{B},$
$\qquad or : \mathbf{B} \times \mathbf{B} \to \mathbf{B},$
$\qquad not : \mathbf{B} \to \mathbf{B},$
$\qquad trim_A^{PC} : A \to PC,$
$\qquad pad_A^{PC} : PC \to A,$
$\qquad pn : A \to \mathbf{N},$
$\qquad np : \{0, \ldots, 8192\} \to PC$
End Algebra.

5.4 Defining the microprogram memory

Informally, each microprogram word consists of 17 fields, of between one and five
bits each, which control various aspects of the controller, memory and datapath,
and also contribute to the machine's output. The fields *rsw, rpc, racc, rir rbuf*
are all one bit long, and control values read by the bus from various sources. The
fields *wpc, wacc, wmar, wir* and *warg* are also one bit long, and control values
written from the bus to various destinations. The field *memctl* is two bits long,
and controls memory reading and writing. The field *aluctl* is also two bits long,
and controls Arithmetic/Logic functions. The field *test* is three bits long and
determines the address of the next microinstruction. The fields *aaddr* and *baddr*
are five bits long and contain alternative next microinstruction addresses. The
fields *ready* and *idle* are one bit long, and control the ready and idle lights. We
will not specify precisely which parts of the microinstruction word correspond
with each field (though this is clearly not difficult, and a full description can

be found in [10]). Rather we will assume, for each separate field, the existence of appropriate boolean functions (in the case of the one-bit fields) or projection functions (in the case of longer fields), as listed in Section 5.3.

Not all possible combinations of control signals are meaningful: we must disallow multiple simultaneous attempts to write to the bus. To do this, we define a *mutual exclusion function* $Mx : \mu IR \to \mathbf{B}$ as follows:

$$Mx(a) = \begin{cases} tt, & \text{if } rsw(a),\, rpc(a),\, rpc(a),\, racc(a), \\ & \quad rir(a),\, rbuf(a),\, memctl(a) = 1 \text{ disjoint;} \\ f\!f, & \text{otherwise.} \end{cases}$$

Informally, we require only one of the possible fields that write to the bus to be true at any one time. We may now define μM to be a subset of $[\mu PC \to \mu IR]$ as follows.

$$\mu M = \{\mu m \in [\mu PC \to \mu IR] \mid \forall \mu pc \in \mu PC,\, Mx(\mu m(\mu pc))\}.$$

5.5   Defining the datapath next-state function

We define the datapath next-state function

$$gdp : Gct \times Gdp \times Mem \times GIn \to Gdp$$

in the manner described in [18]. First, we extend the datapath with the bus, to create a new object Gdp':

$$Gdp' = Gdp \times A.$$

We will define gdp in terms of two subfunctions $gdpwr$ which controls writing to the bus, and $gdprd$ which controls reading from the bus.

$$gdpwr : Gct \times Gdp' \times Mem \times GIn \to Gdp',$$
$$gdprd : Gct \times Gdp' \times Mem \times GIn \to Gdp'.$$

Given definitions of $gdpwr$ and $gdprd$, we may compose them to define gdp as follows.

$$gdp(gc, gd, m, d, sw, b) =$$

$$\pi_g(gdprd(gc, gdpwr(gc, \alpha_g(gd), m, d, sw, b), m, d, sw, b))$$

where $\pi_g : Gdp' \to Gdp$ is a projection function that removes the bus, and $\alpha_g : Gdp \to Gdp'$ is a padding function that pads Gdp with a constant representing the contents of the bus at the start of a machine instruction. What should this constant be? Clearly, any value stored on the bus at the start of a machine instruction will be the result of some computation performed by the previous machine instruction. Such residual information should not affect the current machine instruction in any correct implementation. Hence, we may pad the bus with an arbitrary constant.

It remains to define *gdpwr* and *gdprd*:

$$gdpwr_a(\mu pc, \mu m, a, pc, idle, mar, ir, arg, buf, bus, m, d, sw, b) = a,$$

$$\vdots \qquad\qquad \vdots$$

$$gdpwr_{buf}(\mu pc, \mu m, a, pc, idle, mar, ir, arg, buf, bus, m, d, sw, b) = buf,$$

$$gdpwr_{bus}(\mu pc, \mu m, a, pc, idle, mar, ir, arg, buf, bus, m, d, sw, b) =$$

$$\begin{cases} m(mar), & \text{if } memctl(\mu m(\mu pc)) = 1; \\ sw, & \text{if } rsw(\mu m(\mu pc)); \\ pad_A^{PC}(pc), & \text{if } rpc(\mu m(\mu pc)); \\ a, & \text{if } racc(\mu m(\mu pc)); \\ ir, & \text{if } rir(\mu m(\mu pc)); \\ buf, & \text{if } rbuf(\mu m(\mu pc)); \\ bus, & \text{otherwise}, \end{cases}$$

$$gdprd_a(\mu pc, \mu m, a, pc, idle, mar, ir, arg, buf, bus, m, d, sw, b) =$$

$$\begin{cases} bus, & \text{if } wacc(\mu m(\mu pc)); \\ a, & \text{otherwise}, \end{cases}$$

$$\vdots \qquad\qquad \vdots$$

$$gdprd_{buf}(\mu pc, \mu m, a, pc, idle, mar, ir, arg, buf, bus, m, d, sw, b) =$$

$$\begin{cases} bus + 1, & \text{if } aluctl(\mu m(\mu pc)) = 1; \\ arg + bus, & \text{if } aluctl(\mu m(\mu pc)) = 2; \\ arg - bus, & \text{if } aluctl(\mu m(\mu pc)) = 3; \\ buf, & \text{otherwise}, \end{cases}$$

$$gdprd_{bus}(\mu pc, \mu m, a, pc, idle, mar, ir, arg, buf, bus, m, d, sw, b) = bus.$$

We omit definitions of $gdprd_{pc}, \ldots, gdprd_{arg}$, which are similar to $gdprd_a$ and $gdprd_{buf}$.

5.6 Controller next-state function

We now define the controller next-state function $gct : Gct \times Gdp \times Mem \times GIn \to Gct$:

$$gct(\mu pc, \mu m, mar, pc, a, ir, arg, buf, m, d, sw, b) =$$

$$\begin{cases} baddr(\mu m(\mu pc)), \mu m, & \text{if } test(\mu m(\mu pc)) = 1 \text{ and } b = tt; \\ baddr(\mu m(\mu pc)), \mu m, & \text{if } test(\mu m(\mu pc)) = 2 \text{ and } a = 0; \\ aaddr(\mu m(\mu pc)) + np(d), \mu m, & \text{if } test(\mu m(\mu pc)) = 3; \\ np(op(ir)) + baddr(\mu m(\mu pc)), \mu m, & \text{if } test(\mu m(\mu pc)) = 4; \\ aaddr(\mu m(\mu pc)), \mu m, & \text{otherwise}. \end{cases}$$

To complete the specification of the controller, we must specify an appropriate microprogram. We will not do this here, and the interested reader is referred to [10], and to Section 5.1 for an informal description.

5.7   Memory next-state function

The memory next-state function $gmem : Gct \times Gdp \times Mem \times GIn \to Mem$ is defined as follows.

$$gmem(\mu pc, \mu m, mar, pc, a, ir, arg, buf, m, d, sw, b) =$$
$$\begin{cases} m[a/mar], & \text{if } memctl(\mu m(\mu pc)) = 2; \\ m, & \text{otherwise.} \end{cases}$$

5.8   Output function

The output function $gout : Gct \times Gdp \times Mem \times GIn \to Out$ is defined as follows.

$$gout(\mu pc, \mu m, mar, pc, a, \ldots) = (a, pc, ready(\mu m(\mu pc)), idle(\mu m(\mu pc))),$$

where $ready, idle : \mu IR \to \mathbf{B}$ are functions which project out the appropriate bits of the current microinstruction.

6   Correctness of implementation

We now consider what it means for the programmer's model specification to be simulated by the abstract circuit representation, and outline the proof process. With reference to Section 2.6.2, we construct the following commutative diagram.

$$
\begin{array}{ccc}
T \times Gc \times [T \to In] & \xrightarrow{(GC,OUT)} & Gc \times Out \\
\Big\downarrow{\scriptstyle (\overline{\lambda}, \phi, transch)} & & \Big\uparrow{\scriptstyle (\psi, \chi)} \\
S \times \cdots \times [S \to GIn] & \xrightarrow{(GCT,\ldots,GOUT)} & Gct \times Gdp \times Mem \times Out
\end{array}
$$

We now define λ, ϕ, ψ, h and χ. The output map χ is the identity function, since the outputs in both cases are the same.

The map $\psi : Gct \times Gdp \times Mem \to Gc$ is a projection function defined by

$$\psi(\mu pc, \mu m, a, pc, idle, mar, ir, arg, buf, m) = (a, pc, idle, m)$$

The map $\chi : Out \to Out$ is the identity function (since the representation of output is the same at programmer's level and abstract circuit level).

The map $\phi : Gc \to Gct \times Gdp \times Mem$ is the padding function defined by

$$\phi(a, pc, idle, m) = \begin{cases} (0, \mu m, a, pc, idle, x_{mar}, x_{ir}, x_{arg}, x_{buf}, m), & \text{if } idle; \\ (5, \mu m, a, pc, idle, x_{mar}, x_{ir}, x_{arg}, x_{buf}, m), & \text{if } \neg idle, \end{cases}$$

where μm represents the microprogram memory, and $x_{mar}, \ldots, x_{buf}$ are appropriate *don't care* constants representing the non-canonical elements of

$Gct \times Gdp \times Mem$ (see Section 2.6.3). The microprogram memory μm, and the microprogram counter μpc represent the canonical elements of $Gct \times Gdp \times Mem$ and are initialised to a specific constant (μ_m in the case of the microprogram memory) or are a function of the programmer's level state (in the case of the microprogram counter).

The set C of canonical states of the abstract circuit representation (see Section 2.6.3) is defined as follows:

$$C = \{(\mu pc, \mu m, a, pc, idle, mar, ir, arg, buf, m) \in Gct \times Gdp \times Mem$$
$$\mid mar = x_{mar}, ir = x_{ir}, arg = x_{arg}, buf = x_{buf}\}.$$

Observe that the canonical elements of $Gct \times Gdp \times Mem$ are exactly those representing the state of the controller.

We can now define the function $can : Gct \times Gdp \times Mem \to C$ that maps elements of the abstract circuit state to their canonical equivalents:

$$can(\mu pc, \mu m, a, pc, idle, mar, ir, arg, buf, m) =$$
$$(\mu pc, \mu m, a, pc, idle, x_{mar}, x_{ir}, x_{arg}, x_{buf}, m).$$

The map $h : In \to GIn$ translates input elements for the programmer's level model into appropriate input elements for the abstract circuit level model, and is defined by

$$h(d, sw, b) = \begin{cases} (1, sw, b) & \text{if } d = loadPC); \\ (2, sw, b) & \text{if } d = loadACC); \\ (3, sw, b) & \text{if } d = store); \\ (4, sw, b) & \text{if } d = run). \end{cases}$$

Observe that h simply maps the symbolic representation of the dial position used at the programmer's level, to the corresponding numeric values used in the microprogrammed implementation at the abstract circuit level.

It only remains to define λ, and hence the immersion $\overline{\lambda}$. We may define λ in a number of ways, and our choice will affect the precise nature of any formal verification. For example, in [18], a "weak" definition of λ was chosen. There, λ was defined in terms of the chosen microprogram at the abstract circuit design level. This definition is very flexible, in that changes to the microcode do not require changes to λ. However, it also means that we cannot obtain any concrete statements about how long each instruction will take to execute from any verification, since by definition λ only states that an instruction's execution finishes when the corresponding microprogram sequence ends. Here, we will use a stronger, more concrete, definition of λ, where the number of microinstruction cycles corresponding to each instruction is explicitly stated. This slightly complicates the verification process, since we must now verify that the number of cycles taken is correct in each case, but allows us to make concrete, formal, statements about how long each instruction takes to execute.

6.1 Definition of λ

We wish to exploit the simplified proof method described in Section 2.7.3. Consequently, we require λ to be a uniform retiming. Following the basic method outlined in [18], we define a function $XTIME : Gc \times In \to [T \to \mathbf{N}^+]$ so that

$$\lambda(a, w)(s) = L(XTIME(a, w))(s),$$

where $L : [T \to \mathbf{N}^+] \to Ret(S, T)$ is defined in Section 2.5.2. We define $XTIME$ as follows.

$$XTIME(a, in)(t) = xtime(GC(t - 1, a, in), in(t)).$$

The function $xtime : Gc \times In \to \mathbf{N}$ defines the number of cycles of system clock S required for each instruction clock cycle, for every possible state and input:

$$xtime(a, pc, idle, m, d, sw, b) =$$
$$\begin{cases} 3 & \text{if } idle \text{ and } (b \\ & \text{and } (d = loadPC) \text{ or } d = loadACC); \\ 4 & \text{if } idle \text{ and } (b \text{ and } d = store); \\ 1 & \text{if } (idle \text{ and } \neg b) \text{ or } (\neg idle \text{ and } b); \\ exec(a, pc, f\!f, m), & \text{if } (\neg idle \text{ and } \neg b); \\ exec(a, pc, f\!f, m) + 2, & \text{if } (idle \text{ and } b \text{ and } d = run). \end{cases}$$

We define a sub-function $exec : Gc \to \mathbf{N}^+$ to specify λ for each machine instruction.

$$exec(a, pc, idle, m) = \begin{cases} 5 & \text{if } op(m(pc)) = 0; \\ 5 & \text{if } op(m(pc)) = 1; \\ 6 & \text{if } op(m(pc)) = 2 \text{ and } acc = 0; \\ 7 & \text{if } op(m(pc)) = 2 \text{ and } acc \neq 0; \\ 10 & \text{if } op(m(pc)) = 3; \\ 10 & \text{if } op(m(pc)) = 4; \\ 8 & \text{if } op(m(pc)) = 5; \\ 8 & \text{if } op(m(pc)) = 6; \\ 6 & \text{if } op(m(pc)) = 7. \end{cases}$$

The following lemma is proved in [17]:

Lemma 5. λ *as defined is a uniform retiming.*

6.2 Outline of verification process

In order to verify that the abstract circuit representation of Section 5 correctly implements the programmer's model of Section 4 we must show that the diagram in Section 6 commutes. Alternatively:

$$\begin{aligned} (GC(t, g, i), OUT(t, g, i)) \ =\ & (\psi(GCT(\bar{\lambda}(g, i)(t), \phi(g), transch(\lambda(g, i), h, i)), \\ & GDP(\bar{\lambda}(g, i)(t), \phi(g), transch(\lambda(g, i), h, i)), \\ & GMEM(\bar{\lambda}(g, i)(t), \phi(g), transch(\lambda(g, i), h, i))), \\ & \chi(GOUT(\bar{\lambda}(g, i)(t), \phi(g), transch(\lambda(g, i), h, i)))), \end{aligned}$$

where ϕ, ψ, χ and h are defined in Section 6, and uniform retiming λ is defined in Section 6.1. Given Lemmas 3 and 4, it is sufficient to show

$$
\begin{aligned}
GC(0,g,i) \;=\; &(\psi(GCT(0,\phi(g),transch(\lambda(g,i),h,i)), \\
&GDP(0,\phi(g),transch(\lambda(g,i),h,i)), \\
&GMEM(0,\phi(g),transch(\lambda(g,i),h,i)))),
\end{aligned}
$$

$$
\begin{aligned}
GC(1,g,i) \;=\; &(\psi(GCT(\bar{\lambda}(g,i)(1),\phi(g),transch(\lambda(g,i),h,i)), \\
&GDP(\bar{\lambda}(g,i)(1),\phi(g),transch(\lambda(g,i),h,i)), \\
&GMEM(\bar{\lambda}(g,i)(1),\phi(g),transch(\lambda(g,i),h,i)))),
\end{aligned}
$$

and

$$
\chi(gout(\phi(g))) = out(\psi(\phi(g))),
$$

where $g \in Gc$ is an initial programmer's model state, $i \in In$ is an input stream, *out* is defined in Section 4.3 and *gout* is defined in Section 5.8.

First, we consider the verification of the state functions, and then we consider the output functions.

6.2.1 Verification of the state functions

Our strategy will be to consider each possible sub-case in the programmer's model representation of Section 4, showing that in each case, the programmer's model and the abstract circuit model are equivalent at times $t = 0$ and $t = 1$ for all possible starting states and input values, and that for all possible states σ of the abstract circuit representation at time $s = \bar{\lambda}(g,i)(1)$, that $\phi(\psi(\sigma)) = can(\sigma)$. By inspecting functions gc and *execute* in Section 4.3 we see that there are 23 cases to consider: five cases when no instructions are being executed; nine when instruction execution has just commenced; and nine when instruction execution is ongoing. There are nine instruction execution cases, not eight, because of the JZRO conditional jump. Space prevents a full account of the verification. However, many of these cases are trivial, or similar to each other, making verification a straightforward, if tedious, process.

6.2.2 Verification of the output functions

Finally, we consider the output functions. We require

$$
OUT(t,g,i) = \chi(GOUT(\bar{\lambda}(g,i)(t),\phi(g),transch(\lambda(g,i),h,i))).
$$

From Lemma 4, given $g = (a,pc,idle,m)$, it is sufficient to show that

$$
\chi(gout(\phi(a,pc,idle,m))) = out(\psi(\phi(a,pc,idle,m))).
$$

Observe that $\psi(\phi(a,pc,idle,m)) = a,pc,idle,m$, and

$$
out(a,pc,idle,m) = (a,pc,tt,idle).
$$

Now consider $\chi(gout(\phi(a, pc, idle, m)))$, and observe that given the definitions of χ and ϕ in Section 6 and $gout$ in Section 5.8,

$$\chi(gout(\phi(a, pc, idle, m))) = a, pc, ready(\mu m(0)), idle(\mu m(0))), \text{ or}$$
$$\chi(gout(\phi(a, pc, idle, m))) = a, pc, ready(\mu m(5)), idle(\mu m(5))).$$

We have not formally defined a microprogram memory μm, but examination of the informal microprogram in Section 5.1 reveals that $ready(\mu m(0)) = ready(\mu m(5)) = tt$, which is correct, and $idle(\mu m(0)) = tt$, and $idle(\mu m(5)) = ff$. To complete the verification, we must check the value of $idle$ in each of the 23 sub-cases. However, this is trivial given the verification of the state functions (Section 6.2.1): for example, in the case of the ADD instruction considered above, $idle = ff$, and $\mu pc = 5$, and hence $idle(\mu m(\mu pc)) = ff$.

7   Concluding remarks

We have introduced algebraic tools for the representation of computers at different levels of data and timing abstraction, and for the verification of one level of abstraction against another. We have shown how the process of formal verification can be considerably simplified, for a significant class of digital hardware. This class includes non-pipelined implementations of microprocessors. In addition, we have applied our algebraic tools to a commonly-considered example.

The formal tools and techniques presented in this paper have some advantages. The algebraic tools are independent of specific software systems (for example, theorem provers and proof checkers). It is possible to encode the tools presented here in a range of such tools. Clearly, verification of realistic examples will require machine support. Our models and tools allow us to establish correctness by satisfying considerably simpler proof obligations than are usual in microprocessor verification.

The need for a modular approach to specification and design has been an important consideration in the development of the tools described in this paper, as has the need for a clear mathematical description of the modularisation process. This is addressed in further work on the hierarchical, algebraic structure of specifications and designs. All of these algebraic models can be equationally specified by using initial algebra semantics [18].

The tools presented in this paper are suitable for non-pipelined designs. Modern microprocessor designs are almost invariably pipelined, or superscalar. The tools presented here can be extended to accommodate pipelined and superscalar designs. Extension to pipelined design is straightforward; extension to superscalar design requires a modification to retimings (primarily because of simultaneous, or out-of-order, instruction completion). In addition, other aspects of modern microprocessor design are also being considered, in particular: multiprocessing; exception handling; and more advanced models of memory, including caching and virtual memory.

Acknowledgements

The authors would like to thank A. Fox for work on formal verification in Section 6, and for invaluable comments and corrections on drafts of this paper.

References

1. May, D., Barrett. G. and Sheppard, D. (1992). Designing chips that work. *Mechanized Reasoning and Hardware Design*, Editors: C.A.R. Hoare and M.J.C. Gordon, Prentice-Hall.

2. Birtwistle, G. and Graham, B. (1990). Verifying SECD in HOL. *Formal Methods for VLSI Design*, Editor: J. Staunstrup, North-Holland, 129–177.

3. Bose, B. and Johnson, S.D. (1993). DDD-FM9001: Derivation of a verified microprocessor. *Correct Hardware Design and Verification Methods*, Editors: L. Pierre and G. Milne, *Lecture Notes in Computer Science* **683**, Springer-Verlag, 191–202.

4. Cohn, A. (1987). A proof of correctness of the VIPER microprocessor: the first levels. *VLSI Specification, Verification and Synthesis*, Editors: G. Birtwistle and P.A. Subrahmanyam, Kluwer Academic, 27–72.

5. Cullyer, W.J. (1987). Application of formal methods to the VIPER microprocessor. *IEE Proc.*, **134 E(3)**, 133–141.

6. Cullyer, W.J. (1987). Implementing safety critical systems: the viper microprocessor. *VLSI Specification, Verification, and Synthesis*, Editors: G. Birtwistle and P.A. Subrahmanyam, Kluwer Academic, 1–26.

7. Geser, A. (1989). A specification of the intel 8085 microprocessor: A case study. *Algebraic Methods: Theory, Tools and Applications*, Editors: M. Wirsing and J.A. Bergstra, 347–402, *Lecture Notes in Computer Science* **394**, Springer-Verlag.

8. Goguen, J.A. and Winkler, T. (1988). Introducing OBJ3. *Technical Report SRI-CSL-88-9*, Computer Science Laboratory, SRI International, California.

9. Gordon, M. (1983). LCF-LSM, a system for specifying and verifying hardware. *Technical Report Number 41*, Computer Laboratory, University of Cambridge.

10. Gordon, M. (1983). Proving a computer correct with the LCF-LSM hardware verification system. *Technical Report Number 42*, Computer Laboratory, University of Cambridge.

11. Gordon, M. (1987). HOL: A proof generating system for higher-order logic. *VLSI Specification, Verification and Synthesis*, Editors: G. Birtwistle and P.A. Subrahmanyam, Kluwer Academic, 73–128.

12. Graham, B. (1992). *The SECD Microprocessor: a Verification Case Study*, Kluwer Academic.

13. Graham, B. and Birtwistle, G. (1990). Formalising the design of an SECD chip. *Hardware Specification, Verification and Synthesis: Mathematical Aspects*, Editors: M. Leeser and G. Brown, 40–66, *Lecture Notes in Computer Science*, **408**, Springer-Verlag.

14. Harman, N.A. (1989). *Formal Specifications for Digital Systems*, PhD Thesis, School of Computer Studies, University of Leeds.

15. Harman, N.A. and Tucker, J.V. (1990). The formal specification of a digital correlator I: Abstract user specification. *Theoretical Foundations for VLSI Design*, Editors: K. McEvoy and J.V. Tucker, 161–262. *Cambridge University Press Tracts in Theoretical Computer Science*, **10**.

16. Harman, N.A. and Tucker, J.V. (1993). Algebraic models and the correctness of microprocessors. *Correct Hardware Design and Verification Methods*, Editors: L. Pierre and G. Milne, *Lecture Notes in Computer Science*, **683**, Springer-Verlag.

17. Harman, N.A. and Tucker, J.V. (1994). A model of timing abstraction for synchronous digital hardware. *Technical Report*, University of Wales, Swansea, *Computer Science Report*, (In Preparation).

18. Harman, N.A. and Tucker, J.V. (1996). Algebraic models of microprocessors: Architecture and organisation. *Technical Report, Acta Informatica*, **33**, 421–456.

19. Hunt, W. A formal HDL and its use in the FM9001 verification. *Mechanized Reasoning in Hardware Design*, Editors: C.A.R. Hoare and M. Gordon, Prentice-Hall.

20. Hunt, W. (1994). *FM8501: A Verfified Microprocessor*, *Lecture Notes on Artificial Intelligence*, **795**, Springer-Verlag.

21. Hunt, W.A. (1986). FM8501: A verified microprocessor. *Technical Report*, **47**, Austin Institute for Computing Science, University of Texas.

22. Hunt, W.A. (1989). Microprocessor design verification. *J. of Automated Reasoning*, **5**, 429–460.

23. Joyce, J. (1987). Formal verification and implementation of a microprocessor. *VLSI Specification, Verification and Synthesis*, Editors: G. Birtwistle and P.A. Subrahmanyam, Kluwer Academic, 129–159.

24. Landin, P. (1963). On the mechanical evaluation of expressions. *Computer J.*, **6**, 308–320.

25. Meinke, K. and Tucker. J.V. (1992). Universal algebra. *Handbook of Logic in Computer Science*, Editors: T.S.E. Maibaum, S. Abramsky and D. Gabbay, Oxford University Press, 189–411.

26. Roscoe, W. (1992). Occam in the specification and verification of microprocessors. *Mechanized Reasoning and Hardware Design*, Editors: C.A.R. Hoare and M.J.C Gordon, Prentice-Hall.

27. Staunstrup, J. (1994). IFIP WG 10.2 collection of circuit verification examples. *Technical Report (Draft Version)*, Department of Computer Science, Technical University of Denmark.

28. Stavridou, V. (1993). *Formal Specification of Digital Systems, Cambridge University Press Tracts in Theoretical Computer Science*, **37**.

29. Thompson, B.C. and Tucker, J.V. (1991). Equational specification of synchronous concurrent algebras and architectures. *Technical Report CSR 9.91*, Department of Computer Science, University College Swansea.

30. Tucker, J.V. (1991). Theory of computation and specification over abstract data types and its applications. *Logic, Algebra and Computation*, Editor: F.L. Bauer, Springer-Verlag, 1–40.

31. Tucker, J.V. and Zucker, J.I. (1988). *Program Correctness over Abstract Data Types with Error State Semantics*, North-Holland.

32. Wirsing, M. (1990). Algebraic specification. *Handbook of Theoretical Computer Science: Formal Models and Semantics*, **B**, Editor: J. van Leeuwen, Elsevier, 675–788.

From Program Proving to Formal Design: Lessons Drawn from SACEM

P. Chapront

GEC Alsthom, Saint Ouen, France

1 SACEM goals and principles

The Automatic Train Control System SACEM was initially designed to enhance the passenger carrying capacity of the lines of the RER network in Paris, operated jointly by the French transportation companies SNCF and RATP. The system has been in operation since August 1988 on the east-west line A, the most crowded line. A second application is in operation in Mexico (1991). The system is currently being installed on the three lines of the Hong Kong Metro; it will also be installed on the LAR airport line in Hong Kong and on three metro lines in Santiago (Chile).

Such a system belongs to the class of transmission based systems. It offers automatic train protection, door services, automatic train operations and can be easily linked with automatic train supervision and computer based interlocking. To provide these functions, the system is divided into two subsystems:

- The trackside subsystem which has to collect and transmit to the train the status of track occupancy, the position of points and other signalling information.

- The train borne subsystem which contains all the system intelligence.

On board the train, SACEM equipment interprets received data and computes the safe speed/distance profile. It also determines the operational parameters which are the inputs of the Servo system. Energy saving and local traffic regulation actions can be performed on board. Information for manual driving and for maintenance is produced and displayed.

2 SACEM technology

Microprocessors are used in the different subsystems. Some of them are devoted to safety related functions. These parts must be protected against hardware failures, as well as software errors.

Against hardware failures, the safety is ensured by extensive use of information redundancy and coding, which provides a negligible and provable wrong side failure rate [1,2].

Only a systematic and monitored design process can provide error free software [2]. In this process verification and validation play a significant role. Of course, during validation, functional tests are extensively used. Program proof is prominent in the verification process. This method has been systematically used for the safety related software of SACEM.

3 Program proving

3.1 Hoare method

The method which is used is the Hoare method [3]. The principle of this method is to associate, with each piece of the program (for example a procedure) a pair of predicates named pre- and post-assertion, which acts as the specification of this piece of program by establishing the properties of the data manipulated before and after its execution.

Example 1. $\{A, B \in N^+\}$ *pre-assertion procedure implementing Euclidean division (input A, B – output Q,R)*

$$\{Q, R \in N_0^+ \text{ AND } A = B \times Q + R \text{ AND } R < B\} \text{ post-assertion.}$$

Any programming language can be systematically defined by associating, with each statement of the program an inference rule which establishes how the execution of this instruction transforms its pre-assertion into its post-assertion. The piece of program can be verified by following the transformation of assertions, instruction by instruction, along all the paths which can be used to go from the beginning to the end. The initial pre-assertion is the pre-assertion of the piece of program. The calculated post-assertion is then compared with the specified post-assertion. This work can be done manually if the piece of program is short, but of course we need a tool if we want to prove a complete program. This tool will have to transform the assertions, instruction by instruction, automatically. In fact, for technical reasons, it is more convenient to start from the post-assertions and come back step by step to the beginning. Then the calculated pre-assertions must imply the specified pre-assertions.

3.2 Application to SACEM - results

We have built such a tool that allows us to prove complete programs. In particular:

- about 14,000 lines in Modula 2 for the software of the train borne equipment;

- and about 7,000 lines for the trackside equipment.

That includes non regression checking, related with three successive versions of the software. Using the tool generally reveals about 75% of the total number of errors or problems, the remainder being found during integration tests and functional tests.

4 SACEM specifications using B

4.1 Why a new specification

SACEM was, in France, the first application where software was used to control a safety related system. In order to be convinced that the design and validation process was good, an audit was ordered by the customer to assess the validity of this process. The conclusion of this audit was that the process itself was good but that there was no proof that the basic assertions, which were used for program proving, were not deduced from the program itself. Of course this was not the case, but that can be established only by trusting in the people involved in the validation process.

To remove any doubt it was decided to re-specify the system using a different formal method. Using this method allowed us to verify the basic assertions themselves.

This different method was B.

4.2 What is B

The B method can be considered as a descendant of the Z method. In what follows, we shall review the main theoretical differences between B and Z. For the moment, let us point out that the inventor of the B method, J.R. Abrial, was deeply involved in the design process of the method Z [4], at Oxford University. His goal, when creating the new method, was to obtain a process that allowed us not only to specify but also to produce software by refinement of its specification, while retaining full control of this process, including mathematical proofs.

The principles of the B method are based on three basic requirements:

1. The method must allow us to build a model of the problem by using a basic structure which may be used to split the problem to be solved into smaller pieces which are easier to manage. The syntax of this structure must be rigorous and the properties of entities which can be encapsulated inside it must be well defined, mathematically.

2. The method, and its associated basic structure must allow us to implement a pure top down approach, using progressive refinements with decreasing abstraction. At the same time reusability must be encouraged by allowing us to replace a piece of the problem, as defined by its specification, by an existing implementation.

3. Each activity involved in the method must be systematically proven correct, in the mathematical sense. This includes:

- The structure manipulations.

- The refinement process.

- The properties of the used entities.

The basic structural component of the method is the **abstract machine**. An abstract machine contains two complementary entities:

- the data;

- the operations.

The data are used to model the objects and the attributes of the objects of the real word. They can have a value. All the properties of the data, the values they can take and the relationship between them must be described. The collection of these properties forms the "invariant of the machine". The data can be used through the operations. The operations are used to describe the evolution of the data. When using an operation, the values of some data change. Each operation describes how these values are modified by the operation by establishing the correspondence between the values before and after the operation has been used. Of course the use of operations must comply with the properties of the data, that is to say, it must preserve the invariant of the machine.

In order to describe data, operations and invariant, it is not necessary to create a new language. The use of mathematical notation is safer and more convenient because it is understood by many people. Of course to allow the use of tools a restricted subset of this notation, and a precise syntactic definition of it must be used, but without any semantic modification. The mathematical basis of B is well defined, it uses the Zermelo Fraenkel set theory (a glimpse of which will be given next).

4.3   Link between B and program proving

In our SACEM application the programming language used was Modula 2. Program proving involved the procedures, encapsulated in the "modules", which are the basic structure of the language. In order to re specify the program, and to be able to produce the pre-post-assertion of our pieces of program by using B, we had to split the problem into parts which looked like the modules. The decomposition into abstract machine must reflect closely the decomposition of the program into modules. Of course the formal data must reflect the variables encapsulated in each module. Provided this structural aspect is taken in account, it is possible to deduce the pre and post-assertions from the B specification. Pre-assertions are linked with the invariant and post-assertions are linked with operations. Systematic definition of these links was established which allowed us to produce the assertions with a minimum of manual interventions.

During this re-specification, J.R. Abrial himself was involved in the process. He was our instructor for the method itself and our guide during its applications to SACEM. Thanks to him the process was shortened. This respecification involved ten persons during six months.

4.4 Results and lessons

The results, for us, were very fruitful. First, the verification activity showed us that the used assertions were correct, and when, in a very small number of cases, the assertions produced by the B specifications were different, the differences led to more restrictive constraints which were acceptable in terms of safety. This reinforced our confidence in the system and allowed us to put it into operation with full confidence.

Secondly, we discovered the efficiency of the method, as a design process. It became clear to us that instead of proving that a system is good, after it has been implemented, it is more efficient to build it correctly at the first attempt. We decided to follow this new way for subsequent projects.

5 Designing with the B method

5.1 Mathematical basis

As already stated, B is derived from Z and like it, is based on Zermelo Fraenkel set theory, complemented by the choice axiom. As in Z, all data must have a type, either predefined or defined by the user, and every predicate must be checked as type consistent before its proof. The only basic constructs we need are the most obvious ones, namely:

- the Cartesian product;

- the power set;

- the set comprehension.

The axiomatisation of set theory is then done in a straightforward manner by defining the form taken by set membership on these various constructs. The equality of two sets is expressed, by equality of elements. From there, it is easy to extend the notation by introducing some conditional definitions such as those of:

- the classical operations on sets (inclusion, union, intersection,...);

- the empty set;

- the possibility of defining sets in extension;

- the binary relations and their related operations;

- the functions and their related operations.

In order to construct formally more elaborate mathematical objects such as:

- natural numbers and their related operations;

- finite sequences and their related operations;

- finite trees and their related operations;

we only have to postulate the existence of:

- an infinite set;

- a choice operator on set.

Note that the concept of finiteness can be defined rigorously by means of the previous basic concepts and definitions.

An abstract machine is a construct used to model an element of the real world. The foundations of this abstraction are the data which represent the attributes of the real objects which are pertinent in the problem. All the relevant properties of the data must be specified. These properties are of course the set of values which can be taken, and the invariable relationships existing between the different data. This collection of properties is expressed by using a predicate of the set theory.

The values taken by the data represent the state of the machine. We need some mechanism to express how the state of the machine can change, or, in other words, to be able to animate our model. This mechanism is supplied by the concept of predicate transformer. As introduced by Dijkstra [5], if R is a predicate, and S a predicate transformer, $[S]R$ is a predicate and is the weakest condition necessary to ensure that the transformation of the state modelled by S terminates and the resulting state satisfies R.

The predicate transformer in B is a generalisation of the simple substitution of classical logic which is denoted $x := E$, and $[x := E]R$ is the predicate obtained by replacing in R all the free occurrences of x by E.

Here is the list of predicate transformers (called simply substitutions) and their axioms

$[skip]R \Longleftrightarrow R$	"neutral substitution"
$[P \mid S] \Longleftrightarrow P \wedge [S]R$	"preconditioned substitution"
$[S[]T]R \Longleftrightarrow [S]R \wedge [T]R$	"bounded non deterministic choice substitution"
$[P \Longrightarrow S] \Longleftrightarrow P \Longrightarrow [S]R$	"guarded substitution"
$[@x.S] \Longleftrightarrow \forall x.[S]R$	"unbounded non deterministic choice substitution"

All the possible transformations which characterise the dynamic behaviour of the model are implemented by the operations, each of which consists of a list of substitutions.

The consistency of the model must be verified by proving that each operation preserves the invariant, that is to say that each substitution defining an operation does not modify the invariant when applied to it, which can be expressed by the formula:

$$I(x) \wedge [S] \ true \Longrightarrow [S]I(x),$$

where I is the invariant and S the substitution.

To prove that the model is not empty we have to define a particular operation, termed initialisation, which must also preserve the invariant.

5.2   Structuring rules

In order to build large models, we need to have some rules allowing the decomposition of machine into smaller machines, or on the contrary, the constructing of larger machines by composition of elementary ones. These rules must specify how the invariants can be combined, the visibility of data between one machine to another, the accessibility of operations between one machine and another. It would take too long to enumerate all the rules here. However, what we can say is that this set of rules is guided by the hiding principle, and by the consistency of the proof process.

5.3   Refinements

Refinement is the process which allows us to progress from the specification towards an actual program by decreasing the abstraction level. The refinement notion has been introduced by C.A.R. Hoare [6]. Applied to the substitution, we can say that a substitution T refines a substitution S if $[S]H \Rightarrow [T]H$ (for all predicate H).

Applied to data, the concept is more complicated but can be also reformulated in B using first order predicates. The substitution operators are monotonic with respect to the refinement relation, which implies that every substitution can be replaced by its refinement whatever the context. The refinement relation is transitive; the refinement of a refinement of the specification is a refinement of this specification. These properties allow us to progress, step by step from a first, very abstract model towards a detailed low level model which can be directly translated into a program. The refinement process is checked by a proof process which guarantees the properties of each refinement.

We must show that:

- The initialisation of the refinement refines the specification initialisation:
  $[K]\neg[J]\neg R$:

  where K is the initialisation of the refinement,
  $\quad\quad J$ is the initialisation of the specification,
  $\quad\quad R$ is the predicate defining the change of variable between the specification and its refinement.

- Each operation T in the refinement refines the corresponding operation $P \mid S$ in the specification $I \wedge R \wedge P \Rightarrow [T]\neg[S]\neg R$.

5.4 Practical aspects

In order to help the user, a specific language has been defined to implement the mathematical notation. This language allows easy entry of symbols using a conventional keyboard and provides some verification checks through its syntax, thus avoiding typing errors.

A set of B tools allows basic verification in terms of:

- lexical and syntactic checking;

- check of completeness of variable declaration;

- check of structural aspects;

- proof obligation production;

- proof assistance (automatic proving – whenever possible); and

- configuration management.

5.5 The difficulties in the design process

Amongst the activities introduced by the B method, proving is certainly one of the most difficult:

- The structure choices, the level of abstraction, and the size of each step of refinement (in terms of abstraction) have a great influence on the multiplicity and the complexity of the proof obligations.

- The proof process requires mathematical training and intense intellectual effort.

- Return of investment does not materialise immediately.

5.6 Application results

In GEC Alsthom from 1988 up to now we have made a systematic use of the method for safety critical projects ($\sim$ 10 projects) [7,8]. The size of the produced software varied from 3,000 up to 40,000 lines of Modula 2 or Ada code. During this work we discovered the difficulties, together with the advantages of the process. During these jobs, we were helped by J.R. Abrial, and our co-operation allowed us to get a better understanding of the method, and in some part to improve it. We also experimented with the tools, and participated in their improvement.

We can confirm that, even with the difficulties due to the proving process, the B design method provides us with advantages:

- Global design time is reduced. Reusability is very easy. We have experience of this on three different projects.

- Functional modifications are made easier and non regression checking can be systematically undertaken at minimal cost.

6 Improving the method

6.1 Design conducted by the proof process

It has been clearly shown, during our work, that the proof process must be taken in account, from the very beginning, when the design choices are made. If we do not do that, the proof obligations will be too numerous and too complex and the process will not be manageable. Greater care must be applied to the initial structure choices. We find again the classical trade off between coupling and cohesion. Better structural choice will minimise interface complexity. Also, when specifying and refining the operations the organisation of the control structure must be chosen to reduce the number of proof obligations.

6.2 How to structure, how to refine

The key to process efficiency is to specify at the beginning the fundamental invariant of the system. In this invariant, we have to identify the main properties, among them the safety constraints. Then, remaining at a very abstract level, we specify the main functions of the system by a "black box" substitution, which preserves the invariant. Then, by a data analysis we define the main data and operations allowing the implementation of these "black box" substitutions. When doing that, we must check the complexity of the proof obligations, and iterate if the result is not good. This must be done at the higher level of abstraction. Then, we will reduce the abstraction level by refinement, using additional new variables, while keeping the already refined variables, see example in Table 1. This type of refinement by superposition allows us to introduce hierarchically the data of the problem.

                                   P. Chapront

Table 1. Data refinement

Specification	Refinement
Variables X	Variables X, Y
Invariant I	Invariant I'
Initialisation J	Initialisation $J \parallel K$
Operations $S1, S2, Sn$	Operations $S'1, S'2, S'n$

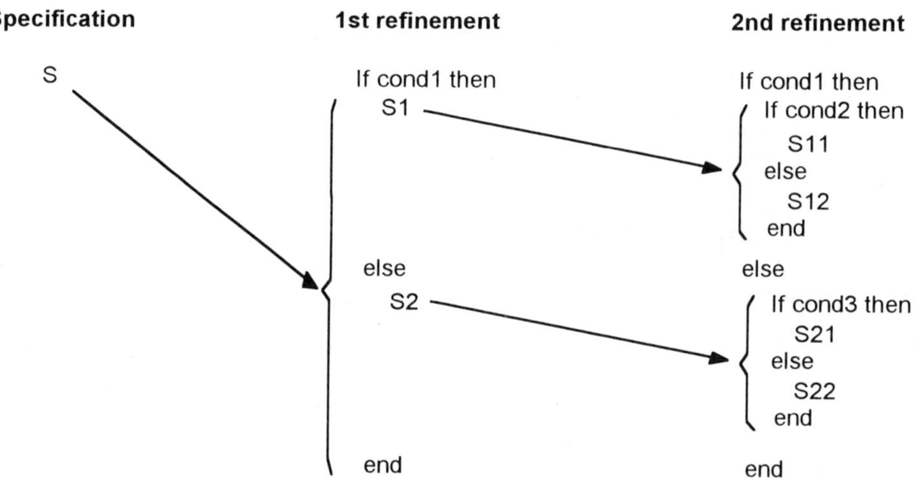

Figure 1. Algorithmic refinement

When refining an operation the process must be conducted in the same way. In each refinement we introduce the new control structure inside the already existing ones (example in Figure 1).

In short, at the upper level of abstraction we concentrate on the basic data of the problem, deferring all the details. Detail is then added progressively and the proof process must be checked to be effective at each step.

7   Results and the future

The last project we worked on proved the efficiency of the method. The publication of a guide book and code of practice is currently in progress, in order to allow beginners to start off in the right way. The B tools have also been modified to help the user more effectively.

What remains to be done?

1. Elaborate a set of rules to help the user to progress more easily from the functional approach to the abstract machine approach.

2. Look at the problem of parallelism, which is not currently taken into account in the method.

These two remaining actions are currently being undertaken within R and D projects supported by the European Commission and the French Ministry of Transport. We can say that progress is good, and that the global method will be ready soon for larger safety related systems.

References

1. Martin, J. (1992). Vital processing by single coded unit. *Safety of Computer Control Systems*, Pergamon Press.

2. Chapront, P. (1992). Vital coded processor and safety related software design. *Safety of Computer Control Systems*, Pergamon Press.

3. Hoare, C.A.R. (1969). *An Axiomatic Basis for Computer Programming.* Comm. ACM, **12**.

4. Spivey, J.M. (1988). *Understanding Z: A Specification Language and its Formal Semantics*, Cambridge University Press.

5. Dijkstra, E.W. (1976). *A Discipline of Programming*, Prentice Hall.

6. Hoare, C.A.R. (1985). *Programs are Predicates in Mathematical Logic and Programming Language*, Prentice Hall.

7. Carnot, M., Da Silva, C., Dehbonei, B. and Mejia, F. (1993). *Error-free Software Development for Critical System Using B Methodology*, IEEE Computer Society Press.

8. Da Silva, C., Dehbonei, B. and Mejia, F. (1993). *Formal Specification in the Development of Industrial Applications: Subway Speed Control System*, North-Holland.

Limitations of Mathematics in Software Engineering

John C. Knight

Department of Computer Science, University of Virginia Charlottesville, USA

Abstract

Although great success has been achieved, software dependability remains elusive and computer-based safety-critical systems continue to fail in service. The need for dependability is wide ranging including well-known applications such as flight control, air-traffic control, weapons systems, nuclear and medical applications and less well-known applications such as banking and telecommunications.

Despite the successful application of mathematics, much of software engineering suffers from the absence of a formal mathematical basis. Formal specification is not able to deal with all aspects of realistic applications, many systems are either difficult or impossible to test, and the complexity of most applications precludes comprehensive application of formal verification.

This paper reviews some of the significant issues in software development that remain to be tackled and examines the role of mathematics in each. Some challenges to the mathematical community are offered in the form of significant areas of software engineering that could benefit from a more solid mathematical basis. Finally, two examples of directions showing promise for helping improve dependability are discussed.

Keywords: Software dependability, software testing, software verification, dependability assessment, software fault tolerance, safety kernel.

1 Introduction

When faced with difficult engineering problems, engineers turn to mathematics in search of solutions. This has been the case in software engineering from the very beginning, and mathematics has made many important contributions to the technology of software development for dependable systems. Although great success has been achieved, software dependability remains elusive. There are many examples of systems failing because of software defects despite the best efforts of the software's developers [1–3]. Computer-based systems fail for a variety of reasons but a significant fraction of failures can be traced to some aspect of software. It is usually not the case that some well-defined programming error is the cause of a failure. More likely are circumstances such as subtle errors in specification and obscure special cases in the timing of events.

Despite the successful application of mathematics, much of software engineering suffers from the absence of a formal mathematical underpinning. The limitations referred to in the title of this paper are the limitations that we face at the present time as a result of this absence. This paper reviews some of the significant issues in software development that remain to be tackled and examines the role of mathematics in each. Some challenges to the mathematical community are offered in the form of significant areas of software engineering that could benefit from a more solid mathematical basis. The limitations should be viewed also therefore as a set of ideas about opportunities for future research.

In considering these topics, it must be kept in mind how extremely important the issue of dependability has become. The need for dependability is actually quite broad and the applications are very sophisticated. Most people are familiar with the importance of software dependability in applications such as flight control, air-traffic control, weapons systems, nuclear and medical applications. But many application domains are such that failure can lead to very serious situations even if human life is not threatened immediately. Consider, for example, the world's financial infrastructure. Countries are linked electronically, and funds are transferred routinely and in vast quantities. Stock trading, check clearing, credit card transactions, and loan originations are all handled by automated systems that we trust. The consequences of certain types of failure in such systems could be catastrophic.

In a similar sense, the global telecommunications system has become a necessity, and it is something in which we routinely place our faith. Loss of telephone service can disrupt business activity causing loss of revenue and can deny rapid access to emergency services. Increased dependence on telecommunications in the future will only make the problem worse particularly as applications that are already safety-critical become dependent on telecommunications. Experiments are already underway, for example, to introduce telemedicine so as to permit rural communities to enjoy medical services from major centers, and remote control of critical services, such as electricity generation and distribution, is becoming routine.

The central difficulty with building dependable software is its complexity. The next section of this paper reviews this issue and itemizes some of the significant sources of complexity. Next the specification and verification phases of software development are discussed and several problem areas reviewed. The paper ends with some techniques that, in the author's opinion, offer some hope of dealing with the problem.

2   System complexity

Complexity is the source of many of the difficulties that we face. Any software system for applications of the type outlined above is a complicated artifact.

This comes about in part because of the size of the software and in part because of its architecture. Some systems requiring high dependability are considered small being perhaps only a few thousand lines long. Despite being this size, such systems are still very difficult to develop. However, many modern critical systems are actually several million lines of source program. Consider for example, any application that employs even a moderately sophisticated graphic user interface. The implementation of the basic facilities used for such interfaces is frequently many hundreds of thousands of lines. These are large programs by any measure.

In considering the size of an "application", it is important to keep in mind that the defects which can affect dependability are sometimes not even in what is generally thought of as the application software. For example, all applications depend on support tools such as compilers, linkers and loaders. During execution, applications depend upon libraries, language run-time support, and an operating system or some sort of monitor (see Figure 1). When a software system fails, it does not matter whether the problem is traced to the application itself or some part of the development or operating environment. In practice, the amount of software that has to work correctly in order to provide a service is far more than what is usually referred to as the application. The consequences of failure can be very serious no matter what the cause.

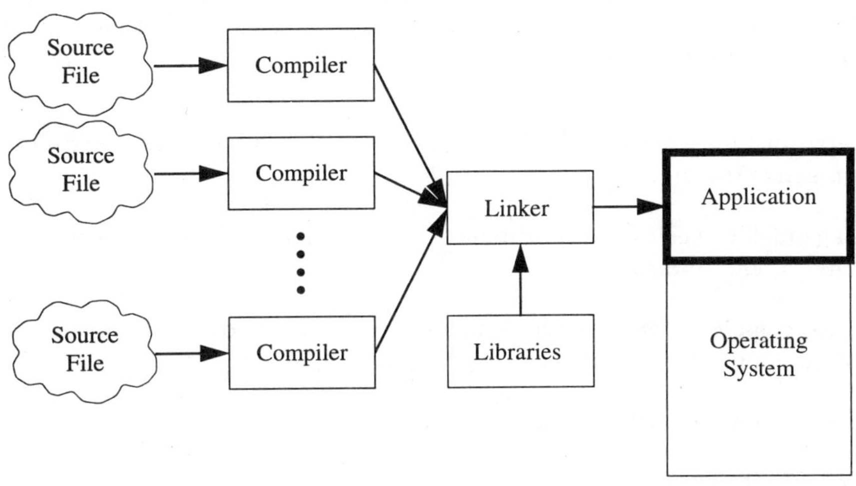

Figure 1. Complex application software context

Architectural complexity is considerable in many modern applications also. For reasons of performance, flexibility, and fault tolerance, many systems execute on distributed platforms and have to deal with the very considerable difficulties of true asynchronous operation as a result [4]. A second source of complexity is the use of highly redundant, parallel hardware systems where the goal is hardware fault tolerance. In that case, the software is often called upon to deal with issues such as voting and hardware resource management. Multi-channel parallel systems employing loose clock synchronization between channels are becoming common in avionics applications, for example.

Making the situation more complex is the fact that some modern systems require multiple dependability characteristics. For example, it is becoming clear that systems of the future will often require high levels of availability and security. In other words, such systems will have to provide continuous service yet include features that provide very high levels of protection against a variety of threats that might try to deny service, take over control, or gain access to sensitive data. An application that clearly requires both availability and security is medical record keeping. Medical records must be available continuously because certain scheduled accesses must be satisfied and there is no way to know when emergency access will be required. But the data within the record system is also sensitive because of its personal nature and because of its financial implications.

In summary, the systems that are required by modern applications are very complex and the complexity has many dimensions. It is likely, for example, that software will be required routinely for safety-critical systems that have the following characteristics (see Figure 2):

- large in the sense of requiring many lines of source text to describe the implementation;

- depend for their development on a variety of tools including compilers, linkers, and libraries;

- have complex user interfaces based on bit-mapped color graphic displays, audio input and output, and other sophisticated devices;

- operate on a distributed target;

- operate in real time;

- use fault tolerant multi-channel processing architectures that require software redundancy management and synchronization.

This is the context in which the mathematics of dependable systems must be discussed. The remainder of this paper discusses certain aspects of software development and the specific challenges that they raise.

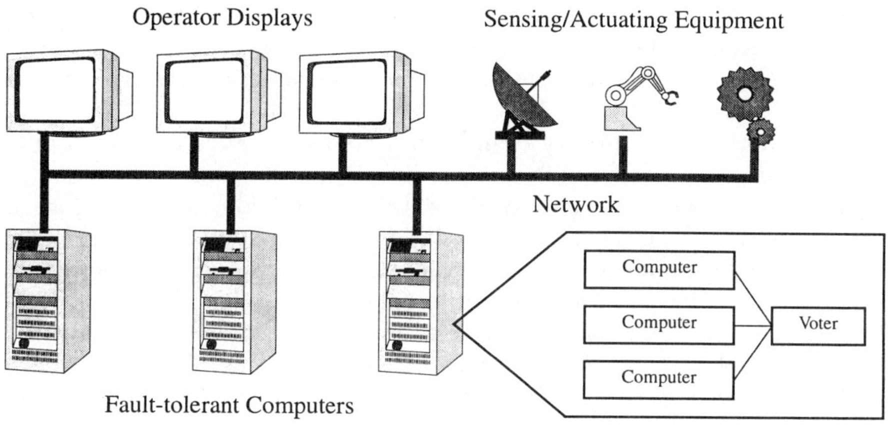

Figure 2. Typical real-time, distributed, fault-tolerant application architecture

3 Specification

There is substantial evidence that the majority of faults in safety-critical systems are actually introduced in the software specification [5]. Faults occur because specifications are incomplete, inconsistent, ambiguous, or just erroneous.

A great deal of research has been done on the problem of specification, much of it in the area of mathematical or formal specification. The success achieved has been considerable. Notations such as Z, VDM, Larch, and Statecharts have precise semantic definitions and this has enabled specifications to be developed for parts of non-trivial systems that permit, (a) very effective communication between engineers, and (b) analysis that demonstrates significant properties of the specifications.

Many difficulties with specification remain, however. First and foremost, it has to be kept in mind that the specification is usually the first formal representation of the requirements for a software system. Prior to the documentation of the specification, the requirements were scattered informally in other documents or were in the minds of the engineers involved. This presents the problem of validation—how is it possible to know whether what is documented in the specification is actually what is needed? Certainly it is possible to check specifications for certain aspects of completeness and consistency but not for intent. Clearly, this is a major source of specification defects yet mathematics cannot deal with issues such as the informality of intent or the ambiguity of natural language.

Although the work on formal specification has yielded many benefits, the available techniques do not deal with all aspects of specification. For example, the precise specification of real-time systems remains elusive although research in the field is promising. Once again a major element of the problem is complexity. Whilst the formal specification of a synchronous real-time system that employs a single frame rate is achievable, the chances are slight of formally specifying an asynchronous system consisting of several concurrent processes that communicate and synchronize in complex ways and which have to meet a variety of deadlines.

In practice the complexity of modern systems demands the use of different specification notations for different parts of a specification. For example, one might choose to use Z to specify the data-manipulation elements of an application, traditional mathematics to define the computational elements, BNF to define the command language presented to the user, Statecharts to specify the reactive elements, and natural language to define the non-functional requirements. There is at present no comprehensive technique that permits such a collection of notations to be analyzed as a single entity. Yet this is essential if significant analysis of the complete specification is to be achieved.

An area of specification that is not presently well served by formal techniques is user interfaces. Although significant progress has been made [6–9], the technology of user interaction is changing rapidly and entire new modes of interaction have to be addressed. For example, virtual reality, telepresence, audio input and output, and mechanical rather than visual displays are being developed and will become quite common even in safety-critical applications. Formal specification of the requirements of such interfaces is essential. Without formal specification, there is the real possibility that informal approaches will lead to implementations of safety-critical systems that do not respond as desired to user commands, that do not display output correctly, or contain defects such as the display of error messages on windows that are covered and hence are not visible to the operator. Even worse is the prospect of interaction between the user interface and the rest of the system. This occurred, for example, when a windowing system failed to release the processor in a computer-controlled respirator that was connected to a patient. The effect was to deny the patient breathing assistance while the operator was changing the size of a window on the screen.

A second aspect of user interfaces that presents significant problems is ergonomics. In safety-critical applications, appraising human operators of significant events and dependable communication of routine information is essential. Many accidents have been attributed to defects in information displays. This area seems unlikely to yield to mathematical analysis to any great extent. Yet, given its importance in securing dependability, it seems wise to try.

In summary, since specification is perhaps the most significant source of software defects, the challenge for mathematics is to develop approaches to formal specification that can cope with the size of modern applications, their real-time aspects, their sophisticated user interfaces, and the need to have seamless analysis of the various notations used. This has to be done also with a view to restricting to the extent possible the major limitations of validation and user-interface ergonomics.

4 Verification

Verification is an area in which mathematics has been applied successfully. Although not yet at the stage of routine use, many significant properties of software systems have been demonstrated in a mathematical framework.

Once again, however, significant challenges remain. The technique that is referred to as formal verification frequently is able to conclude that a software system possesses a certain useful property *provided certain assumptions hold*. These assumptions are often subtle and their significance is not always appreciated.

An example of this is arithmetic. Consider the following simple assignment statement in a Pascal-like programming language:

$$a := b + c;$$

If a, b, and c are floating-point variables, this statement merely instructs a computer to fetch the values of the variables b and c, compute their sum, and replace the value of a with this sum.

Unfortunately, it is common to equate the arithmetic being requested with real arithmetic. This is common for two reasons. First, computer arithmetic is "close" to real arithmetic in a sense, and second the realities of computer arithmetic are so complex that one is tempted to ignore them whenever possible. This is very dangerous since it is precisely the differences between computer arithmetic and real arithmetic that are the cause of many subtle failures in software systems.

How does the addition in the simple statement above differ from addition in real arithmetic? There are three differences:

- the sum could be larger than the available representation supports and yield an unrepresentable result - a situation commonly called overflow;

- the sum could be smaller than the available representation supports and yield an unrepresentable result - a situation commonly called underflow;

- the sum could lie between the available discrete values that are representable and thereby have to be represented inaccurately - an effect commonly called rounding error.

This is a serious situation and yet for some floating-point operations things are actually worse. Where an operator is commutative in real arithmetic, the corresponding machine implementation is often not commutative.

Programmers have to deal with the realities of arithmetic since they see the effects of the programs that they write. Dealing with these effects has lead to the realization that computerized operations such as floating-point addition are usually implemented as *partial* functions. If either of the first two circumstances arise in practice, the offending program is usually terminated.

In an effort to deal with the partial-function nature of computer arithmetic, programming language designers have introduced awkward mechanisms such as exception handling. An exception is just a euphemism for a branch in the flow of program control. The effect of an exception is to cause a branch in a program at a point where an arithmetic operation appeared and where in both the source and the object programs there is no indication of a branch instruction whatsoever.

The combination of floating-point arithmetic not matching real arithmetic and having a direct but implicit effect on flow of control makes analysis of floating-point arithmetic extremely difficult. Formally verifying desired properties of something as complex as a program to invert matrices in which floating-point arithmetic is modelled completely is well beyond the state of the art.

When other forms of verification fail, software engineers turn to testing. Testing in software engineering differs significantly from testing in other branches of engineering. Consider, for example, the development of mechanical structures. The performance of most structures is predicted using techniques such as finite-element analysis. Testing a structure, for example stressing an aircraft's wing to destruction, is undertaken to confirm existing analysis not to assess some aspect of performance like strength.

In software engineering, testing is an experimental approach to verification. The hope is always that the result of testing software can be extrapolated so that general conclusions can be drawn. In many cases, this has to be done no matter how little confidence one actually has in the conclusion because there is no alternative. In some cases this is quite a stumbling block because prescribed levels of performance have to be shown. Butler and Finelli [10] have shown how significant this can be where the prescribed level of performance is in the ultra dependable region.

The mathematical challenges that arise from this situation with software testing are twofold. First, general software verification techniques that use testing for confirmation would be very valuable, and, second, mathematical theories of testing that permit general conclusions to be drawn about significant applications based on testing would have immediate applicability.

An application domain that is not even amenable to extensive testing is expert systems. Although expert systems can be executed on sample problems, the number of tests that can be run this way is tens at best. Even when tests are run, it is often not clear what the output should be. If an expert system disagrees with an expert, is that because it is defective or because its knowledge base led to a different conclusion? Verification of expert systems is an important aspect of their development, and, given their increasing role in safety-critical systems, a mathematical framework for their verification would be very valuable. The development of such a framework seems unlikely at this point.

5 Process

Software development is an engineering process. Most engineering disciplines develop artifacts using processes that are well-defined, refined, and immersed in formalism; for the most part, software engineering does not because the required technology is not available. The vast majority of software is developed using ad hoc techniques that have no real scientific basis.

Some processes are not ad hoc but, even where a process is established and repeatable, it is usually not clear what effect the application of such a process will have on the resulting software. In part, this is the reason that the various processes that have been developed are not widely adopted—engineers are not sure what the benefits might be. As an example, consider the software inspection technique made popular by Fagan [11]. It is known that the use of this technique tends to be beneficial in that it tends to reduce defects in the inspected work product. But the problem faced by developers of safety-critical systems is quantifying the benefit—just how much of a benefit is obtained?

What is required is a theory associated with development processes that will permit quantification of the effects of the process. Naturally, absolute quantification in the process area is rare and unlikely to be found in software development. Under such circumstances a statistical approach is required. It is useful to know that a specific technique will have an effect on a population (at some confidence level) even if the effect on a single sample cannot be predicted. The problem in software engineering is that the replication and controls inherent in the statistical process require resources well beyond those typically available. Consider for example, attempting to determine by experiment whether the use of object-oriented design improves some measure of dependability. This would require the parallel development of sufficient systems to randomize independent variables under managed circumstances using object-oriented design together with development of a similar number of controls using some other design method. Once developed, all of these systems would have to be evaluated in service. For realistic applications, such an approach is obviously out of the question.

The challenge in this area is clear. Statistical techniques are needed that permit sound conclusions to be drawn where replicates are either very few or non-existent and where comparisons are drawn against other documented development activities rather than traditional experimental controls.

6 Promising directions

To deal with the problems with which we are faced, there are several technologies that seem to offer hope for improvement and that will benefit the most from stronger mathematical bases. Two of these technologies, reuse and isolation, are reviewed here as examples.

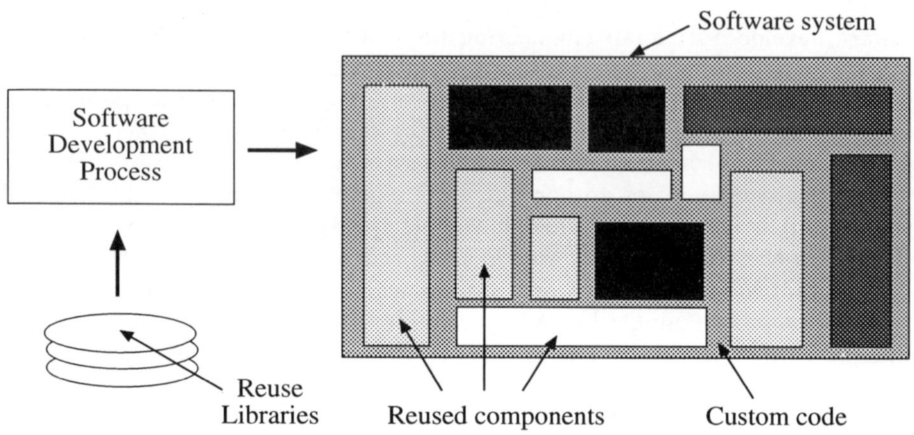

Figure 3. Component-based software reuse

6.1 Reuse

The commonly cited incentive for reuse in software development is improved productivity [12]. But in the field of dependability, reuse of an artifact permits the reuse of any properties related to dependability. In the simplest case, a software system designed for one application could be used unchanged in another. If great care is exercised in how this is done, any dependability achieved in the first application will be achieved in the second. Irrespective of the productivity gain, this could be very useful and raises intriguing possibilities.

In a more complex case, a new software system might be constructed from components that were developed to be reused (see Figure 3). In that case, the potential exists for viewing the components as black boxes and developing arguments about the dependability of the product from the known dependability properties of the components. This is similar in some ways to using existing theorems and lemmas to prove new theorems.

This approach could be key to managing the complexity of large systems and the challenge in this case is to develop the necessary mathematics to permit the analysis of systems constructed via reuse. This is a daunting task but the payoff could be considerable.

6.2 Isolation

An approach to providing one form of dependability, security, is the security kernel [13]. The reason the security kernel architecture is attractive is that it isolates the secure information from the remainder of the software. Thus, provided the security kernel works correctly, there will be no breach of security irrespective of what the rest of the application software does. The system might fail and thereby deny service because of some inadequacy of the software outside of the kernel but the security requirements are not violated in that case.

This isolation approach is quite attractive because it limits the amount of software that has to work correctly for a system to be dependable. In practice, the amount of software in a security kernel can be several orders of magnitude less than in the entire application.

Security kernels are not a panacea for a number of reasons. They are difficult to build, difficult to verify, and the concept does not scale up well to distributed targets. The kernel concept deserves attention, however, because of the benefits that it bestows. Rushby suggested that the concept might be applied to safety systems [14] and this idea has been pursued recently [15]. The initial results are encouraging. To make the kernel concept successful in safety systems and other areas of dependability requires generalization of many of the results in verification obtained in the security field together with new results in verification of certain aspects of traditional operating systems.

7 Conclusion

Dependability is important and becoming increasingly so as more and more critical applications are developed using computers. These applications are very complex employing lots of software on distributed, fault-tolerant hardware platforms. In many cases, developers have to be sure that critical dependability levels have been reached. Software engineering does not have the tools to deal with these systems and the only hope for serious improvement is the application of mathematics.

This paper has explored what have been referred to as limitations of mathematics in software engineering. In some areas, mathematical approaches are possible in principle and have been demonstrated on sample problems but are significantly short of routine application on typical applications. In other areas, software development poses challenges for which mathematical solutions appear impossible to achieve.

To a certain extent, the different aspects of complexity can be analyzed separately. But a software system, like a chain, is only as strong as its weakest link. Ultra dependability in one element of a system is of little value if other elements are weak. Presently, no mathematical techniques are capable of analyzing comprehensively systems such as those outlined in this paper. The overall challenge to the mathematical community is to develop ways by which the extraordinary complexity of the software systems we build now and wish to build in the future can be managed. It is the author's opinion that this challenge will not be met at any time in the foreseeable future.

References

1. Garman, J.R. (1981). The bug heard round the world. *ACM Software Engineering Notes*, **6**, 3–10.

2. Leveson, N.G. and C.S. Turner (1993). An Investigation of the therac-25 accidents. *IEEE Computer*, **26**, 18–41.

3. Neumann, P.G. (Editor). Risks to the public. *Software Engineering Notes*.

4. Cristian, F. (1991). Basic concepts and issues in fault-tolerant distributed systems. *Operating Systems of the 90s and Beyond*, Springer Verlag, Berlin, 118–149.

5. Potter, B. et al. (1991). *An Introduction to Formal Specification and Z*, Prentice Hall.

6. Abowd, G. and Dix, A. (1994). Integrating status and event phenomena in formal specifications of interactive systems. *ACM SIGSOFT*, 44–52.

7. Foley, J., Kim, W., Kovacevic, S., and Murray, K. (1989). Defining interfaces at a high level of abstraction. *IEEE Software*, **6**, 25–32.

8. Sufrin, B. and He, J. (1990). *Specification, Analysis, and Refinement of Interactive Processes, Formal Methods in Human-Computer Interaction*, Editors: M. Harrison and H. Thimbleby, Cambridge University Press, 153–200.

9. Jacob, R. (1983). Using formal specifications in the design of a human-computer interface. *Communications of the ACM*, **26**, 259–264.

10. Butler, R.W. and Finelli, G.B. (1993). The infeasibility of quantifying the reliability of life-critical real-time software. *IEEE Transactions on Software Engineering*, **19**, 3–12.

11. Fagan, M.E. (1986). Advances in software inspections. *IEEE Transactions on Software Engineering*, **SE12**, 744–751.

12. Prieto-Daz, R. (1993). Status report: Software reusability. *IEEE Software*, **10**, 61–66.

13. Jr. Ames, S.R., Gasser, M. and Schell, R.R. (1983). Security kernel design and implementation: An introduction. *IEEE Computer*, **16**, 14–22.

14. Rushby, J. (1989). Kernels for safety? *Safe and Secure Computing Systems*, Editor: T. Anderson, Blackwell Scientific Publications, 210–220.

15. Wika, K. (1995). Safety kernel enforcement of software safety policies. *Ph.D. Dissertation*, University of Virginia, Charlottesville, Virginia.

A Methodology for Reliability Analysis of Fault-Tolerant Systems with Repairable Subsystems[1]

Olof Bridal

Department of Computer Engineering, Laboratory for Dependable Computing, Chalmers University of Technology, Göteborg, Sweden

Abstract

When safety-critical systems are designed, reliability analysis is required in the early phases if adequate design decisions are to be made. For repairable systems, such analysis is difficult to perform with conventional reliability evaluation tools since the reliability model complexity requires that the models be solved numerically; numerical values of various system parameters are usually not known before the system has been designed. A methodology which permits symbolic evaluation of the reliability of complex repairable fault-tolerant systems is presented in this paper. The methodology is based on considering each succession of events leading to failure by itself and then combining the results of these analyses into a closed-form reliability approximation with known error bounds.

Keywords: dependability, reliability, safety, repairable, markov, fault tolerance, approximation.

1 Introduction

Safety-critical control systems with ultra-high reliability requirements are being introduced into a variety of applications. For example, it is expected that many safety-critical functions in automobiles, such as steering and braking, will be controlled by microprocessor-based systems in a way that makes the safety of the vehicle highly dependent on the operation of these control systems. The successful design of such systems requires that dependability attributes can be modelled and analyzed in a way that enables the design to be tailored to the dependability requirements. Ideally, it should be possible to analyze the models without detailed knowledge of all the model parameters. This is precisely what the methodology described in this paper aims for.

The goal of the methodology is to obtain a closed-form expression which approximates the reliability or safety of a repairable system with known bounds

---

[1] This work was partially funded by the Swedish National Board for Industrial and Technical Development (NUTEK) under contract 93-3199.

on the approximation error. This is in contrast to most earlier research efforts in the area of reliability analysis which are directed at reducing the computational complexity of reliability models. Examples of such techniques are given in [1–3]. Although a number of methods for reducing the model complexity have been devised [4–8], these can not be used to obtain closed-form approximations to the reliability of non-trivial systems with known approximation error bounds.

Compared to numerical solution techniques, the symbolic approach has the advantage of clearly showing how different parameters affect the reliability of the system. Even though numerical sensitivity studies can provide similar information, the results of such analysis is considerably more difficult to interpret; complex interdependencies between the effects of a large number of variables on system reliability are hard to trace in numerical output.

2 The reliability model

The starting point for the methodology is a time-homogenous continuous-time markov chain (CTMC) model of the system of concern. CTMC models allow the modeling of state-dependent event rates which is not possible with such techniques as fault trees and reliability block diagrams. Since the models considered are time-homogenous, all transition rates are constant with respect to time. A more realistic model would allow inter-transition times to be arbitrarily distributed, resulting in a semi-markov model. While such a model is more powerful in terms of modeling capability, it would be much harder to analyze. The employment of a markov model with constant transition rates is believed to be an acceptable trade-off between modeling power and simplicity of analysis.

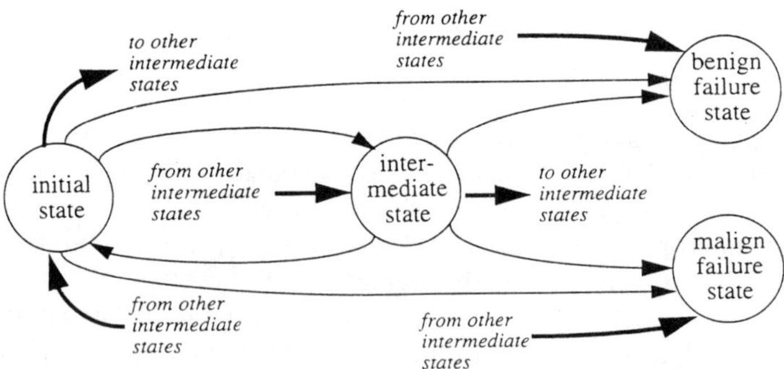

Figure 1. General dependability model

For the methodology described in this paper to be applicable, the model should have an initial state representing the fault-free state, a number of faulty intermediate states from which the system can return to the initial state as the result of a repair action, and a number of absorbing states corresponding to various types of system failure. Typically, an absorbing state corresponds to one of two types of failure: benign or malign. Considering the types of states in the model (shown in Figure 1), we find the following:

- From the initial state, the transitions to the benign failure states represent safe shutdown of the system. While the shutdown of a fault-free system may seem to be a strange action, it could correspond to an exponentially distributed mission time; if the system completes its mission before it fails, the system is obviously safe. These transitions could also represent the case when the system shuts itself down as a result of an erroneous indication of an error when no error is present.

- Transitions from the initial state to the malign failure states represent events that cause the system to fail in a way that jeopardizes the safety of the system. The corresponding events could be permanent hardware faults that are not covered by the fault tolerance capabilities or transient faults from which the system fails to recover sufficiently fast. Since faults in well-debugged software usually manifest themselves as transient faults [9], software bugs can also be accounted for in the model.

  Regarding the modeling of transient faults, a model of the error detection and recovery procedure can be constructed and evaluated for each state in the model. An expression for the probability that the system fails to recover in a sufficiently short time from such an error may be established from an analysis of this model. Such coverage models are discussed in [10]. The rate of covered transient faults, i.e. faults from which the system recovers fast enough, can be neglected in the model whereas the rate of uncovered faults should be included in the transition to the malign failure state.

- In the fault-free state, the system has some fault tolerance capabilities. The events that cause the system to change state to a state with reduced capability to tolerate faults are represented in the model by transitions from the initial state to various intermediate non-failed states. Typically, these transitions represent permanent hardware faults.

- From the intermediate states, three types of transitions may occur. An uncovered permanent or transient fault could make the system fail in a benign or malign way. The mechanisms behind these transitions are equivalent to those described above concerning direct failure from the initial state. Alternatively, an event - typically a permanent hardware fault - may occur which causes the system to enter another intermediate state, further reducing the fault tolerance capabilities. It is also possible that the system returns to the initial state by means of a repair action.

In the models considered in this paper, the repair rates from all the intermediate states to the initial states are equal. In other words, regardless of the number and types of permanent faults present, the expected repair time is always the same. This is certainly an unusual assumption. However, it is a very reasonable one. If the model is taken to represent an on-line maintainable system, the process of actually repairing or replacing the faulty components is in many cases quite short compared to the time between the occurrence of the fault and the start of the actual repair. Clearly, this supports the assumption of equal repair rates. Alternatively, the model could be viewed as describing a system which is shut down when a permanent fault is detected. With this view, the repair rate could correspond to the time to shutdown which may be assumed to be independent on the number and types of faults present. In this case, time is considered to stand still between the instant of shutdown and the restart of the system after repair. With this interpretation of the reliability model, the benign failure state becomes superfluous as the initial state represents both the true fault-free operating state and the shutdown state.

3   Transformation of the model

In order to facilitate a structured reliability analysis, the model should be rearranged so that each possible succession of events leading from the initial state to a failure state is separated from any other such succession. This allows each event succession to be analyzed separately. This model rearrangement, or transformation, should be made such that the state probability are the same before and after transformation.

To aid in the description of the model transformation procedure, a few definitions related to the described type of markov model are needed:

Definition 1. *A merging state is a state, other than the initial one, which has more than one input transition.*

Definition 2. *A forking state is a state which has more than one output transition, excluding the repair transition to the initial state.*

Definition 3. *A path is a sequence of transitions from the initial state, via any number (including zero) of intermediate states, to an absorbing state.*

As shown in [11], each merging state may be split into a number of substates without altering the state probabilities of the system. The resulting state diagram will look like the one in Figure 2. Although only one path is actually shown in the figure, the tree structure of the diagram should be evident. The

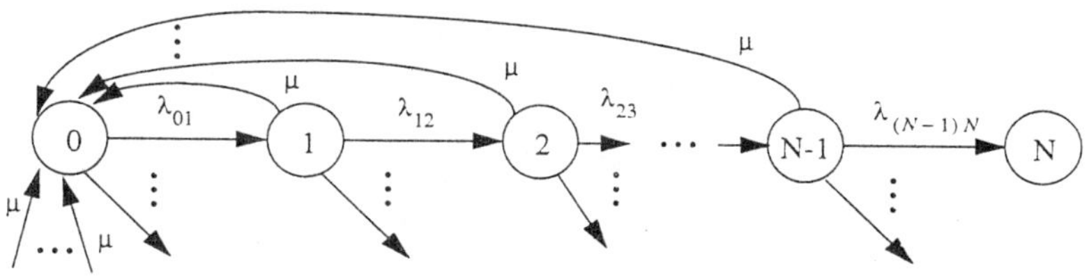

Figure 2. One path of the general dependability model

transition rates $\lambda_{01}, \lambda_{12}, \lambda_{23}, \ldots, \lambda_{(N-1)N}$ in this model are identical to those of the corresponding path in the original state diagram. Thus, the rates of any path can be found in the original diagram by tracing the path from the initial state to its absorbing state.

In order to construct a model in which the states of the different paths are separated from each other, except for the initial state, the forking states $1, 2, \ldots, N-1$ should also be transformed. Through recursive application of the transformation method described in [11], the model may be transformed into the one shown in Figure 3 without altering the state probabilities. In Figure 3, state $1'$ represents a substate of state 1, state $2'$ represents a substate of state 2, etc. The transition rates λ_j, with $j \in [1, 2, \ldots, N-1]$ equal the sum of all transition rates, excluding the repair transitions, from state j in the model shown in Figure 2. The rate λ'_{01} of the initial transition of the path is given by:

$$\lambda_{01}' = \lambda_{01} \prod_{j=1}^{N-1} \frac{\lambda_{j(j+1)}}{\lambda_j}. \tag{3.1}$$

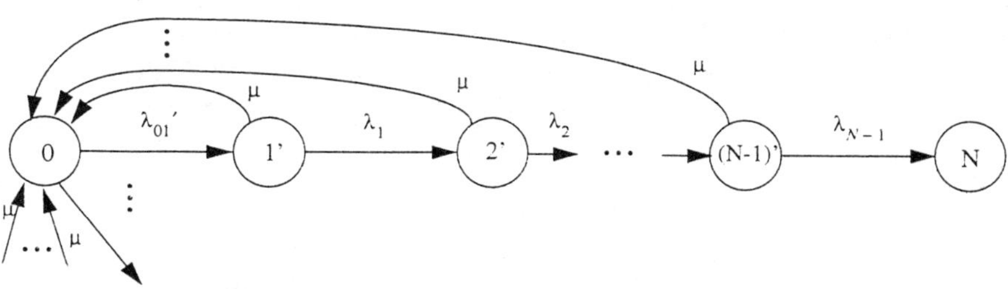

Figure 3. The result of separating one path from the others

O. Bridal

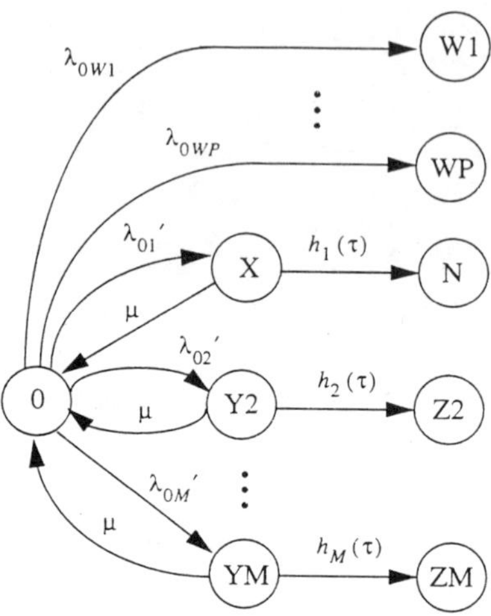

Figure 4. Transformed dependability model

To see how the path studied so far fits into the overall model of the system, we consider Figure 4. In this figure, state X represents the concatenation of states $1', 2', \ldots, (N-1)'$ of Figure 3. The transition rates from intermediate to absorbing states are no longer constant, which is indicated by the $h_j(\tau)$ transitions with τ denoting the time elapsed since the last transition from state 0. Thus, this is a semi-markov model. The paths to state Zk, with $k \in [2, 3, \cdots, M]$, are of the same general structure as the path to state N. In other words, each of these paths may be drawn as shown in Figure 3, albeit with different transition rates and different number of intermediate states. States W1-WP represent different types of failure, thus generalizing the notion of benign and malign failures to an arbitrary number of failure types.

Owing to the simplicity of the model transformation technique presented in this section, it can easily be automated. A computer program can analyze the original transition model and establish a path as shown in Figure 3 for every path to an absorbing state of the original state transition diagram.

4 Absorbing state probability bounds

For each absorbing state of the model shown in Figure 4, upper and lower bounds on the state probability as functions of time may be derived. For the state transition diagram in Figure 3, with λ_{01}' given by Equation 3.1, it has been shown in [12] that an upper bound on the probability of state N can be expressed as:

$$P_N(t) \leq \frac{\prod_{j=0}^{N-1} \lambda_{j(j+1)}}{\mu^{N-1}} t. \tag{4.1}$$

By combining the results obtained in [11,12], a lower bound on this probability may also be found:

$$P_N(t) \geq (1-\rho)\cdot\left[1-\sum_{S\neq 0} (\text{upper bound on probability of state} S)\right]\cdot\frac{\prod_{j=0}^{N-1} \lambda_{j(j+1)}}{\mu^{N-1}} t \tag{4.2}$$

where the summation is to be taken over all states except state 0 in the model in Figure 4. According to [12], the parameter ρ is given by:

$$\rho = \frac{\lambda_{01}' + \lambda_1 + \lambda_{01}' \cdot \lambda_1 \cdot t + \frac{1}{t}}{\mu} \qquad \text{for } N = 2$$

$$\rho = \frac{\lambda_{01}' \cdot t}{2} + \frac{N-1}{\mu \cdot t} + (N-1)\frac{\lambda_{01}' + \sum_{j=1}^{N-1} \lambda_j}{\mu} \quad \text{for } N \geq 3. \tag{4.3}$$

If Equation 4.2 is to be useful, the state probability bounds on its right-hand side have to be found. An upper bound on the sum of the state probabilities of the intermediate states $X, Y2, \cdots, YM$ in Figure 4 can be found by concatenating these states into a single state with an input transition rate equal to the sum of all λ_{oi}' rates (with $i = 1, 2, \cdots, M$) from state 0 and with output transition rates μ and $h_{total}(\tau)$, respectively. The $h_{total}(\tau)$ can be expressed as a function of the transition rates of the model in Figure 4, but for our purposes that is not necessary here[2]. The important point is that from the simplified model with all intermediate states concatenated, the sum of their probabilities can easily be shown to be bounded by:

$$\sum_{\substack{\text{all intermediate states}}} P_{\text{state}} \leq \frac{\sum_i \lambda_{oi}'}{\mu + \sum_i \lambda_{oi}'}. \tag{4.4}$$

For the probabilities of states W1-WP, it is easily seen that:

$$P_{Wj}(t) \leq 1 - e^{-\lambda_{0Wj}t} \leq \lambda_{0Wj} \cdot t \quad \text{for} \quad j = 1, 2, \cdots, P. \tag{4.5}$$

Upper bounds on the probabilities of states Z2-ZM can be obtained by studying these paths in the same way as has been done for the path to state N above. Thus, Equation 4.2 applies for these paths as well if the transition rates in this equation are replaced by those of the considered path.

For the states W1-WP that may be entered via a direct transition from the initial state, upper bounds are given by Equation 4.5. By making use of

---

[2] In fact, none of the $h_{index}(\tau)$ functions are used in any calculation in this paper. They merely provide a means of indicating that the corresponding transitions are not independent of the time elapsed since the last state transition.

the results obtained in [11], lower bounds on these state probabilities can be established as:

$$P_{Wj}(t) \geq \left(1 - \frac{\lambda_{0Wj} \cdot t}{2}\right)$$

$$\left(1 - \sum_{S \neq 0} (\text{upper bound on probability of state } S)\right) \lambda_{0Wj} \cdot t. \tag{4.6}$$

To conclude this section, we note that closed-form expressions for upper and lower bounds on the probability of every absorbing state in the model in Figure 4 can be established from Equations 4.1–4.6. Once these bounds have been established, the probabilities of the absorbing states may be compared to each other. Since each absorbing state of a given type corresponds to a certain event succession leading to this type of failure, the relative contributions of various event successions to this failure type can easily be evaluated. If it is found that some of these contributions are very small compared to others, they may be neglected by the reliability analysis. However, they should still be considered in the analysis of the approximation error that occurs when they are ignored.

5   Methodology example

As an example of how to apply the reliability analysis methodology on a system, we will consider the simple reliability block diagram in Figure 5. The corresponding configuration consists of four units, logically connected as two pairs, for example two processors and two memories. Basically, each pair is operational if at least one of the units in the pair is operational. Single points of failure are accounted for by the inclusion of the "component" having fault rate λ_C. This "component" represent all the events that cause the system to crash immediately. When a model of a system is constructed, care must be taken to ensure that such single points of failure are modelled well. It is often tempting to assume that single points of failure do not exist, but this assumption should not be made unless a thorough analysis reveals that the corresponding fault rate is insignificant.

For the example system, the state transition model in Figure 6 can be drawn. In this figure, error detection coverage and transient faults have been accounted for. The parameters shown in the figure are:

- $\lambda_A, \lambda_B, \lambda_C$: rates for the occurrence of a permanent fault in a unit of type A, B or C, respectively.

- c_A, c_B: coverage for the detection and successful handling of a permanent fault in a unit of type A or B, respectively. Thus, c_A is the conditional probability that a fault in an A type unit is handled such that the unit is effectively disconnected from the system and the remaining units can continue to operate, given that a permanent fault exists in that A type unit.

- $\lambda_{TA}, \lambda_{TB}$: rates of occurrence of uncovered transient faults in a unit of type A or B, respectively. An uncovered transient fault is a transient fault that the system does not recover from within a sufficiently short time. Typically, these rates can be determined from a model of the transient fault occurrence, detection and recovery process.

- μ: the repair rate. It may be interpreted as discussed in Section 2.

Following a transformation of the state-space model according to the method presented in Section 3, the model in Figure 7 is obtained. In order to facilitate the reading of the figure, the repair transitions with rate μ from states 1a, 1b, 2a, 2b, 3a and 3b to state 0 are not shown.

Table 1 shows upper and lower bounds on the absorption state probabilities, obtained from Equations 4.1–4.6.

By summing all the upper bounds an upper bound on the system failure probability is obtained. If the upper bounds given in Table 1 are interpreted as approximations of the corresponding state probabilities, an examination of them may show that some of these probabilities are very small compared to others. For instance, states Fd and Fe may be considered insignificant if it is expected that the repair rate μ is much higher than the λ_A and the λ_B rates. Similarly, it is possible that the parameters are such that the failure state probability contribution from the path to state Fc is, say, much less than the contribution from the path to state Fb. If that is the case, the unreliability U (=1-Prob[failure]) could be approximated by $\overline{U}$ given by:

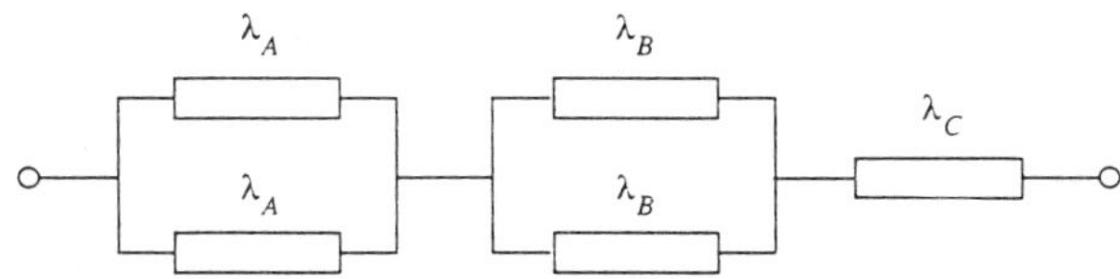

Figure 5. Example system

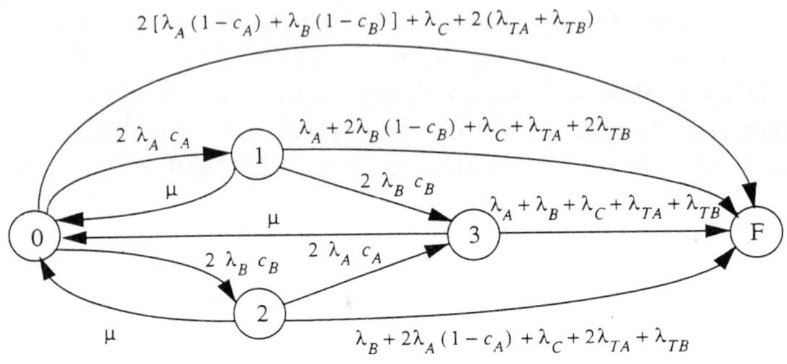

Figure 6. State-space model of the example system

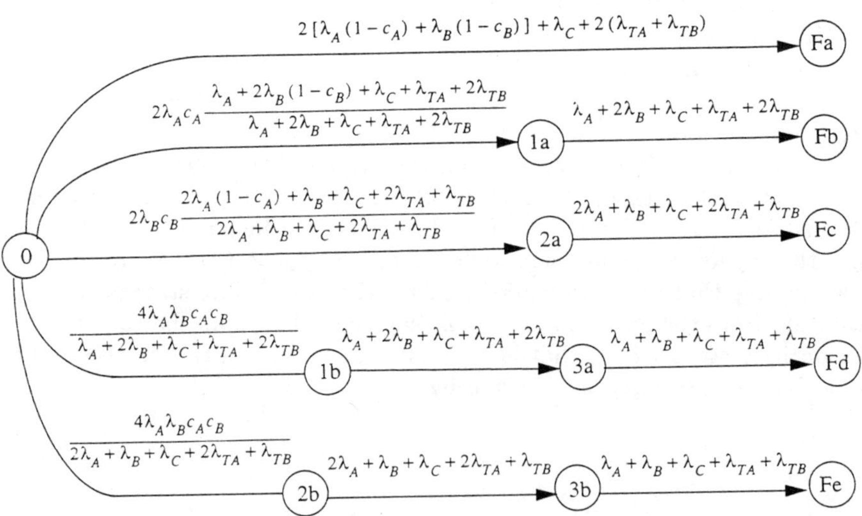

Figure 7. Transformed state-space model of the example system (note that the repair transitions from the intermediate states are not shown

State	State Probability Upper Bound (UB_{state})	State Probability Lower Bound (LB_{state})[a]
Fa	$[2[\lambda_A(1-c_A)+\lambda_B(1-c_B)]+$ $\lambda_C+2(\lambda_{TA}+\lambda_{TB})]\cdot t$	$UB_{Fa}\cdot\left[1-\dfrac{UB_{Fa}}{2}-2\cdot\dfrac{\lambda_A c_A+\lambda_B c_B}{\mu}-\sum_{i=a,b,c,d,e}UB_{Fi}\right]$
Fb	$\dfrac{2\lambda_A c_A[\lambda_A+2\lambda_B(1-c_B)+\lambda_C+\lambda_{TA}+2\lambda_{TB}]}{\mu}\cdot t$	$UB_{Fb}\cdot\left[1-\rho_{Fb}-2\cdot\dfrac{\lambda_A c_A+\lambda_B c_B}{\mu}-\sum_{i=a,b,c,d,e}UB_{Fi}\right]$
Fc	$\dfrac{2\lambda_B c_B[2\lambda_A(1-c_A)+\lambda_B+\lambda_C+2\lambda_{TA}+\lambda_{TB}]}{\mu}\cdot t$	$UB_{Fc}\cdot\left[1-\rho_{Fc}-2\cdot\dfrac{\lambda_A c_A+\lambda_B c_B}{\mu}-\sum_{i=a,b,c,d,e}UB_{Fi}\right]$
Fd	$\dfrac{4\lambda_A\lambda_B c_A c_B(\lambda_A+\lambda_B+\lambda_C+\lambda_{TA}+\lambda_{TB}]}{\mu^2}\cdot t$	$UB_{Fd}\cdot\left[1-\rho_{Fd}-2\cdot\dfrac{\lambda_A c_A+\lambda_B c_B}{\mu}-\sum_{i=a,b,c,d,e}UB_{Fi}\right]$
Fe	$\dfrac{4\lambda_A\lambda_B c_A c_B(\lambda_A+\lambda_B+\lambda_C+\lambda_{TA}+\lambda_{TB}]}{\mu^2}\cdot t$	$UB_{Fe}\cdot\left[1-\rho_{Fe}-2\cdot\dfrac{\lambda_A c_A+\lambda_B c_B}{\mu}-\sum_{i=a,b,c,d,e}UB_{Fi}\right]$

a. Note: ρ_{state} is given by Equation 4.3 applied to the path to state *state* in Figure 7.

Table 1. Upper and lower bound on absorbing state probabilities

$$\overline{U} = P_{Fa,UB} + P_{Fb,UB} = [2[\lambda_A(1-c_A)+\lambda_B(1-c_B)]+\lambda_C+2(\lambda_{TA}+\lambda_{TB})+$$

$$\frac{2\lambda_A c_A[\lambda_A+2\lambda_B(1-c_B)+\lambda_C+\lambda_{TA}+2\lambda_{TB}]}{\mu}]\cdot t \tag{5.1}$$

where $P_{Fa,UB}$ and $P_{Fb,UB}$ are the upper bounds on the probabilities of states Fa and Fb, respectively, as given in Table 1.

The error associated with the approximation given by Equation 5.1 can be evaluated by noting that the following holds for the theoretically correct unreliability U:

$$\sum_{i=a,b,c,d,e} LB_{Fi} \leq U \leq \sum_{i=a,b,c,d,e} UB_{Fi} \tag{5.2}$$

with these bounds given by Table 1. It must be realized that the evaluation of the approximation error $\overline{U} - U$ can usually be carried out without any great accuracy as its purpose is only to show that the approximation is acceptable. In the error analysis, the bounds given by Table 1 may therefore be simplified as long as these simplifications do not result in significant overestimations of the approximation accuracy. The choices made in these simplifications clearly depend on the assumptions made, or knowledge possessed, regarding the relative magnitudes of the parameters involved. Ideally, the methodology should be supported by an interactive software tool that permits an analyst to supply basic information such as very rough ranges for the parameters involved. The software then examines the reliability model and identifies possibly insignificant paths. The remaining paths are then analysed and perhaps approximated further. The results of such an analysis of the example given above could for instance be:

- Unreliability approximation: $2 \cdot \left[\lambda_A(1 - c_A) + \lambda_B(1 - c_B) + \lambda_{TB} + \frac{\lambda_A^2}{\mu} \right] \cdot t.$

- Relative approximation error: $< 5\%$.

Such a software tool would obviously be very useful in that it would enable reliability analysis at an early phase of the design process when only limited information on the design is available. This limited knowledge is thus used to identify which failure mechanisms are important to the system reliability and which ones are not.

It is interesting to study how well the technique scales to system models of higher complexity. From the example it is clear that the upper bound on the unreliability has the form:

$$UB = t \cdot \sum_i \mathrm{term}_i. \tag{5.3}$$

For a complex model, the number of elements in the sum in Equation 5.3 becomes prohibitively large, seemingly reducing the usefulness of the methodology. However, an inspection of the sum often reveals that the elements of the sum differ by several orders of magnitude. An approximation may then be established by ignoring the smallest terms of the sum. Typically, the contributions from state transitions involving more than two independent faults are candidates for such exclusion. Thus, the proposed method is feasible for system models of much higher complexity than in the given example.

6 Summary

A methodology for the stepwise analysis of a certain type of markov model is presented. The model type considered corresponds very well to a reliability model of a repairable fault-tolerant system. Application of the methodology facilitates the making of well-founded design decisions early in the design process, before design details are known. Typically, the method can be used to help the designer choose between a number of fault-tolerance strategies. An interactive software tool that implements the methodology could simplify the reliability analysis process. The different steps of the methodology can be summarized as shown below.

1. Draw a state transition diagram of the system. Make sure that imperfect coverage and single points of failure are accounted for and that they are

accurately modelled. Coverage can be calculated in separate models describing the error detection and error handling process. In these models, real-time aspects such as maximum allowed time to recovery can be considered. Permanent as well as transient faults should be included in the model.

2. Transform the state transition diagram into an equivalent model where each path to failure is separated from the others.

3. Establish closed-form expressions for the bounds on the absorbing states probabilities. The contributions of the different paths to the failure probability may now be compared to each other. Depending on the purpose of the modeling, the analysis either stops here with an understanding of which failure mechanisms that are important or goes on with steps 4–5 below to arrive at an approximate expression for the reliability of the system.

4. Identify insignificant paths to failure by comparing the probabilities of the absorbing states to each other. Insignificant paths can be excluded from the model. Their contributions, however, should be included in the approximation error that results when their contributions are neglected.

5. For each type of failure, establish an approximate expression for the failure probability. The error associated with this approximation can be expressed from the knowledge gained in the previous steps of the methodology.

References

1. Balakrishnan, M. and Raghavendra, C.S. (1993). An analysis of a reliability model for repairable fault-tolerant systems. *IEEE Trans. Computers*, **42**, 327–339.

2. Bobbio, A. and Trivedi, K.S. (1986). An aggregation technique for the transient analysis of stiff Markov chains. *IEEE Trans. Computers*, **C-35**, 803–814.

3. Dyer, D. (1989). Unification of reliability/availability/repairability models for Markov systems. *IEEE Trans. Reliability*, **R-38**, 246–252.

4. Balakrishnan, M. and Reibman, A. (1993). Characterizing a lumping heuristic for a Markov network reliability model. *Proc. 23rd Ann. IEEE Int. Sym. on Fault-Tolerant Computing*, 56–65.

5. Bon, J.L. and Collet, J. (1994). An algorithm in order to implement reliability exponential approximations. *Reliability Engineering and System Safety*, **43**, 263–268.

6. Butler, R.W. (1992). The SURE approach to reliability analysis. *IEEE Trans. Reliability*, **R-41**, 210–218.

7. Pagès, A. and Gondran, M. (1986). System reliability, evaluation and prediction in engineering. Springer-Verlag, 189–230.

8. Takaragi, K., Sasaki, R. and Shingai, S. (1985). A method of rapid Markov reliability calculation. *IEEE Trans. Reliability*, **R-34**, 262–268.

9. Laprie, J-C., Arlat, J., Béounes, C. and Kanoun, K. (1990). Definition and analysis of hardware-software-fault-tolerant architectures. *IEEE Computer*, **23**, 39–51.

10. Bechta Dugan, J. and Trivedi, K.S. (1989). Coverage modeling for dependability analysis of fault-tolerant systems. *IEEE Trans. Computers*, **38**, 775–787.

11. Bridal, O. (1994). Safety and reliability analysis of repairable systems. *Technical Report Number: 197*, Dept. of Computer Engineering, Chalmers University of Technology, Göteborg, Sweden.

12. Bridal, O. (1994). Reliability estimates for repairable fault-tolerant systems. *Technical Report Number 194*, Dept. of Computer Engineering, Chalmers University of Technology, Göteborg, Sweden, and *Proc. of the Nordic Seminar on Dependable Computing Systems*.

Reliability Models for Hard Real-Time Systems

C.S. Perkins and A.M. Tyrrell

Department of Electronics, University of York

Abstract

We present a new reliability model for hard real-time systems. This is
an extended Markov model, derived from an analysis of the generic properties of hard real-time systems subject to a simple random-fault model.
Our model permits analysis of the run-time behaviour of a system, in order
to derive the probability profiles of the system's completion/failure times.
The model is applied to the analysis of a simple sequential recovery block
system, and illustrative examples based on this system are provided. The
paper concludes with a discussion of the application of such accurate completion profile information to the design of embedded software systems.

Keywords: Real-time system, Recovery block, Markov model, completion probability profile.

1   Introduction

Before fault-tolerant features can sensibly be incorporated in a system, there is
a need to determine the effects they have on the reliability and failure modes
of the system as a whole. In particular, it is important that an accurate fail-
ure/reliability model is available during the design of fault-tolerant and safety
critical systems, whether those systems comprise hardware, software or some
combination of the two. This paper will describe a new approach to reliability
modelling for embedded software systems, with emphasis on the applicability of
this technique to hard real-time safety critical systems.

The reliability models which have been developed in the literature may be
split into two groups: functional models which describe the system from a
time-independent viewpoint, and dynamic models which describe the run-time
behaviour of a system. Time-independent models [1,9,18,21] are typically based
around a Markov-chain or other probabilistic process which is used to describe
the behaviour of the system either neglecting information about execution time
or providing a partial ordering of events only. Such models enable the probability
of failure for a particular structure to be calculated, but do not provide for the
calculation of the timing properties of the system. Whilst this is undoubtably
of value, its usefulness in the analysis of hard real-time systems must be questioned, since these systems require not only functionally correct behaviour, but

also *temporally* correct behaviour. The timing properties of a hard real-time system are as important as its functional properties in ensuring correct operation and, unfortunately, this class of model is not able to describe this with sufficient rigour.

In contrast, time-dependent models are much less well developed [4,7]. Although some work has been conducted into finding algorithms to derive the mean execution time of a set of processes in the presence of failure [20], there has been little work undertaken to determine the probability distribution of the system's execution time. Much of the research conducted with hard real-time systems has focussed on scheduling problems [2,8,16,22,24] and typically requires knowledge of the execution time bounds of a process to enable efficient schedules to be calculated. With the introduction of fault-tolerant procedures, the execution time bounds of the system will change. It is therefore important that a means of deriving an expression for the execution time of a system with fault-tolerant processes is found, and it is this problem which is addressed in this paper.

It is therefore noted that:

1. whilst time-independent reliability models are useful, they do not address a number of important problems which must be resolved before these techniques will be of use in designing hard real-time systems; and

2. it is of great importance to be able to derive the probability distribution of process completion times, in order to have some means of developing an execution schedule to meet all required deadlines, even in the presence of failures and error recovery.

Taken together these points illustrate a problem with current approaches to designing hard real-time systems. It is usual for the timing properties of a hard real-time system to be abstracted away so as to give each process a maximum execution time. Provided such a maximum time can be assigned to each process, it is then possible to devise scheduling algorithms which, given sufficient resources, will ensure that all deadlines are met. These algorithms are, however, pessimistic because they rely on the upper bound of a process execution time, where as in real-systems, the probability of errors occurring is low and the execution time of most processes is typically much less than the maximum. The system therefore operates with much slack-time, implying low efficiency but high reliability. The thesis of this paper is that, if the probability distribution of the process execution times is known, it is possible to design a system which relies on this to attain much improved efficiency, whilst still managing to operate within a tolerable level of risk.

The remainder of this paper is split into the following sections. Section 2 describes the motivation behind this work, and places it in the context of other published literature. Sections 3 and 4 describe the underlying mathematical model used as a basis for the work, whilst Sections 5 and 6 describe the application of this to the modelling of a sequential recovery block structure. Finally Section 7 summarises the work.

2   Background

It is desired to model the execution of a system in such a manner that the probability distribution of the execution time can be determined, together with the system reliability. This section will propose a scheme by which this can be accomplished.

A number of experimental studies have been conducted into the failure characteristics of software systems [10,15]. These studies, together with theoretical results such as those presented in [7,11,12,13,14] seem to indicate that it is possible to achieve a reasonably accurate prediction of the failure characteristics of a software system using very simple models, and indeed, it has often been proposed that a random-fault model will suffice. Such a model is of use because of its ease of application and similarity to hardware reliability models, allowing similar techniques to be applied to the modelling of both hardware and software.

The notion of software faults occurring randomly is not intuitively obvious. In particular, a software system is typically thought of as being purely deterministic – given a specific set of inputs a certain output will arise, and that same output will arise whenever that set of inputs is presented to the system. How can such a system conform to a random-fault model?

The simple answer is, of course, that it cannot. However, it can be seen that although the underlying faults do not occur randomly, their manifestation can appear to follow the random-fault model. A typical embedded control system will comprise a set of interacting software processes, together with a number of hardware devices. Interactions occur not only between software processes, but also between software processes and hardware devices and between hardware devices. In addition, interactions may occur between different parts of the system due to the flow of information through the external environment. This is illustrated in Figure 1.

The software comprising an embedded system such as this will have a large input space. It is directly affected by software-software interactions and software-hardware interactions and also indirectly affected by hardware-hardware interactions and the influence of the external environment. As the number of inputs to the system increases, and more and more external devices are included, it becomes increasingly difficult to determine the system boundary and the number of possible interactions increases rapidly. Furthermore, it is typical that embedded systems have a temporal dimension to their input space. Identical inputs may well produce different outputs at different times.

It can readily be seen that, for all but the simplest of systems, the input space is so large, and the interactions which occur are so subtle and complex, that it is effectively impossible to predict the path the system will take through its input space [13]. From the above arguments, it seems reasonable to model the system's path through its inputs as a random-walk in a multi-dimensional space. This is transformed by the system to provide a path through the output space which is necessarily also modelled as a random walk. This is illustrated in Figure 2.

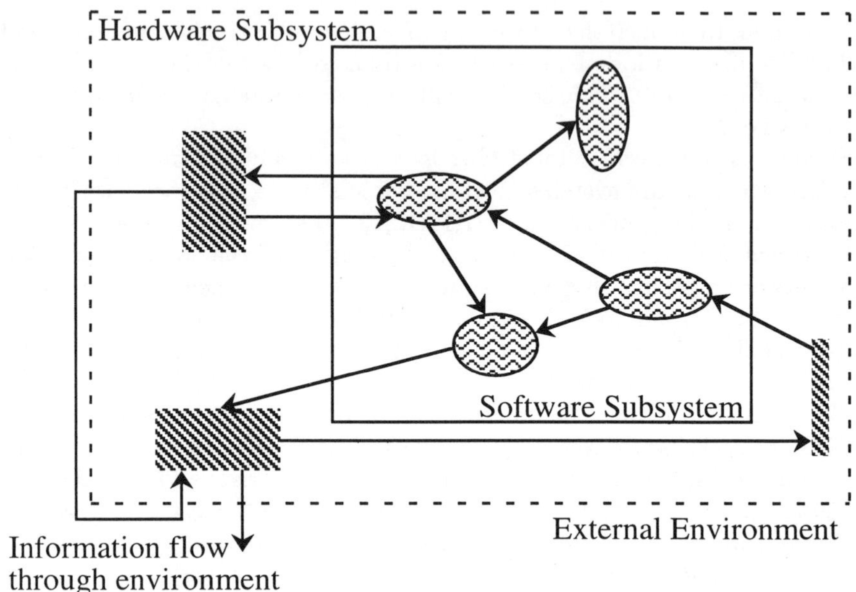

Figure 1. The structure of a typical embedded control system

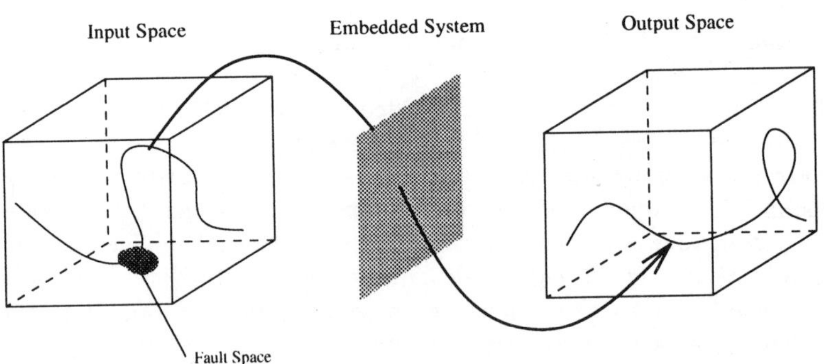

Figure 2. Random walk through the system's input space

There are typically a number of points in the input space which will give rise to faults in the system, and those faults may, eventually, cause errors to manifest themselves. Such errors, if untreated, may cause system failures. It is noted that faults which are close in the input space will not necessarily give rise to faults which are close in the output space.

This then is the basis for the system model to be used in this paper. It will be assumed that the system's input space is sufficiently large, and the tasks to be undertaken sufficiently complex, that a random-fault model such as this is applicable. It is considered that such an assumption is not unrealistic, indeed it is the basis for a number of other models [12-14], and certain experimental data [6,15] has been collected which appears to confirm the validity of this approach. The work conducted by Laprie [11] also lends support to this, when it is noted that

> "...the constancy of the hazard rates, although it is an *a priori* unrealistic hypothesis, turns out to be satisfactory."

It is further noted that a study made of the reliability logs of Tandem systems [6] provides evidence for this claim, as indeed does the work of Musa at Bell Laboratories [14,15], and that of the European Space Agency [5], where it is noted that

> "Software failure is a process that appears to the observer to be random, therefore the term reliability is meaningful when applied to a system which includes software and the process can be modelled as stochastic."

It can therefore be seen that the random-fault model as applied to software and combined hardware-software systems provides a reasonable fit with experimental data with a relatively simple theoretical background.

3 Underlying mathematical model

The underlying mathematical model detailed here is a stochastic model, derived primarily from Markov chain theory [23], with modifications to allow for simple process interactions. The underlying network model borrows a number of concepts from Petri net theory [17], not least the notation used. Despite the notational similarities, however, this is primarily a Markov model, not a Petri net system.

The basis of the model comprises a multi-graph consisting of a set of *places* and a set of *transitions* connected by directed arcs. The system state is defined by the probabilistic distribution of a set of tokens amongst these places. Changes in the system state are indicated by movement of tokens along these arcs, from place to place by means of the intermediate transitions. All tokens move at once, in step-time. A transition cannot fire until it has a token in each of its input places, and when it does fire it sends a single token to one of its output places, determined probabilistically by the *transition probabilities* labelled on the arcs leading away from the transitions. A place may have multiple input arcs and hence, may receive multiple tokens. A place will output a token down each of its output arcs. A place will therefore create or destroy tokens as required.

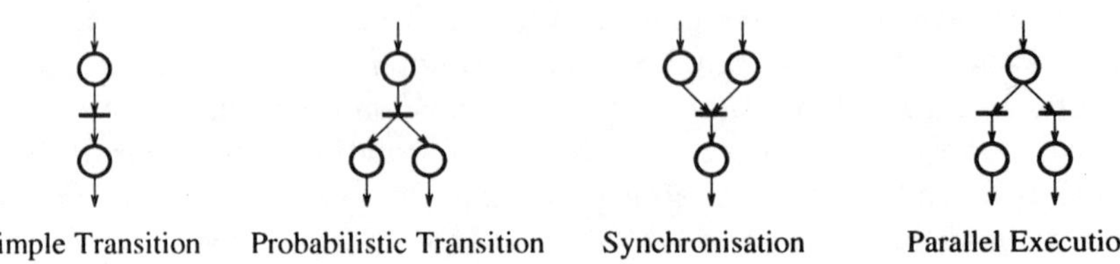

Figure 3. Basic modes of execution

The basic modes of execution of the model are shown in Figure 3. The *simple transition* and *probabilistic transition* modes correspond to a standard Markov chain model. Tokens are neither created or destroyed. In these modes the system shows multiple possible paths of execution – it can perform *one* action from a choice of many possibilities – this is modelled as a *transition* with multiple output arcs.

A system which permits concurrent execution of multiple paths is also possible, and is modelled by a *place* with multiple output arcs. This is the parallel execution mode, and shows token creation. Further, it is possible to model synchronisation among these concurrent processes by means of transitions with multiple input arcs. Such transitions cannot fire until all their input places contain tokens, and so they introduce synchronisation into the execution of the system, and destroy excess tokens.

It is the ability to model both probabilistic and concurrent execution with ease which sets this model apart from traditional Markov models.

A formal definition of this model is provided in Section 4, whilst details of the application of this model to problems in real-time system design are discussed in Sections 5 and 6.

4   Formal definition of the model

4.1   Basic network model

The basis of the model is a set of places with probabilistic movement of tokens between them. This is defined by a four-tuple

$$C = (\Theta, \Lambda, I, O), \tag{4.1}$$

where

- $\Theta = \{\theta_1, \theta_2, \ldots, \theta_n\}$ is a finite set of *places* with $n \geq 2$ representing the system state.

- $\Lambda = \{\lambda_1, \lambda_2, \ldots, \lambda_m\}$ is a finite set of *transitions* with $m \geq 1$, representing the possible movements between states.

- The *input function*, I, and the *output function*, O, define the following mappings between Θ and Λ:

  * Transition to place:
  $$I : \Lambda \mapsto \Theta, \qquad (4.2)$$
  $$O : \Lambda \mapsto \Theta. \qquad (4.3)$$

  * Place to transition:
  $$I : \Theta \mapsto \Lambda, \qquad (4.4)$$
  $$O : \Theta \mapsto \Lambda. \qquad (4.5)$$

  * Transition to transition:
  $$I : \Lambda \mapsto \Lambda, \qquad (4.6)$$
  $$O : \Lambda \mapsto \Lambda. \qquad (4.7)$$

  It is noted that no mapping is defined for $\Theta \mapsto \Theta$. Furthermore, it is seen that I and O can be regarded as defining arcs connecting the places and transitions of the network. These arcs are weighted, with all arcs having weight $w = 1.0$, with the exception of the arcs defined by $O : \Lambda \mapsto \Theta$ and $O : \Lambda \mapsto \Lambda$ which together define the transition probabilities $T_{i,j}^{(n)}$ (see below), and have weight $w : 0 \leq w \leq 1$. It is noted that the sum of the arc-weights for arcs leaving any state must be unity.

The following restrictions are made

- The set of places, Θ, and the set of transitions, Λ, are disjoint:
$$\Theta \cap \Lambda = \emptyset. \qquad (4.8)$$

- Two places θ_i and θ_j may be connected by at most *one* single-step transition:
$$|O(\theta_i) \cap I(\theta_j)| \leq 1. \qquad (4.9)$$

- A transition may take input from a set of places *or* a set of transitions, but not both:
$$I(\lambda_i) \cap \Theta \neq \emptyset \Rightarrow I(\lambda_i) \cap \Lambda = \emptyset, \qquad (4.10)$$
$$I(\lambda_i) \cap \Lambda \neq \emptyset \Rightarrow I(\lambda_i) \cap \Theta = \emptyset. \qquad (4.11)$$

- A transition can take input from at most one other transition:

$$|I(\lambda_i) \cap \Lambda| \leq 1. \tag{4.12}$$

- A transition which has output to one or more other transitions can have at most one input:

$$\forall \lambda_k : O(\lambda_k) \cap \Lambda \neq \emptyset, |I(\lambda_k)| \leq 1. \tag{4.13}$$

These definitions provide the basic system structure.

4.2   Single-step execution rules

The *time-independent single-step transition probability* between places θ_i and θ_j is denoted by $T_{i,j}^{(1)}$. This is the probability that a movement can occur from place θ_i to place θ_j provided that there is a single-transition, λ_k, linking these two places. It can be seen that $T_{i,j}^{(1)}$ is the weight of the arc linking places Θ_i and Θ_j.

In order for a single transition, λ_k, to link two places, that transition must be an element of the set of output transitions of one of the places, and an element of the set of input transitions of the other place:

$$\lambda_k = O(\theta_i) \cap I(\theta_j). \tag{4.14}$$

If $\lambda_k = \emptyset$ then no single-step transition is possible between states θ_i and θ_j. However, if $\lambda_k \neq \emptyset$ then a single-step transition is possible, and the set λ_k holds the transition by which that movement is made.

It is now necessary to define the *time-dependent single-step transition probability* between places θ_i and θ_j at time t. This is the probability that a single-step transition will occur, based around the system state at a specified time. It is not possible for a transition to fire until all its input places are enabled; and a place is said to be enabled if there is a non-zero marking for that place. Hence, the time-dependent single-step transition probability is defined as:

$$\pi_{i,j}^{(t)} = T_{i,j}^{(1)} \prod_{I(\lambda_k)-\theta_i} P_k(t), \tag{4.15}$$

where λ_k is defined in Equation 4.14 and $P_k(t)$ is the marking for place θ_k at time t, is defined later by Equation 4.21. The time-independent single-step transition probability, $T_{i,j}^{(1)}$, is multiplied by the product of the probabilities that each of the input places to that transition are enabled, with the exception of the input place from which the transition is made. This exception is made for two reasons: firstly, if the place θ_i is not included, then a system with only single input arc becomes equivalent to a simple Markov chain model. Second, if the input from place θ_i is included then the definitions required by the model become mutually recursive and are impossible to evaluate.

4.3 n-step execution rules

In Section 4.1 it was specified that movement can occur between two transitions, λ_i and λ_j, subject to certain restrictions on topology. This allows time-independent n-step transitions between places to be described. These transition probabilities are denoted by $T_{i,j}^{(n)}$ and indicate a movement from place θ_i to place θ_j which passes through n transitions, where $n > 1$, and which *does not* pass through any intermediate places. As for the single-step transition probabilities, $T_{i,j}^{(1)}$, these n-step transition probabilities are formed by the product of the weights of the arcs traversed. Given this definition, and the definitions of Section 4.2, it is possible to derive an expression for the *time-dependent* n-step transition probability, $p_{i,j}^{(n,t)}$, between places θ_i and θ_j at time t.

It is noted that the n-step transition probabilities *for a Markov chain* are given by:

$$p_{i,k}^{(n)} = \sum_j p_{i,j} p_{j,k}^{(n-1)}, \tag{4.16}$$

where

$$p_{j,k}^{(0)} = \left\{ \begin{array}{l} 0 \text{ if } j \neq k \\ 1 \text{ if } j = k \ . \end{array} \right. \tag{4.17}$$

It is also noted that this probability is *time-independent*, and allows only n-step movements which pass through other intermediate places, since Markov chains do not allow for mappings $\Lambda \mapsto \Lambda$.

This definition can be extended by allowing n-step movements which use only transitions, $T_{i,j}^{(n)}$, although it is *not* possible to simply add $T_{i,j}^{(n)}$ to the above equation, since there may be other indirect paths by which a movement may occur, consisting of an m step transition-only movement, and an $(n - m)$ step movement using intermediate places. This, therefore, leads to the following expression for the n-step transition probabilities:

$$p_{i,k}^{(n)} = \sum_j p_{i,j} p_{j,k}^{(n-1)} + \sum_{m=2}^{n} \sum_j T_{i,j}^{(m)} p_{j,k}^{(n-m)}, \tag{4.18}$$

where $p_{j,k}^{(0)}$ is defined as in Equation 4.17. This consists of the transition probability as if the direct multi-step transitions were not present, specified by the first summation term, with the addition of the probability of making the transition by any combination of direct, $T_{i,j}^{(m)}$, and indirect, $p_{j,k}^{(n-m)}$, routes.

It is then a simple matter to add timing information to this; the time independent single step transition probability, $p_{i,j}$, is replaced by the time-dependent probability, $\pi_{i,j}^{(t)}$ (see Equation 4.15), and a timing parameter is added into the definition of the n-step transition probability, $p_{i,k}^{(n)}$. This provides an expression for the time-dependent n-step transition probability as follows:

$$p_{i,k}^{(n,t)} = \sum_j \pi_{i,j}^{(t-n)} p_{j,k}^{(n-1,t)} + \sum_{m=2}^{n} \sum_j T_{i,j}^{(m)} p_{j,k}^{(n-m,t)}, \qquad (4.19)$$

where

$$p_{j,k}^{(0,t)} = \left\{ \begin{array}{l} 0 \text{ if } j \neq k \\ 1 \text{ if } j = k \ . \end{array} \right. \qquad (4.20)$$

4.4   Markings and system state

The system marking function is defined to be the *absolute probability distribution*, $P_i(t)$ representing the probability that there is at least one token at place θ_i at time t.

The definition of this is based around the equivalent definition for a Markov chain system, modified to allow for time-dependent transition probabilities (as detailed in Section 4.2), and to allow for direct n-step transitions, as detailed in Section 4.3. This leads to a definition for the absolute probability as follows:

$$P_i(t) = \sum_j P_j(0) p_{j,i}^{(t,t)}, \qquad (4.21)$$

where $P_i(0)$ denotes the initial probability distribution for the system. The marking is a vector which changes with time, based upon the execution rules of the system, and is therefore a representation of the system state at a particular time.

5   Generic hard real time system model

The mathematical framework described in Sections 3 and 4 allows the behaviour of real-time systems to be modelled. From this basic framework a lattice structured model is developed that models the progress of a computation from its initial state to one of several final states; completed, detectable fault, hidden fault, and failed. This model allows for both the functional and temporal properties of a hard real-time system to be represented and is derived from generic properties of hard real-time systems, thus being independent of any specific design/implementation technique for such systems. We now discuss the development of this model in some detail.

In order for a system to be classified as *hard real-time* it must have certain properties. In particular, the system must have well-defined execution time bounds, and the probability of the system exceeding those bounds must be known. Given this information, and in the absence of faults, such a system may be modelled as a simple state chain with probabilistic transition to a *completed* state which can only occur during a specified time period (Figure 4).

Completed

Figure 4. Basic state chain

It is noted that the transition probabilities to the completed state must match the completion profile of the system in the absence of failures. In general therefore it is expected that these transition probabilities will not be uniform.

Such a model is, of course, overly simplistic and must be extended in order to account for the presence of faults within the system. We divide such faults into two classes:

1. those which cause run-time errors and so are detectable *before* normal system completion; and

2. those faults which do not cause such errors, and so can only be detected by examining the final system state.

The first such class of fault may be modelled by the addition of a *detectable fault* state to the model describing the system. A transition is made from each state in the basic state chain to this *detectable fault* state, with probability determined as using a random fault model (Section 2), this is illustrated in Figure 5. Since the system obeys a random-fault model, the transition probability for each of these paths is uniform. It is noted that faults which would cause a time over-run fall into the detectable category, and so there is no need to further model a process which can exceed its time bounds.

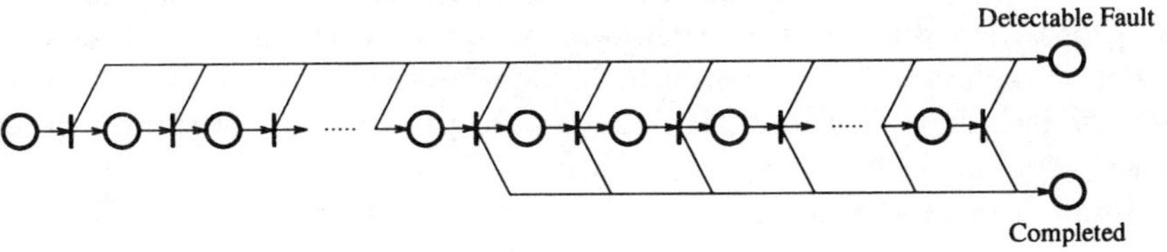

Figure 5. System model with detectable faults

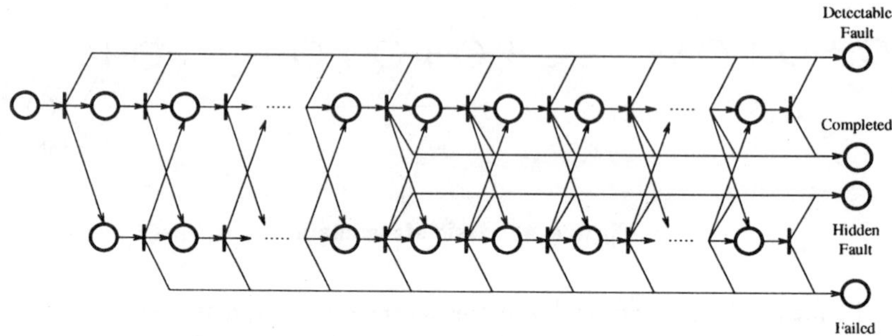

Figure 6. System model with undetectable faults

The second class of fault leads to a more complex model, requiring a parallel state chain to represent a system which is still functioning, but with a hidden fault. These parallel states mimic the function of the original state chain, and lead to the *hidden fault* and *failed* states (Figure 6). The transition probabilities for this parallel set of states mirror those of the original, fault-free, states. That is, the transition probabilities into the *hidden fault* state equal those for transitions into the *completed* state, and the transition probabilities into the *failed* state equal those for the *detectable fault* state. The transitions to/from this parallel set of states have uniform probability, according to the random-fault model.

This then leads to our final model definition, comprising two parallel state chains, representing normal execution and execution with a hidden fault. These are interconnected with a lattice structure which models hidden fault occurrence and recovery. This model may then be subjected to analysis as described in Section 4, leading to the determination of the marking function (Equation 4.21) for the four final states of this model. It is this marking function which represents the system behaviour in time.

Our model may therefore be used to determine *both* the functional and the temporal correctness of a system. The *functional* correctness is indicated by the probability distribution of the system between the four final states of our model; completed, detectable fault, hidden fault, and failed. The *temporal* correctness is indicated by plotting the timing profile to show the distribution of these probabilities with respect to time.

Implicit in the above discussion has been the precise nature of the transition probabilities, $T_{i,j}^{(1)}$, of the lattice model. We divide these into four categories:

- **Probability of completion, p_c** This is the probability that the system completes execution at any given time step. It is independent of the occurrence of faults, and must be derived from knowledge of the algorithm used by the process and/or test data. This is the transition probability for the arcs leading to the *completed* and *hidden fault* states.

- **Probability of detectable fault, p_d** This is the probability that the system fails in such a manner that can be detected before the normal completion. It may be estimated from test data, or from experience with similar systems. This is the transition probability for arcs leading to the *detectable fault* and *failed* states.

- **Probability of hidden fault, p_f** This is the probability that a fault occurs which does not give rise to an error detectable at run-time. Such a fault may be detected after completion of the process, and hence may be estimated based on the results of a system acceptance test. This probability, together with the probability of hidden recovery, defines the transition probabilities on the arcs interconnecting the two main state chains of our model.

- **Probability of hidden recovery, p_r** This is the probability that the system recovers silently from a hidden fault. May be estimated in a similar manner to the probability of a hidden fault.

With the exception of the completion probability, p_c, these transition probabilities are expected to be uniform, and to follow a random-fault model.

It is therefore seen that the parameters required by our model may readily be estimated based on test data from a real system. Our model is therefore of use in a predictive role; given preliminary test data for a component we derive a reliability and timing prediction. A number of these may then be combined to predict the behaviour of an entire system.

There is, of course, the question of granularity: at which level is it envisaged that our model will be applied? A typical system will consist of a number of fault-tolerant components; perhaps recovery blocks, atomic transactions, or N-version systems with voters. Each of these components will consist of a number of diverse alternates. We feel that our model may best be employed to model the behaviour of these alternates, since these are relatively small systems from which parameters may be readily derived. Techniques such as those discussed in Section 6 may then be employed to extend the model to the component level.

Such a model may then be used as a design aid during schedulability analysis. In particular, it may be used to derive a schedule which takes into account the probability distribution of the system's execution time; allowing the reliability/performance trade off to be made explicit.

6 Application to recovery block systems

The recovery block [19] is a technique which uses multiple versions of a program block to attempt to ensure success in the presence of system failures. The first version is known as the *primary* and the second and subsequent versions are known as *alternates*. The primary is executed, and an acceptance test evaluated. If this fails, the alternates are executed in series until one succeeds. In order for

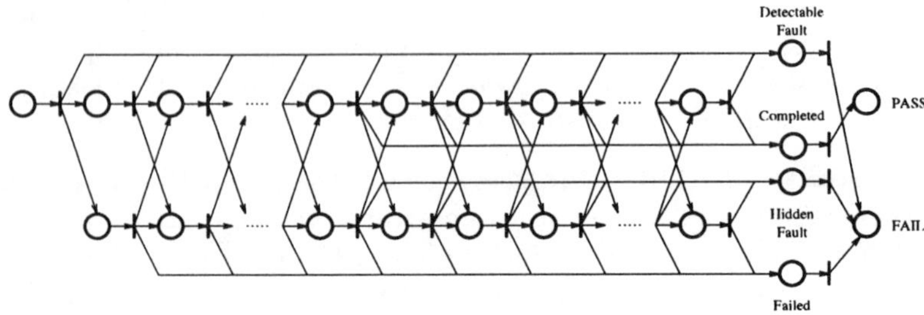

Figure 7. Alternate model with acceptance test

the entire system to operate successfully under hard real-time constraints, it is necessary for each alternate to operate under such constraints. Each alternate in the recovery block may, therefore, be viewed as a generic hard real-time system, and the model developed in Section 5 is applicable. In order to model the full recovery block, an acceptance test model is also required. This must map from the output states of the alternate to the final pass/fail states. A generic acceptance test will be fallible, that is, it will not correctly classify all systems, and will take a finite amount of time. For reasons of simplicity and tractability of the analysis, the test modelled here will, however, be assumed *infallible* [3], and will take unit time. The study of systems with fallible acceptance tests is the subject of current research. This combined alternate and acceptance test model is illustrated in Figure 7.

Several such systems may be combined in order to model a complete recovery block. This is illustrated in Figure 8 for a recovery block consisting of a primary and two alternates.

In order to illustrate the applicability of our model, a system such as that in Figure 8 has been analysed. For the purpose of this example, the primary and the two alternates were selected as follows (these systems are illustrated in Figure 9):

- **Primary** A slow but reliable system, where the completion probability increases with time. For example some form of iterative solution or stepwise refinement technique.

- **1st Alternate** A fast but unreliable system. For example a naive linear interpolation algorithm applied to a nonlinear system.

- **2nd Alternate** A reliable, medium speed system. The completion profile of this system follows a "bell-shaped" curve. For example an algebraic solution to a set of equations, where the completion time is somewhat data dependent.

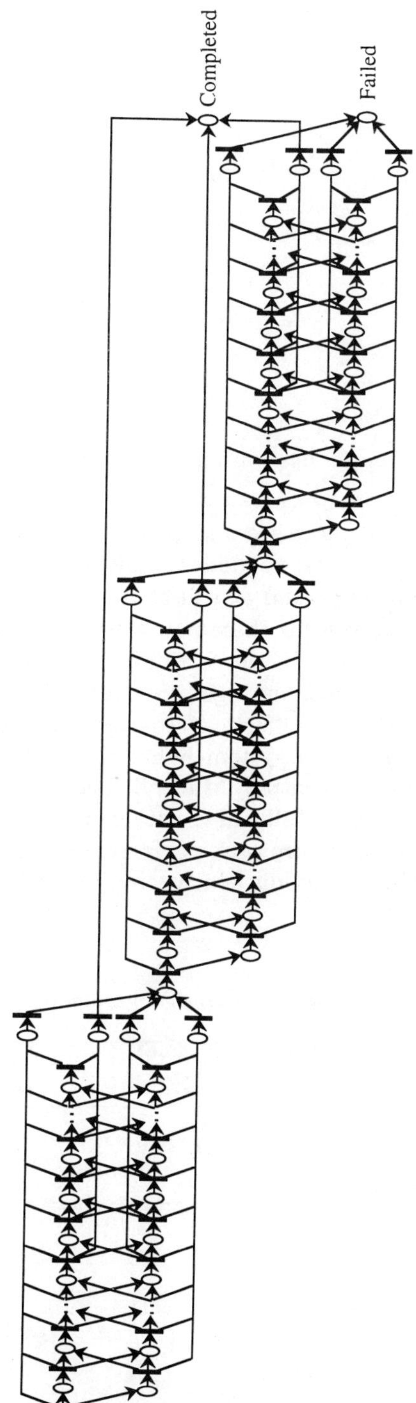

Figure 8. Recovery block model

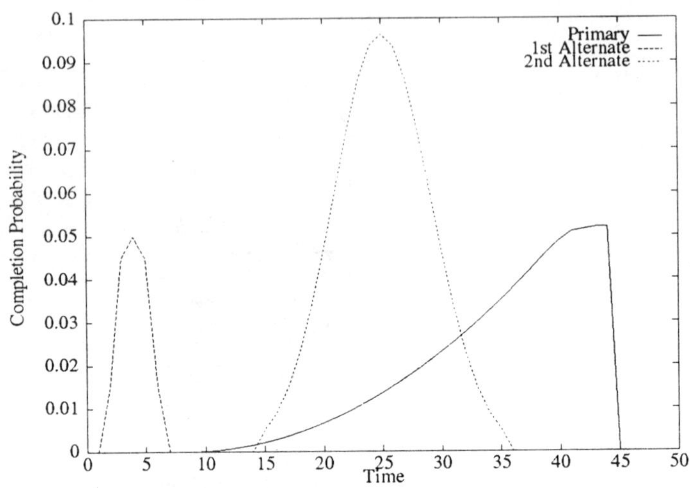

Figure 9. Basic alternate completion profiles

There are three other parameters to the alternate model: probability of detectable fault, p_d; probability of hidden fault, p_f; and probability of hidden recovery, p_r. In these tests p_f and p_r will be fixed for each alternate, and p_d will be varied. The values chosen for these parameters are shown in Table 1.

The results of the analysis in the form of completion/failure profiles for different values of p_c are shown in Figures 10 and 11. The completion profile (Figure 10) clearly shows the effects of changing the value of p_c, the forward failure rate. For small p_c the system behaves as if the primary and the two alternates are executing sequentially. Indeed this is so, because the majority of failures occuring are due to an alternate exceeding its time bounds, and not due to forward failures. As the failure rate, p_c, increases, the shape of the completion profile also changes. Those systems which complete successfully do so sooner, but

Table 1. Alternate parameters

	Probability hidden fault, p_f	Probability hidden recovery, p_r
Primary	0.001	0.001
1st Alternate	0.010	0.010
2nd Alternate	0.010	0.005

the completion probability decreases also. Further, the three alternates become less distinguishable.

The failure profile (Figure 11) shows a related trend. For low failure rates, most failures occur towards the end of the system's life, due to exhaustion of alternates in the recovery block. As the forward failure rate increases systems are increasingly likely to fail sooner in their life.

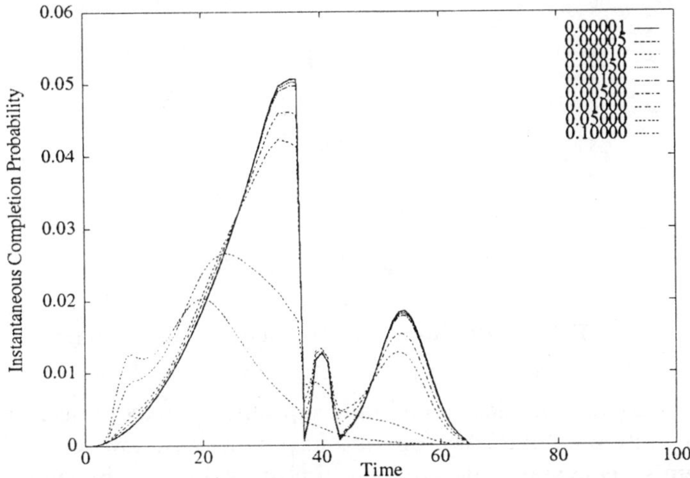

Figure 10. Recovery block completion profile

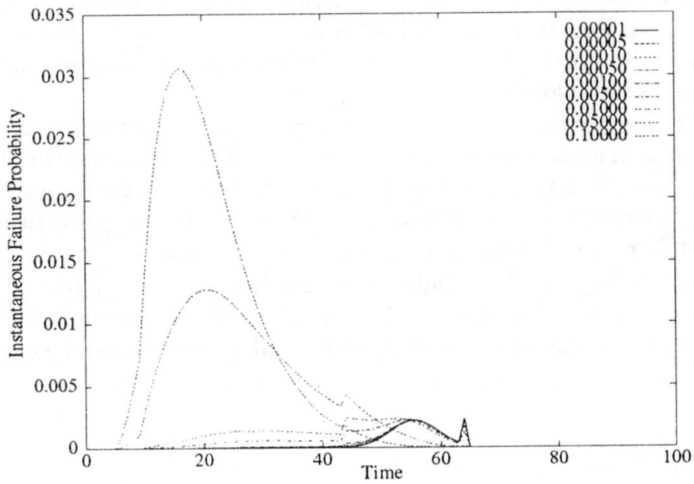

Figure 11. Recovery block failure profile

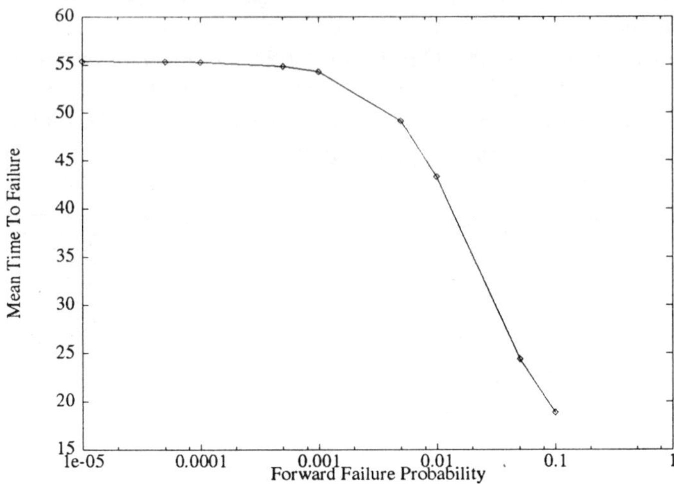

Figure 12. Recovery block mean-time-to-failure

Comparing the completion and failure profiles, it may be seen that the recovery block system exhibits two operational modes. At low forward failure rate, the system's behaviour is determined almost exclusively by time-overrun of alternates, and eventual exhaustion of alternates towards the end of the system's life. As the failure rate increases, we see a transition to a mode where alternates rarely complete their execution and the system failure rate increases dramatically. Such a mode change is confirmed also by a plot of the mean-time-to-failure (Figure 12) derived from the failure profile. Such a plot shows a sharp decline around the point where the mode change may be observed on the completion/failure profile plots.

Given this information, and a knowledge of the expected use of the system, the designer is in a position to make an informed decision on whether the absolute worst-case execution time must be used, or whether a reduced set of bounds can be chosen, with a specific risk that the system will fail to perform within these bounds. It is believed that in many cases the absolute worst-case behaviour is sufficiently unlikely, and the failure probabilities of other parts of the system are sufficiently large, that the increased probability of time-bound over-run will be acceptance. Application of this model will provide greater confidence that software can be designed to a specific, *tolerable*, level of risk.

7　Conclusions

In this paper we have introduced a new reliability model for the analysis of hard real-time systems which are subject to faults. The advantage of our technique compared to other published models is its ability to model the completion and failure profiles of hard real-time systems as probability distributions with respect to system execution time. The model described is based upon the concept of a random-failure model as applied to an embedded software system, with few parameters. All system parameters should be readily observable from real systems.

The new model has been used to analyse a simple recovery block system. The results illustrate that the model is sufficient for describing such systems. The concept of bounded completion profiles has been introduced, and the use of this technique in system design has been discussed briefly.

Future work will report on the effects of fallible acceptance tests on the system completion profile, and on the application of this model to systems other than the recovery block. In particular, evaluation of concurrent systems requiring synchronisation is a priority.

8 Acknowledgments

This research was supported by the UK Engineering and Physical Sciences Research Council.

References

1. Arlat, J., Kanoun, L. and Laprie, J.-C. (1988). Dependability evaluation of software fault-tolerance. *Proc. 18th Int. Sym. on Fault-Tolerant Computing*, IEEE.

2. Balaji, S., Jenkins, L., Patnaik, L.M. and Goel, P.S. (1989). Workload redistribution for fault-tolerance in a hard real-time distributed computing system. *19th Int. Sym. on Fault-Tolerant Computing*, IEEE, 366–373.

3. Csenki, A. (1993). Reliability analysis of recovery blocks with nested clusters of failure points. *IEEE Trans. on Reliability*, **42**, 34–43.

4. Dimitrov, B., Khalil, Z., Kolev, N. and Petrov, P. (1991). On the optimal total processing time using checkpoints. *IEEE Trans. on Software Engineering*, **17**, 436–442.

5. European Space Agency. (1988). Software reliability modelling study. Invitation to tender AO/1-2039/87/NL/IW.

6. Gray, J.N. (1986). Why do computers stop and what can be done about it? *Proc. 5th Sym. on Reliability in Distributed Software and Database Systems*, 3–12.

7. Grnarov, A., Arlat, J. and Avizienis, A. (1980). On the performance of software fault-tolerance strategies. *Proc. 10th Int. Sym. on Fault-Tolerant Computing*, IEEE.

8. Haban, D. and Shin. K.G. (1990). Application of real-time monitoring to scheduling tasks with random execution times. *IEEE Trans. on Software Engineering*, **16**.

9. Helvik, B.E. (1988). Modelling the influence of unreliable software in distributed computer systems. *Digest of papers: 18th Int. Sym. on Fault-Tolerant Computing*, IEEE, 136–141.

10. Knight, J.C. and Leveson, N.G. (1986). An experimental evaluation of the assumption of independence in multiversion programming. *IEEE Trans. on Software Engineering*, **SE-12**, 96–109.

11. Laprie, J.-C. (1984). Dependability evaluation of software systems in operation. *IEEE Trans. on Software Engineering*, **SE-10**, 701–714.

12. Laprie, J.-C. and Kanoun, K. (1992). X-ware reliability and availability modelling. *IEEE Trans. of Software Engineering*, **18**, 130–147.

13. Littlewood, B. (1981). Stochastic reliability-growth: A model for fault-removal in computer programs and hardware designs. *IEEE Trans. on Reliability*, **R-30**, 313–320.

14. Musa, J.D. (1979). Validity of execution-time theory of software reliability. *IEEE Trans. on Reliability*, **R-28**, 181–191.

15. Musa, J.D. (1980). Software reliability data. *Technical Report*, Bell Telephone Laboratories. Report obtainable from DACS, Rome Air Development Centre, Rome, New York.

16. Park, C.Y. (1993). Predicting program execution times by analysing static and dynamic program paths. *Real-Time Systems*, **5**, 31–62.

17. Peterson, J.L. (1981). *Petri Net Theory and the Modelling of Systems*, Prentice-Hall.

18. Pucci, G. (1992). A new approach to the modelling of recovery block structures. *IEEE Trans. on Software Engineering*, **18**, 159–167.

19. Randell, B. (1975). System structure for software fault tolerance. *IEEE Trans. on Software Engineering*, **SE-1**, 220–231.

20. Ranganathan, A. and Upadhyaya, S. (1993). Performance evaluation of rollback-recovery techniques in computer programs. *IEEE Trans. on Reliability*, **42**, 220–226.

21. Scott, R.K., Gault, J.W. and McAllister, D.F. (1987). Fault-tolerant software reliability modelling. *IEEE Trans. of Software Engineering*, **SE-13**, 582–592.

22. Shepard, T. and Gagné, J.A.M. (1991). A pre-run-time scheduling algorithm for hard real-time systems. *IEEE Trans. on Software Engineering*, **17**.

23. Takács, L. (1962). *Stochastic Processes*, Methuen.

24. Xu, J. and Parnas, D.L. (1993). On satisfying timing constraints in hard-real-time systems. *IEEE Trans. on Software Engineering*, **19**, 70–84.

Applying Space Based Modelling Techniques to Dependable Systems[1]

Sue Haines and Tom Longshaw

DRA Malvern, Worcestershire

Abstract

This paper proposes a novel approach to the validation of safety properties for dependable systems. This approach, which we call space based modelling, has its roots in the work by Pawlak on Rough Sets [5]. To illustrate this technique, we apply our space based modelling approach to a mine drainage control system and compare our results with that of a conventional approach. The paper concludes with an assessment of the technique and its applicability to dependable systems.

Keywords: rough sets, system modelling, safety.

1 Introduction

Dependable systems need to undergo validation at every stage in their development. In this paper we are interested in exploring the validation requirements at the earliest stages in the development cycle when there is a high degree of uncertainty associated with many parameters of the system. This sort of early validation is necessary in order to reduce life-cycle costs, as finding non-compliances later in the life-cycle of a system increases the cost of rectifying them. Indeed, in extreme cases where a proposed system design is infeasible the earlier this is discovered the better.

There are many properties of a system which require validation. The properties of primary interest to us here are safety and availability requirements. These properties are often intimately related, as relaxations in safety requirements often improve availability of a system (at least in the short term). Thus early in system development, trade-offs need to be made between acceptable levels of safety and economic viability of the system (which is related to the availability of the system). In order to make these trade-offs, some kind of system model needs to be constructed and analysed to determine their affect on the proposed system. To see how uncertainty affects these properties we shall consider a classic example from real time control – namely a mine drainage control system.

---

2   Mine drainage control system

The mine drainage control system which we shall consider is based on that described in [1]. It has two main requirements. The first is to maintain the water level present in the mine at a safe level through the operation of a pump. The second requirement is to only operate the pump when it is environmentally safe to do so. Each of these requirements is examined in more detail below.

The control of the water level in the mine requires the presence of two sensors; one to detect when the water rises above a critical high water level and the other to detect when the water falls below a critical lower water level. The output from these sensors is used to determine when to turn the pump on and off respectively.

The safety constraints also require the presence of three sensors which measure the level of certain gases in the mine atmosphere and the level of airflow through the mine. The gases which are of concern are methane and carbon monoxide. When the level of methane exceeds a specified level the pump must stop operating. In addition, when the level of carbon monoxide exceeds a specified level or the depth of water becomes too great work must cease in the mine and the personnel be evacuated.

In addition to these two principal requirements, there is a secondary requirement to maintain system records. These should contain a record of the environment status, a record of the water level and the operational status of the pump.

Now, given such a system and a particular mine there are many questions which we could pose. In this paper we are interested in the interaction of safety in the mine and its availability for coal cutting. Thus, given an initial set of environmental parameters for the mine we want to determine if it is economically viable to work a certain shift. Here a shift is said to be economically viable if the length of time that it is safe to cut coal exceeds a specified threshold. Thus if the predicted availability of the mine shaft is below this threshold then the shift will be cancelled. We need to determine a lower bound on the availability of the shaft for a particular set of environmental parameters.

In order to obtain bounds on the system's behaviour, a model of the system needs to be built. Traditionally this model has then been subjected to Monte Carlo testing to provide the answers required. In the next section we shall describe this conventional approach and highlight its weaknesses.

3   Conventional approach

Monte Carlo methods exercise a system model by selecting random samples from the input space of the model. Thus if the model has n variable parameters, then a set of n random values will be used to stimulate the model. The random values chosen should reflect any knowledge the modeller has about the bounds of the input space. For example, for the system above, the *water arrival rate* is part of the input space for the mine and so would be modelled as a random variable.

At each time step in the execution of the model a value would be selected, from a predetermined range, to be used as the value of water arrival rate during that time step.

These methods cannot guarantee coverage of all the model's behaviours since they cannot guarantee a "representative" sample of the input space (representative in the sense that all the model's behaviours will be exercised by the sample chosen). Thus Monte Carlo methods are what we term a subset approach to modelling, as they provide only a subset of the possible behaviours of the system. For example, in a mine control system, there may exist behaviours of the system where the water depth increases more rapidly than has been observed in the model. However if a behaviour is exhibited by a Monte Carlo simulation, then it is guaranteed to be a possible behaviour of the system.

The accuracy and coverage of a Monte Carlo method can be improved by performing more sample runs and collecting statistics about the set of runs. However, due to the random nature of the sampling technique, Monte Carlo methods cannot provide absolute error bounds on the answers produced using them. They can provide a confidence interval for the answer, but many samples are required for a "reasonable" level of confidence to be achieved.

In the next section we shall look at superset modelling techniques. These techniques provide the modeller with a superset of the possible behaviours of a system. Thus a superset model will exhibit all possible behaviours of the system, but may also exhibit some impossible ones. For a system to be described as dependable one must ensure that it functions correctly in all cases, not just in a random subset.

4 Space based modelling

The failure of the conventional Monte Carlo models to answer the type of questions described in the previous section is due to the method's inability to cover all behaviours of the system. Thus the Monte Carlo approach may be termed a subset method as it provides only a subset of the possible behaviours of a system. Now in order to answer such questions we need a superset method which will guarantee coverage of the system's behaviour space. Such a method, which we shall refer to as a space based modelling technique, is outlined below with the aid of a very simple example. We call it space based because the data is represented by a space rather than a point (Monte Carlo modelling) or an interval (interval arithmetic).

Coverage. Consider a system, S, which has two variables x and y. Initially these variables are each independently distributed in $[0, 100]$. Thus S can be described as shown in Equation 4.1.

$$S = \{x \in [0, 100], y \in [0, 100]\}. \tag{4.1}$$

The Monte Carlo approach to such a model would randomly select a pair of values from S for each execution of the model (that is one random value to represent x and the other to represent y). In our approach we manipulate the random distributions of x and y rather than single values. However, as we shall show, simply manipulating each of these distributions independently is not always sufficient. We also need to maintain dependencies between variables.

Dependencies. Suppose we take our original system S and add the extra constraint that $y < (x/5)^2$. Let us call this new system S'. Now if we simply look at x and y as ranges, then all we can say about this constraint is that $x > 0$ as shown in the second line of Equation 4.2.

$$\begin{aligned}
S' &= \{(x,y) \in S \wedge (y < (x/5)^2)\}, \\
S' &\subseteq \{x \in (0,100], \quad y \in [0,100]\}.
\end{aligned} \qquad (4.2)$$

However, simply selecting random pairs from S' will produce pairings which violate the constraint so we need to find a more refined description of S'. Such a description could be provided by describing the distribution of x and y as a closed shape in two dimensional space. Then all the pairs of x and y which satisfied the constraint would lie inside the shape, while those pairs which violated the constraint would lie outside the shape.

Spaces. Figure 1 shows two spaces representing S and S' respectively. This method of describing an n dimensional system gives more information about the relationship than the previous definition, where the upper and lower bounds of x and y were known only in isolation. However it can be easily be appreciated that the description of such a space in terms of its boundary rapidly becomes too complex to manipulate. Thus we need an approximation for such a space which lies as a "half way house" between the complex boundary equation and the n dimensional bounding box provided by a set of n ranges. Such an approximation is provided by the application of rough sets [5] (and fuzzy rough sets).

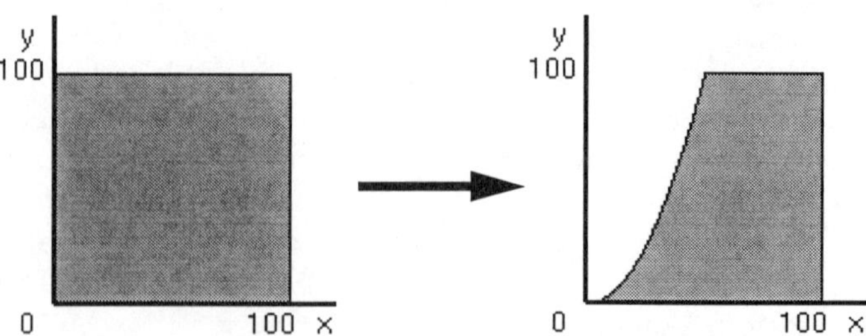

Figure 1. The spaces S and S'

Figure 2 shows a fuzzy rough set approximation of the space S. Now adding the original restriction that $y < (x/5)^2$ yields a new space, which is also shown on the right of the figure.

This space is computed by applying a test to each of the hypercubes in the original fuzzy rough set. This results in those hypercubes which wholly satisfy the constraint remaining unaltered, those which wholly violate it being discarded, and finally those which partially satisfy the constraint having their membership grades modified. It can be seen that this does indeed yield a "half way house" between spaces and sets of ranges.

The membership grade of a hypercube allows us to reason about the relative likelihood of values in the space. In Figure 2, in the initial space we have assumed that values closer to the mean are more likely than those at the edges. This is signified by a darker shading and higher membership grade to the hypercube.

Thus our spaced based modelling approach uses fuzzy rough sets to approximate the state of our models (and submodels). The use of this technique is described in more detail in [4]. This approach requires the provision of several specialised operations on fuzzy rough sets. These are beyond the scope of this paper, but are described in [3]. In the rest of the paper we shall examine how such techniques can be exploited in the area of dependable system validation. We shall use the mine drainage system outlined previously as a vehicle for this examination.

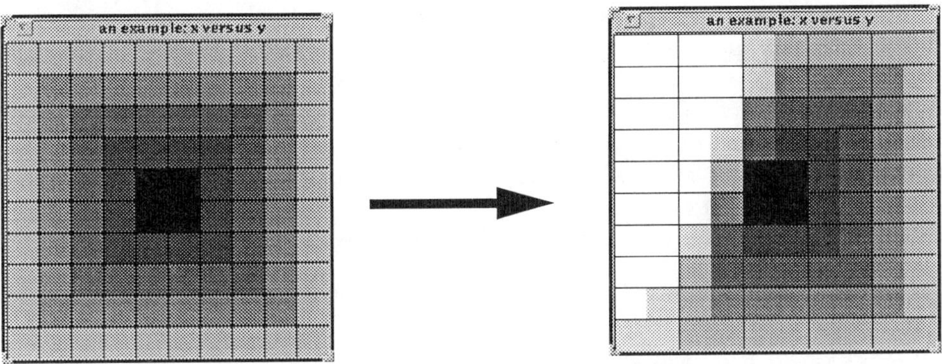

Figure 2. Fuzzy rough set approximation of the spaces S and S'

5   Model structure

The mine drainage system described earlier is most naturally modelled as four communicating objects. These are; a pump, its controller, the environment, and its monitor. Each of these is described in outline below.

Pump. This object models those aspects of the pump installed in the mine which are relevant to the study of the operation of the control system. The pump has the following attributes:

1. Water arrival rate – the observed rate of change of water depth in the mine when the pump is not functioning. This attribute may be uncertain.

2. Depth – the current depth of water in the mine.

3. Pump out rate – the change in depth of water when the pump is operating and the water arrival rate is zero.

Pump controller. This object models the control system for the pump. Its role requires it to ask the environment monitor if it is safe to operate the pump. This request is sent each time unit. The model has two attributes:

1. High water level – this is the minimum water depth which will cause the pump to restart operations if it is environmentally safe to do so.

2. Low water level – this is the maximum water depth at which the pump ceases to operate.

Environment. This object models those aspects of the mine environment which are relevant to the study of the control system. The environment has the following attributes all of which may have uncertain values:

1. Methane level – the current level of methane in the mine's atmosphere.

2. Carbon monoxide level – the current level of carbon monoxide in the mine's atmosphere.

3. Methane growth rate – the observed growth rate of methane in the mine's atmosphere.

4. Carbon monoxide growth rate – the observed growth rate of carbon monoxide in the mine's atmosphere.

Environment monitor. This object models that part of the control system which is responsible for monitoring the environment. In this role it is required to respond to requests from the pump controller. These requests relate to the environmental safety constraints for the pump system. In order to satisfy these requests the monitor must poll its sensors.

The model has two attributes:

1. Critical methane level – this is the level of methane in the mine's atmosphere above which it is no longer safe to operate the pump.

2. Critical carbon monoxide level – this is the level of carbon monoxide in the mine's atmosphere above which it is no longer safe for personnel to be present in the mine.

The values assigned to the attributes described above come in two different forms, crisp and fuzzy. Crisp values, such as pump out rate, occur where a simple real value is assigned to an attribute, such as -5. Fuzzy values, such as initial depth, occur where the modeller wishes the attribute to have an interval of values assigned to it. Such an interval may be graded to show that some parts have a greater possibility of occurring associated with them. For example arrival rate has the interval [0,3] assigned to it; if we wish to indicate that the central region from 1 to 2 is more possible that the outer regions then we will assign a higher membership value to the central part of the original interval that to its extremities.

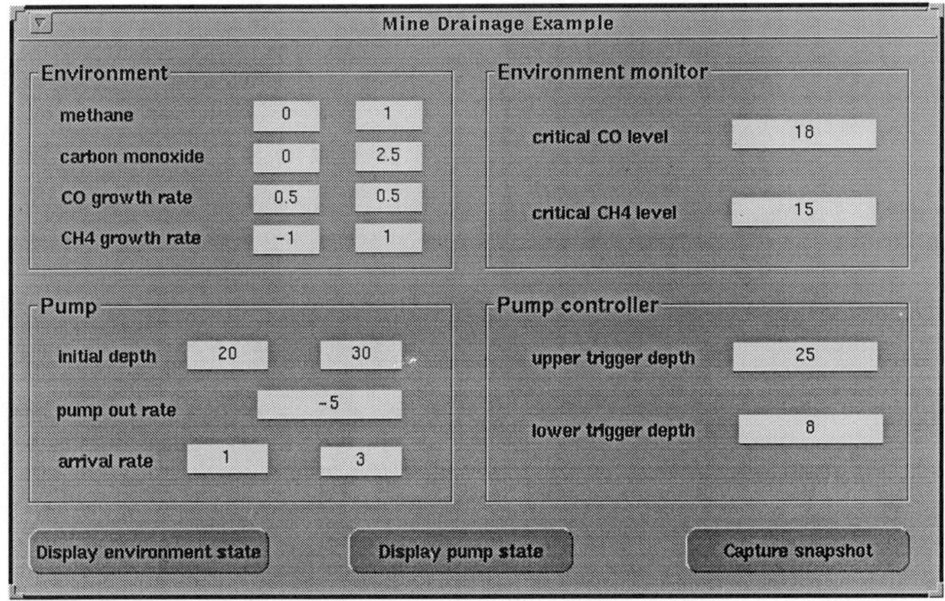

Figure 3. Panel showing a sample set of input values for the mine drainage system model

The initial values chosen for these attributes are shown in Figure 3. Here uncertainties associated with the change in water depth have all been associated with the water arrival rate, thus leaving the pump out rate as a crisp value. Due to the structure of the model, this simplification leads to the same overall behaviour as splitting the uncertainty between these two attributes. Additionally, the critical water depth for evacuation was set to be 50. With these values assigned to the attributes, the system model was ready to be executed. The results obtained are discussed below.

6   Results

The previous section dealt with the structure of the model and its attributes. The following presents the results of the subsequent model execution. In order to set the scene we present the results of a conventional Monte Carlo modelling exercise first and then use these as a starting point for discussing the output from the space based modelling approach.

Conventional. With the model structure described above and the initial values shown in Figure 3, the following plots were obtained using the conventional Monte Carlo techniques. The model was exercised over 60 time units for 100 sample runs.

Figure 4 shows the evolution of the pump state (depth on the y axis) over time (x axis). Here the y axis has been broken up into 0.5 metre intervals, while the x axis shows whole time steps. d_c denotes the critical depth at which the mine must be evacuated.

Figure 5 shows the evolution of the carbon monoxide level (y axis) over time (x axis). Here l_c denotes the critical level of carbon monoxide at which the mine must be evacuated. t_c is the minimum time at which this evacuation needs to occur. The Monte Carlo results suggest its value is 33.

Space based results.   With the model structure described above and the initial values shown in Figure 3, plots were obtained using our prototype modelling tool, the fuzzy rough scheduler [2]. These are shown in Figures 6 and 7. Here the black areas of the plot represent behaviours which are definitely possible, the white areas represent behaviours which are impossible, and finally the grey areas represent behaviours which may be possible (that is it is not certain whether these behaviours are definitely possible or impossible).

Figure 6 shows the evolution of the water level (depth on the y axis) over time (x axis). Here the y axis has been broken up into 0.5 metre intervals, while the x axis shows whole time steps. The model was exercised for 35 time units. The space describing the pump state is three dimensional. The third dimension being the operational status of the pump. Thus this space can be divided into two regions, that where the pump is operating and that where it is not operating. Each of these sub-states is shown separately. Once again d_c

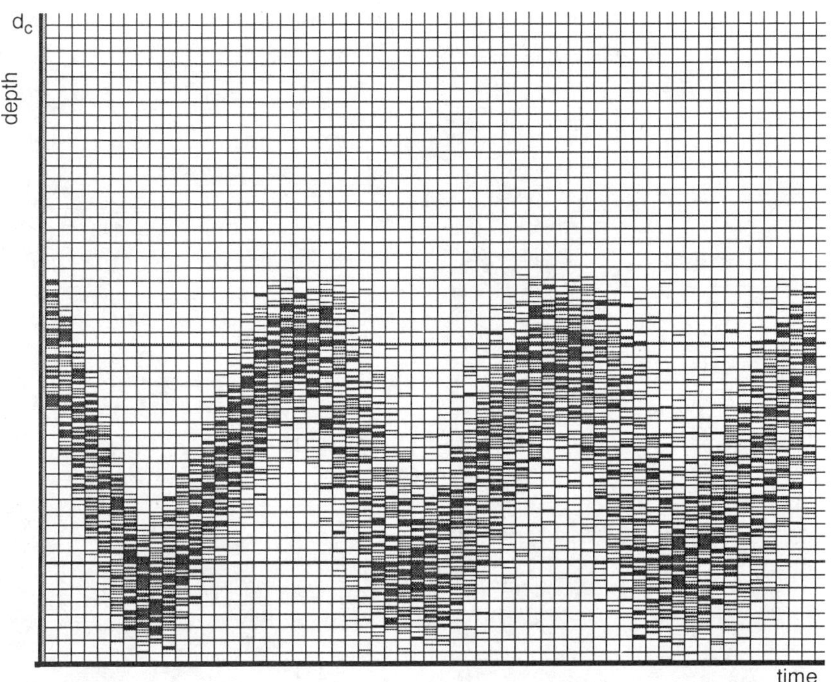

Figure 4. Conventional model – depth of water plotted against time

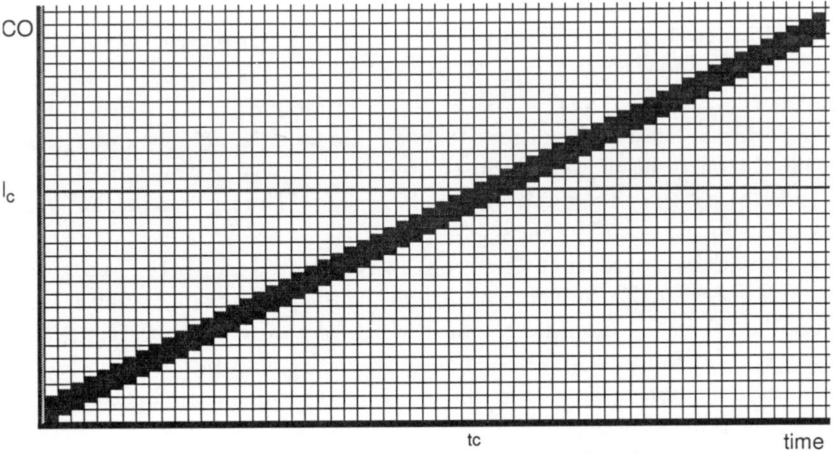

Figure 5. Conventional model – CO level plotted against time

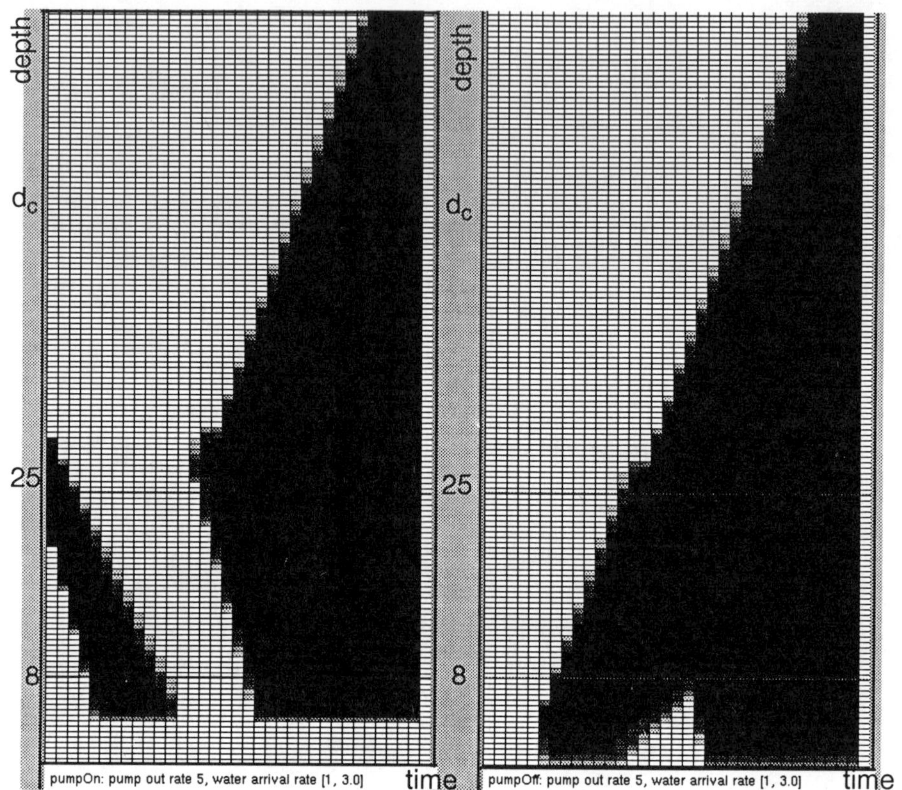

Figure 6. Spaced based model – depth of water plotted against time

denotes the critical depth at which evacuation must take place. However, in contrast to the conventional model, here this value is achieved at $t_m = 23$. The region on the right of the graph relates to the part of the model where there is a possibility that the environment is unsafe. Thus the depth of water grows unchecked in part of the space.

It should be noted that the "run away" behaviour to the right of the plot does not occur in the conventional model plot. This is due to the relatively low probability that the boundary values of the environmental distributions will be chosen by the random number generator in the conventional model. It is the possibility of this extreme case occurring which causes the behaviour exhibited by the space based model.

Figure 7 shows the evolution of the carbon monoxide level (y axis) over time (x axis). Here l_c denotes the critical level of carbon monoxide at which the mine must be evacuated. t_c is the minimum time at which the critical level of carbon monoxide is exceeded. The minimum safe evacuation time can be calculated

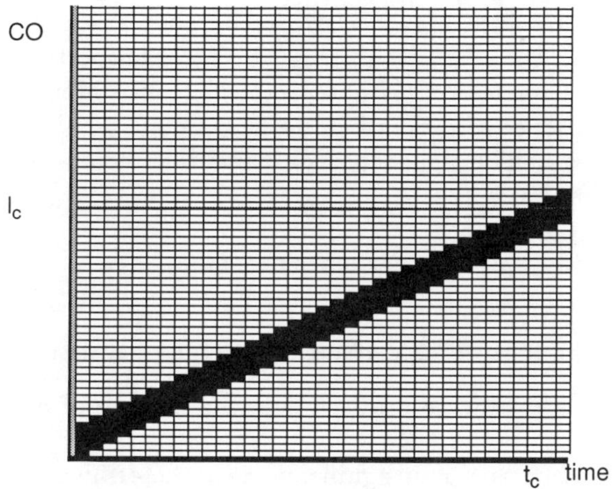

Figure 7. Spaced based model – CO level plotted against time

as the minimum of t_m and t_c. Thus in the space based model the minimum evacuation time is determined by water depth whereas in the conventional model it appears to be dependent solely on the build up of carbon monoxide.

7   Conclusions

The study described in the preceding sections of this paper had the aim of demonstrating the applicability of space based modelling techniques to dependable systems. In this section we review the progress which has been made and assess the strengths and weaknesses of our technique.

Advantages. The space based modelling technique has three main advantages over Monte Carlo techniques. These are:

1. maintenance of dependency between variables whilst manipulating ranges of values;

2. guarantees path coverage – works with ranges of values rather than "representative" random points;

3. requires a single execution of the model.

In particular, Monte Carlo models can only be analysed for the existence of properties in the system. This holds for properties of the form "it is possible that ...", but not for properties of the form "for all behaviours it is true that ...". This is because Monte Carlo techniques are a subset approach to modelling. However, the real system may also have properties which the model does not exhibit. Therefore, it is not practical to use Monte Carlo models to demonstrate the absence of properties in the system.

Disadvantages. The space based modelling technique has three main disadvantages. These are:

1. does not readily prove the existence of system behaviours – due to superset properties;

2. grid size of the fuzzy rough sets is determined heuristically;

3. performance is related to grid size, via the number of hypercubes.

The grid size issue is not insignificant as it determines the granularity of information processed by the system. Thus a reduction in grid size increases the accuracy of the model's approximation (that is reduces the number of behaviours exhibited by the model which are not present in the real system). This increase in accuracy is paid for in terms of increased memory usage and increased run-time.

References

1. Burns, A. and Lister, A.M. (1991). A framework for building dependable systems. *Computer J.*, **34**, 173–181.

2. Haines, S.L. (1994). Fuzzy scheduler architecture. *Technical Report*, DRA Malvern, DRA/CIS(SE2)/N9DAC001/TR/1/1.0.

3. Haines, S.L. (1994). Operations on fuzzy rough sets. *Technical Report*, DRA Malvern, DRA/CIS(SE2)/N9DAC001/TR/2/1.0.

4. Haines, S.L., Longshaw, T.B. and Magee, G.A. (1994). The practical application of rough sets to semantics and simulation. *Rough Sets and Soft Computing 94*.

5. Pawlak, Z. (1982). Rough sets. *Int. J. of Computer and Information Sciences*, **11**.

A Bayesian Model that Combines Disparate Evidence for the Quantitative Assessment of System Dependability

Bev Littlewood and David Wright

Centre for Software Reliability, City University, London

Abstract

For safety-critical systems, the required reliability (or safety) is often extremely high. Assessing the system, to gain confidence that the requirement has been achieved, is correspondingly hard, particularly when the system depends critically upon extensive software. In practice, such an assessment is often carried out rather informally, taking account of many different types of evidence—experience of previous, similar systems; evidence of the efficacy of the development process; testing; expert judgement, etc. Ideally, the assessment would allow all such evidence to be combined into a final numerical measure of reliability in a scientifically rigorous way. In this paper we address one part of this problem; we present a means whereby our confidence in a new product can be augmented beyond what we would believe merely from testing that product, by using evidence of the high dependability in operation of previous products. We present some illustrative numerical results that seem to suggest that such experience of previous products, even when these have shown very high dependability in operational use, can improve our confidence in a new product only modestly.

1   Introduction

Critical systems are coming to depend more and more upon the correct functioning of software to ensure their safe operation. At the same time, the size and complexity of these software subsystems is increasing as designers take advantage of the extensive functionality that software makes possible—functionality that sometimes enhances different aspects of safety.

There are important unresolved questions concerning how one might go about designing such systems so that they will be sufficiently safe in operation. In this paper, however, we shall concentrate upon the difficult problems of *evaluation* that they pose. In particular, we shall be concerned with the problem of how to measure the reliability of such a software system when that reliability is likely to be very high.

In several recent papers different authors have pointed out some of the basic difficulties here, [1,5]. They show that, if we are only going to use the evidence obtained from operational testing of the software, we shall only be able to make quite modest claims for its reliability. For example, Littlewood and Strigini show that even in the most favourable situation of all, that of a system that has not failed during x hours of statistically representative operational testing, we can draw only the weak conclusion that there is a 50:50 chance that it will survive failure-free for the same time x in the future.

The limitations here seem intrinsic; they arise from the relative paucity of evidence (when compared with the stringency of the reliability level that needs to be demonstrated) and will not be ameliorated significantly by better statistical models. To make a very strong claim—that a particular system is ultra-reliable— needs a great deal of evidence. If that evidence comprises only observation of failure-free behaviour, then the length of time over which such behaviour is observed needs to be very great. To assure the reliability goals of certain proposed and existing systems, for example the 10^{-9} probability of failure per hour for the "fly-by-wire" computer systems in civil aircraft [8], would clearly require the systems to be observed *and show no failures* for lengths of time that are many orders of magnitude greater than is practicable.

Faced with these limitations to what can be claimed from merely observing the system in operation, it has been suggested that we should instead base our evaluations upon *all* the disparate kinds of evidence that are available. These include, in addition to the operational data discussed above, evidence of the efficacy of the development methods utilised, experience in building similar systems in the past, competence of the development team, architectural details of the design, etc. Most of these other sources of evidence about the dependability of a system will involve a certain amount of engineering judgement in the evaluator, which might itself introduce further uncertainty and potentiality for error. In addition, there are serious unresolved difficulties in *combining* such disparate evidence in order to make a single evaluation of the overall dependability and thus to make a judgement of acceptability.

In this paper we shall consider only a small part of this problem. We shall treat in detail the situation where we wish to augment the evidence that can be gained from the operational testing of a particular product, by also taking into account the success (or not) in building "similar" products in the past. An important special case, of course, is that where there is unreserved good news from these previous products—i.e. none of them has failed during operational use up till the present time.

It should be emphasised that the goal in all this work is to obtain a *quantification* of the reliability of a product. The model that is proposed in the next sections, therefore, requires us to make certain assumptions about the failure process, and about how we represent our beliefs about certain model parameters. We acknowledge that these assumptions can be questioned, and are certainly very difficult to validate. However, we believe that they are reasonably plausible. More importantly, our main aim is to demonstrate that this kind of evidence can only improve our confidence in the reliability of a product quite modestly. Thus, we would regard a critique of our results on the grounds that they are not sufficiently conservative as being in the spirit of our own aims; suggestions, on the other hand, that the assumptions here can be modified in order to arrive at much higher confidence in product reliability we would regard with suspicion. It seems to us that, particularly in the case of safety-critical applications, it is safest to adopt a conservative view of the informativeness of evidence unless there are scientifically valid reasons to believe the contrary.

2　Modelling approach

When we use evidence we have obtained from building and operating previous products in order to try to improve the accuracy of the predictions that we can make about the reliability of a novel product, we must take account of two kinds of uncertainty. In the first place, there will be uncertainty concerning the actual reliabilities that have been achieved by these earlier products. Even in those cases where there is extensive operating experience, we shall never know the true reliability of a product and will have to use an estimate based upon the data collected during its operation. In those situations where we are dealing with products that are likely to be very reliable, we shall probably only see a small number (or even none at all) of failures even in quite extensive periods of operation.

The second source of uncertainty will concern the "similarity" of the products that have been observed in the past, and the "similarity" of the one under study to these past products. In what follows, we shall assume that the probabilities of failure of the different products, past and present, can be assumed to be realisations of independent and identically distributed random variables. This assumption, although an idealisation, captures the essentials of what we mean by "similarity". Thus, it means that the actual reliabilities of the different products will be different, as is clearly the case in reality. We would not expect the reliabilities of, say, two versions of a software-based telephone switch to be identical, even though we might be prepared to agree that the problems posed, and the quality of the processes deployed in their solution, were similar. The notion of "similarity" in the eye of an observer here seems to be equivalent to a kind of "indifference". You might agree that two different products were similar for the purposes of the current exercise if you were indifferent between them in reliability terms: if you were asked to predict which would be the most reliable, before seeing them in operation, you would have no preference. This is represented by their probabilities of failure being identically distributed random variables: any probability statements you would make about the reliabilities of products A and B will be identical. The important point here is that this interpretation of "similarity" in terms of indifference does not mean that you believe that the two products will have identical reliabilities [4] - indeed you will know that the actual reliabilities of the products will differ.

The two sources of uncertainty here are both important. However, it is the nature of the uncertainty concerning "how similar" the products actually are that will be most difficult to estimate in practice, since this requires us to see as many different products as possible. It is far more likely that we have large quantities of information about a few products, than that we have information on many products.

Consider first the failure process of a *single* software product $\mathcal{A}$. Assume a Bernoulli trials process model of the failures of this product in a sequence of "demands" with neither debugging, maintenance, nor significant variation in the "stressfulness" of the software's operational environment. Thus, in the first n trials of product $\mathcal{A}$, let R be the random number of failures occurring and p be the probability of failure on demand. Then the distribution of R for fixed n and p is

$$R \,|\, n, p \sim \binom{n}{r} p^r \, (1-p)^{n-r} . \tag{2.1}$$

Now think of p as unknown and construct a Bayesian model by assuming that p is a realisation of a random variable P having a parametric distribution

$$P \,|\, \theta \sim f_p(p|\theta).$$

with parameter θ. Here we can think of this distribution for P as representing the general reliability of products in a particular *product family*, perhaps produced by a single development team, using a common development method, and for similar applications. For example, a family of products known to have highly variable reliability levels would correspond to a distribution $f_p(p|\theta)$ with a large variance, whereas for another product family a high "average" product reliability would correspond to a small mean for $f_p(p|\theta)$. If we fully understood the true variation in reliabilities of the products in each of these two product families then we could describe the two families by specifying two different P-distributions having the required characteristics and index these P-distributions with two different θ-values, θ_1 and θ_2, say. More generally, our parameter space $\mathcal{S}$, say, for θ, could be said to represent a set of different conceivable reliability characteristics each of which potentially characterises a different *family of similar products*. That is, given sufficient data on the reliability variation amongst the products of a particular family, a value of θ (and hence a particular distribution $f_p(p|\theta)$) could in principle be assigned as descriptive of that variation. In this way, we have defined a model in which θ can be thought of as a product-family-characterising parameter. For a product chosen at random from those of a particular family of similar products (i.e. particular θ) and observed for a sequence of n demands, it follows that (R, P) has joint distribution

$$(R, P) \,|\, n, \theta \sim \binom{n}{r} p^r \, (1-p)^{n-r} \, f_p(p|\theta), \tag{2.2}$$

given n and θ. Integrating Equation 2.2 over p gives the conditional distribution of R given n and θ as

$$R \,|\, n, \theta \sim \binom{n}{r} \int_0^1 p^r \, (1-p)^{n-r} \, f_p(p|\theta) \, dp \tag{2.3}$$

or, expressed in terms of moments of $f_p(\cdot|\theta)$,

$$R|n,\theta \sim \binom{n}{r} \mathbf{E}\big(P^r(1-P)^{n-r}|\theta\big) \ . \tag{2.4}$$

If we *observe* that $R = r$ failures actually occur during n demands, then we can condition on this data by normalising Equation 2.2 to give the updated distribution

$$P|r,n,\theta \sim \frac{p^r\,(1-p)^{n-r}\,f_p(p|\theta)}{\int_0^1 p^r\,(1-p)^{n-r}\,f_p(p|\theta)\,dp} \tag{2.5}$$

of the probability of failure on demand for this program, given θ, n and the observation r.

The last three equations describe properties of a general mixture of Bernoulli trials processes, where $f_p(\cdot|\theta)$ is the mixing distribution. Note that although exchangeability[1] of the original Bernoulli trials process has not been lost by mixing the processes, the property that non-intersecting sections of the process are independently distributed does not hold in general for the resulting mixed process. In fact the number R' of failures in a subsequent set of n' demands on the same product now has an updated distribution obtainable from Equation 2.5 as

$$\begin{aligned}
R'|r,n,n',\theta \ &\sim\ \binom{n'}{r'}\frac{\int_0^1 p^{r+r'}\,(1-p)^{n+n'-r-r'}\,f_p(p|\theta)\,dp}{\int_0^1 p^r\,(1-p)^{n-r}\,f_p(p|\theta)\,dp}\ , \\[2mm]
&=\ \binom{n'}{r'}\frac{\mathbf{E}\Big(P^{r+r'}(1-P)^{n+n'-r-r'}|\theta\Big)}{\mathbf{E}(P^r(1-P)^{n-r}|\theta)}
\end{aligned} \tag{2.6}$$

given n, r.

The distributions which we have considered up till this point are parameterised by θ. We now adopt a Bayesian approach to handling this parameterisation by supposing a prior distribution

$$\Theta \sim \mathrm{Prior}_\theta(\theta)\ ,$$

with support set $\theta \in \mathcal{S}$. If we plan to observe and predict reliability only of a single software product, this extension adds very little to the model as so far described, since, by integrating over θ, the model is reduced to a degenerate ($|\mathcal{S}| = 1$) case of the assumptions described earlier. (Simply replace $f_p(p|\theta)$ by $\int_{\theta \in \mathcal{S}} f_p(p|\theta)\mathrm{Prior}_\theta(\theta)\,d\theta$ in the distributions above.)

---

[1] i.e., the property that any permutation of a portion of the binary success-failure sequence has the same probability as the unpermuted sequence. Equivalently, we can say that the probability of a precise sequence of successes and failures during a specified interval of discrete time (say from the 10th to the 20th demand, inclusive) can be expressed as a function of the *number*, only, of successes during that interval.

The idea of a prior distribution for θ becomes a useful concept, however, if we wish to address the problem of *learning* about a *distribution* of product reliabilities by observing the failure behaviour of *multiple* software products from a single family $\langle \mathcal{A}_i \rangle$, say, of similar products. We can then represent a conservative[2] version of a *process* concept for the trend of their reliabilities, from one product to the next, by modelling these products' individual failure processes as above with *different* p_i, and an assumption that each of these p_i arises *independently given* θ for some *unknown, common* parameter value θ characterising the entire family of products.

Thus θ and p now play distinct roles in terms of the model concepts: Whereas each p_i still captures a property of a single software product, θ now represents a common unknown characteristic of the whole family of similar products. To obtain the value of θ would be to capture the reliability-relevant characteristic which these software products all have in common. For this *multi*-product model, there is now a real purpose behind including separate distributional assumptions for firstly θ, and secondly p_i given θ. In the following, we do not in fact assume that θ can ever be known[3]. However, we assume that we hold *probabilistic prior beliefs about* θ (i.e. beliefs about the possible distributions $f_p(\cdot|\theta)$ of reliabilities of products belonging to the family $\langle \mathcal{A}_i \rangle$). Then, any observation of failure behaviour of any subset of the sequence $\langle \mathcal{A}_i \rangle$ can be regarded as information about θ which we will use in order to learn about θ by the usual Bayesian learning mechanisms. Thus the second stage of our doubly stochastic model is to represent our prior beliefs about a subjective random variable Θ of which the true value θ for our particular product family is a single unknown realisation.

Observe now that, conditionally given θ and $\langle n_i \rangle_{i=1}^{k}$, our independence assumption for the $\langle P_i \rangle$ tell us that the first k terms of our $\langle R_i \rangle$ sequence are jointly distributed

$$\langle R_i \rangle_{i=1}^{k} \big| (\langle n_i \rangle_{i=1}^{k}, \theta) \sim \prod_{i=1}^{k} \binom{n_i}{r_i} \int_0^1 p^{r_i} (1-p)^{n_i - r_i} f_p(p|\theta) \, dp \,. \qquad (2.7)$$

Once we have executed these k software products and observed their failure behaviour (i.e., r_i failures out of n_i trials for each product $\mathcal{A}_i$) then we can regard Equation 2.7 as the likelihood function $L\big(\theta; \langle n_i, r_i \rangle_{i=1}^{k}\big)$ of the parameter θ given this failure data. $L\big(\theta; \langle n_i, r_i \rangle_{i=1}^{k}\big)$ is a product involving combinatorial terms together with moments of the parametric distribution $f_p(\cdot|\theta)$

---

[2] In the sense that we desist from making any stronger assumption of any kind of systematic development of reliability from one product to the next. For example, we do not assume an increasing trend in reliabilities of different products in the family.

[3] Loosely, we can say that in order to *know* the value of θ characterising a family $\langle \mathcal{A}_i \rangle$ of products, we would require a very large amount of operational failure data on *each* of a very large number of products belonging to that family.—So that we could accurately describe from empirical data the shape of the distribution $f_p(\cdot|\theta)$.

$$\langle R_i \rangle_{i=1}^{k} \big| (\langle n_i \rangle_{i=1}^{k}, \theta) \sim \prod_{i=1}^{k} \binom{n_i}{r_i} \mathbf{E}\big(P^{r_i}(1-P)^{n_i-r_i} \big| \theta\big) \ . \tag{2.8}$$

In Section 3 we make use of the factor of this likelihood which depends on θ,

$$
\begin{aligned}
L_k(\theta) &= \prod_{i=1}^{k} \mathbf{E}\big(P^{r_i}(1-P)^{n_i-r_i} \big| \theta\big) \\
&= \prod_{i=1}^{k} \int_0^1 p^{r_i}(1-p)^{n_i-r_i}\, f_p(p|\theta)\, dp.
\end{aligned}
\tag{2.9}
$$

3 Bayesian updating of distributions in the general case

To implement the Bayesian learning about Θ given observation of $\langle r_i \rangle_{r=1}^{k}$ we would like to calculate the posterior distribution of Θ. Recalling that the prior for Θ is denoted Prior_θ, for θ lying in $\mathcal{S}$, then the required posterior distribution is proportional to the product of the prior distribution for Θ and the likelihood function evaluated as Equation 2.7

$$\Theta \big| \langle n_i, r_i \rangle_{i=1}^{k} \sim c L_k(\theta)\, \mathrm{Prior}_\theta(\theta)$$

where c is a function of $\langle r_i, n_i \rangle$ not involving θ, i.e.

$$\Theta \big| \langle n_i, r_i \rangle_{i=1}^{k} \sim \frac{\left[\prod_{i=1}^{k} \int_0^1 p^{r_i}(1-p)^{n_i-r_i}\, f_p(p|\theta)\, dp \right] \mathrm{Prior}_\theta(\theta)}{\int_{\theta \in \mathcal{S}} \left[\prod_{i=1}^{k} \int_0^1 p^{r_i}(1-p)^{n_i-r_i}\, f_p(p|\theta)\, dp \right] \mathrm{Prior}_\theta(\theta)\, d\theta}. \tag{3.1}$$

Equation 3.1 moves the focus of attention away from failure probabilities P_i of products $\mathcal{A}_i$ by the integrations over p. It is now of great interest to know an up-to-date distribution for P given what has been observed (in order to make predictions about a particular new product, for example). Then our learning could be expressed directly in terms of the changing nature of the current uncertainty about a failure probability of some particular product. At this stage it is instructive to distinguish between four different stages in our learning about one of the failure probabilities, say P_k. The first of these is the prior marginal distribution of P_k

$$P_k \sim \int_{\theta \in \mathcal{S}} f_p(p_k|\theta) \mathrm{Prior}_\theta(\theta)\, d\theta \ , \tag{3.2}$$

which represents our initial state of uncertainty concerning the reliability of any given product, $\mathcal{A}_k$, prior to any observation either of that or of any other product's behaviour.

The second most trivial case—observing only the past failure behaviour of the specific product of interest—has effectively already been covered by Equation 2.5. Substituting $\int_{\theta \in \mathcal{S}} f_p(p|\theta)\mathrm{Prior}_\theta(\theta)\,d\theta$ for $f_p(p|\theta)$ in Equation 2.5 gives a conditional distribution

$$P_k\,|\,n_k, r_k \sim \frac{p_k^{r_k}(1-p_k)^{n_k-r_k}\displaystyle\int_{\theta \in \mathcal{S}} f_p(p_k|\theta)\mathrm{Prior}_\theta(\theta)\,d\theta}{\displaystyle\int_{\theta \in \mathcal{S}}\int_0^1 p^{r_k}(1-p)^{n_k-r_k}\,f_p(p|\theta)\,dp\,\mathrm{Prior}_\theta(\theta)\,d\theta} \tag{3.3}$$

for P_k given n_k and r_k.

Thirdly, replacing k by $k-1$ in Equation 3.1 and then substituting this distribution in place of $\mathrm{Prior}_\theta(\theta)$ in Equation 3.2 (or, alternatively, directly substituting $n_k = r_k = 0$ in Equation 3.5) gives the distribution

$$P_k\,\big|\,\langle n_i, r_i\rangle_{i=1}^{k-1} \sim \frac{\displaystyle\int_{\theta \in \mathcal{S}} f_p(p_k|\theta)\left[\prod_{i=1}^{k-1}\int_0^1 p^{r_i}(1-p)^{n_i-r_i}\,f_p(p|\theta)\,dp\right]\mathrm{Prior}_\theta(\theta)\,d\theta}{\displaystyle\int_{\theta \in \mathcal{S}}\left[\prod_{i=1}^{k-1}\int_0^1 p^{r_i}(1-p)^{n_i-r_i}\,f_p(p|\theta)\,dp\right]\mathrm{Prior}_\theta(\theta)\,d\theta}$$

$$\tag{3.4}$$

of P_k given observation of the failure behaviour $\langle n_i, r_i\rangle_{i=1}^{k-1}$ *only* of *other* products $\langle \mathcal{A}_i\rangle_{i=1}^{k-1}$.

Finally, replacing k by $k-1$ in Equation 3.1 and then substituting this distribution in place of $\mathrm{Prior}_\theta(\theta)$ in Equation 3.3 gives the distribution

$$P_k\,\big|\,\langle n_i, r_i\rangle_{i=1}^{k} \sim$$

$$\frac{p_k^{r_k}(1-p_k)^{n_k-r_k}\displaystyle\int_{\theta \in \mathcal{S}} f_p(p_k|\theta)\left[\prod_{i=1}^{k-1}\int_0^1 p^{r_i}(1-p)^{n_i-r_i}\,f_p(p|\theta)\,dp\right]\mathrm{Prior}_\theta(\theta)\,d\theta}{\displaystyle\int_{\theta \in \mathcal{S}}\left[\prod_{i=1}^{k}\int_0^1 p^{r_i}(1-p)^{n_i-r_i}\,f_p(p|\theta)\,dp\right]\mathrm{Prior}_\theta(\theta)\,d\theta}$$

$$\tag{3.5}$$

for P_k given observation both of the failure behaviour $\langle n_k, r_k\rangle$ of the product $\mathcal{A}_k$ itself and *also* the failures $\langle n_i, r_i\rangle_{i=1}^{k-1}$ of other products $\langle \mathcal{A}_i\rangle_{i=1}^{k-1}$.

4   The no-failures case

Consider the special case in which no failures at all have been observed—neither of the product for which we wish to predict reliability, nor of other products within the same product family. This case is of particular importance since it provides an upper limit for the reliability levels which can be objectively measured in a given amount of observation time purely from observation of failure behaviour. Specialising the equations of Section 3 to this case is simply a matter of substituting $\langle r_i \rangle = \langle 0 \rangle$. If we similarly specialise the form of our *predictions* by considering the Bayesian predictive probability of a *further* period of failure-free operation, we find that these predictions can be expressed in rather a simple form as the expectations of products of higher non-central moments of a particular conditional distribution. So, conclusions about the reliability levels measurable using this model turn out to depend crucially on our decision about what may be considered realistic model assumptions for these moments. Thinking in terms of the probability $Q_i = 1 - P_i$ of successful completion of an individual demand, and assuming that we do believe that our product family is highly reliable, then the conditional distribution of Q_i given θ will be concentrated very close to 1 (for all except, perhaps, some values of the product-family parameter θ which we consider to be highly unlikely, i.e. that are assigned small probability (density) values $\mathrm{Prior}_\theta(\theta)$ by our prior for θ). Defining μ'_m to be the mth non-central moment of this conditional distribution of Q_i given θ makes μ'_m a deterministic function of θ

$$\mu'_m = \int_0^1 (1-p)^m f_p(p|\theta) \, dp. \tag{4.1}$$

We now take the expectation of Q_k^n with respect to each of the three updated distributions Equations 3.3–3.5 for P_k. This yields three expressions representing the Bayesian predictive probability that the next n demands on $\mathcal{A}_k$ will be failure-free given previous observation of failure-free execution of respectively: $\mathcal{A}_k$ only; $\langle \mathcal{A}_i \rangle_{i=1}^{k-1}$; or, lastly, all of $\langle \mathcal{A}_i \rangle_{i=1}^{k}$:

$$\mathbf{E}(Q_k^n \,|\, R_k = 0) = \frac{\mathbf{E}\left(\mu'_{n_k+n}\right)}{\mathbf{E}\left(\mu'_{n_k}\right)}, \tag{4.2}$$

$$\mathbf{E}\left(Q_k^n \,\middle|\, \langle R_i \rangle_{i=1}^{k-1} = \langle 0 \rangle\right) = \frac{\mathbf{E}\left(\mu'_n \prod_{i=1}^{k-1} \mu'_{n_i}\right)}{\mathbf{E}\left(\prod_{i=1}^{k-1} \mu'_{n_i}\right)}, \tag{4.3}$$

$$\mathbf{E}\left(Q_k^n \,\middle|\, \langle R_i \rangle_{i=1}^{k} = \langle 0 \rangle\right) = \frac{\mathbf{E}\left(\mu'_{n_k+n} \prod_{i=1}^{k-1} \mu'_{n_i}\right)}{\mathbf{E}\left(\prod_{i=1}^{k} \mu'_{n_i}\right)}. \tag{4.4}$$

These predictive probabilities of n consecutive successful demands on $\mathcal{A}_k$ should be compared with the unconditional

$$\mathbf{E}(Q_k^n) = \mathbf{E}(\mu'_n) \tag{4.5}$$

which is the probability that the next n demands on $\mathcal{A}_k$ will be failure-free given *no* conditioning observation of either $\mathcal{A}_k$ or any other products—i.e. based solely upon the prior belief.

5　An example of a particular choice of prior distributions for P given Θ, and for Θ

We shall retain throughout what follows our original assumptions that each product $\mathcal{A}_i$ fails as a Bernoulli trials process with unknown parameter P_i, and that the $\langle P_i \rangle$ sequence is i.i.d. conditionally given an unknown product-sequence-characterising parameter θ. To generate particular cases of our model we are then left with the tasks of choosing the distribution family $\{f_p(\cdot|\theta)\,;\,\theta \in \mathcal{S}\}$ and the single prior distribution Prior_θ over this family.

The beta-family of distributions

$$f_p(p|\theta) = \frac{p^{a-1}(1-p)^{b-1}}{\beta(a,b)}, \quad \theta = \langle a,b \rangle, \quad a,b > 0 \tag{5.1}$$

is conjugate [2] to both the binomial and the negative binomial (including geometric) distributions, and is thus in some sense a "natural" choice. If we use this as our f_p distribution family, we obtain a mixed process for the failures of a single product for which the probability of r failures in n demands is given from Equation 2.4 to be

$$R|n,a,b \sim \frac{\binom{n}{r}\beta(r+a,n-r+b)}{\beta(a,b)}, \tag{5.2}$$

obtained by integrating over p the joint distribution of Equation 2.2 which would be

$$(R,P)|n,a,b \sim \frac{\binom{n}{r}p^{r+a-1}(1-p)^{n-r+b-1}}{\beta(a,b)} \tag{5.3}$$

in this case.

The likelihood Equation 2.8 resulting from observation of k products in operation is

$$\langle R_i \rangle_{i=1}^k \big| (\langle n_i \rangle_{i=1}^k, a, b) \sim \prod_{i=1}^k \binom{n_i}{r_i} \frac{\beta(a+r_i, b+n_i-r_i)}{\beta(a,b)} \tag{5.4}$$

with

$$L_k(a,b) = \prod_{i=1}^k \frac{\beta(a+r_i, b+n_i-r_i)}{\beta(a,b)} \tag{5.5}$$

as defined in Equation 2.9.

Having decided to investigate the beta f_p, the choice of Prior_θ over $\mathcal{S}$, the positive quadrant[4], remains problematic. In real life there would be an "expert" from whom we would wish to elicit the distribution that truly reflects his a priori belief. This is not an easy task in such a complex model, and the expert may find it difficult to represent his beliefs in a distribution for $\langle a, b \rangle$. A way out of this difficulty is to assume that the expert is "ignorant", and use that prior distribution which represents ignorance. Even this is a non-trivial task. As an example we consider the simple case of distributions uniform on some finite rectangle with sides parallel to the a and b axes,

$$\text{Prior}_\theta(a, b) = \begin{cases} \frac{1}{(a_2 - a_1)(b_2 - b_1)}, & \text{if } a_1 < a < a_2,\ b_1 < b < b_2 \\ 0, & \text{elsewhere.} \end{cases} \tag{5.6}$$

Firstly we can examine characteristics of the prior distribution Equation 3.2 for P_k implied by these model assumptions,

$$P_k \sim \int_{a_1}^{a_2} \int_{b_1}^{b_2} \frac{p^{a-1}(1-p)^{b-1}}{\beta(a, b)} \frac{db\, da}{(a_2 - a_1)(b_2 - b_1)}. \tag{5.7}$$

The first and second non-central moments of $P\,|\,a, b$ are $\frac{a}{a+b}$ and $\frac{a(a+1)}{(a+b)(a+b+1)}$. These may be integrated analytically with respect to $f_p(p|a, b)$ (first expanding in partial fractions with respect to b in the case of the second moment) to give the expressions,

$$\mathbf{E}(P) = \frac{1}{2} +$$

$$\frac{(a_1^2 - b_1^2)\log(a_1 + b_1) - (a_2^2 - b_1^2)\log(a_2 + b_1) - (a_1^2 - b_2^2)\log(a_1 + b_2) + (a_2^2 - b_2^2)\log(a_2 + b_2)}{2(a_2 - a_1)(b_2 - b_1)}$$

and

$$\mathbf{E}(P^2) = \frac{2}{3} + \frac{t(a_1, b_1) - t(a_2, b_1) - t(a_1, b_2) + t(a_2, b_2)}{6(a_2 - a_1)(b_2 - b_1)} \tag{5.8}$$

where $t(a, b) = s(a, b) - s(a, b + 1)$, where

$$s(a, b) = (2a^2 - 2ab + 2b^2 + 3a - 3b)(a + b)\log(a + b). \tag{5.9}$$

The prior reliability function is given from Equations 4.1 and 4.5 by

$$\mathbf{P}(X_k > n) = \mathbf{E}(\mu'_n) \;=\; \int_{a_1}^{a_2} \int_{b_1}^{b_2} \frac{\beta(a, b+n)}{\beta(a, b)} \frac{db\, da}{(a_2 - a_1)(b_2 - b_1)}$$

$$=\; \int_{a_1}^{a_2} \int_{b_1}^{b_2} \frac{b(b+1)...(b+n-1)}{(a+b)(a+b+1)...(a+b+n-1)} \tag{5.10}$$

$$\frac{db\, da}{(a_2 - a_1)(b_2 - b_1)},$$

---

[4]Possibly extended to include points representing $a, b \to \infty$ with a/b constant, and $a, b \to 0$ with a/b constant, to include all the limiting cases of the beta family

where the *first* failure of $\mathcal{A}_k$ occurs on the X_k^{th} demand.

These expressions can be thought of as different ways of expressing *a priori* belief about the reliability of a product. Now we explore the effects on these beliefs of learning from observation. We examine the realisations under these particular distributional assumptions of both the posterior distributions for P_k given by Equations 3.3–3.5, and the predictions of X_k, the time to next failure of $\mathcal{A}_k$ using Equations 4.2–4.4. In the most general case of arbitrary periods of observation of some finite number of previous products, each of the probabilities entailed by these questions takes the form of the ratio of a pair of integrals (over the chosen rectangle in the $\langle a, b \rangle$-plane), where the integrands in the numerator and denominator are each equal to some product of terms of the form

$$
\mathbf{E}(P^r(1-P)^{n-r}\,|\,a,b) \;=\; \int_0^1 p^r(1-p)^{n-r}\frac{p^{a-1}(1-p)^{b-1}}{\beta(a,b)}\,dp = \frac{\beta(a+r,b+n-r)}{\beta(a,b)}
$$

$$
=\; \frac{a(a+1)...(a+r-1)b(b+1)...(b+n-r-1)}{(a+b)(a+b+1)...............(a+b+n-1)} \;.
$$

$$(5.11)$$

In practice, since this kind of inference is most likely to be called for in dealing with very high reliability systems, the values n_i of n in these products are likely to be rather large, and the values of r are likely to be small, and ideally zero. So some very large products will be involved in the above term. We shall report elsewhere on the mathematical difficulties that arise as a result of this. Here we show only some illustrative numerical results based upon the observation of three previous products, each of which has been exposed to 10^7 demands without a single failure. In Table 1 we can see how various different assumptions for Prior$_\theta$ affect the strength of the inferences concerning a fourth product in the same family which can be drawn from this sort of evidence of high reliability of previous, similar products.

All the results in Table 1 involve assuming uniform distributions over different regions of the $\langle a, b \rangle$–space. We have excluded values of b smaller than one, since these entail beta distributions with infinite density at 1; but we have allowed values of a smaller than one, since infinite density at the origin seems plausible. The region in the positive quadrant where a and b are both large can also be ruled out, since any point here corresponds to a beta distribution with very small variance—that different products will have essentially identical probabilities of failure upon demand, which runs counter to the spirit of this whole exercise.

The first nine rows of Table 1 involve several rectangles of the kind described above. The ninth row shows a small rectangle, effectively approximating to a known point value for $\langle a, b \rangle$. Rows 10 to 12 show thin "wedges" adjacent to the b-axis. The informal reasoning here is that it may be reasonable to believe a priori that the mean $\mathbf{E}(P\,|\,a,b)$ of the distribution of probability of failure on demand does not exceed a certain value $0 \leq \mathbf{E}(P\,|\,a,b) \leq M < 1$, say, and this is equivalent to the restriction to $\frac{a}{b} \leq \frac{M}{1-M}$. We used $M = 10^{-3}$, 10^{-5}, and 10^{-7}. Once again, all points in the wedge are given equal weight.

Table 1. Effect on reliability predictions of observation of non-failure of previous products

Region of Uniform Prior				Given no Data		Given no Failure of this Product		Given no Failure of Previous Three Products		Given Failure Neither of this nor of Previous Three Products	
a_1	a_2	b_1	b_2	$E(P_4)$	$R(10^7)$	$E(P_4)$	$R(10^7)$	$E(P_4)$	$R(10^7)$	$E(P_4)$	$R(10^7)$
0	1	1	2	.2384	.6229E-1	.3966E-1	.9585	.1388E-1	.7498	.1047E-1	.9893
0	1	1	10	.1037	.6828E-1	.1577E-1	.9547	.5398E-2	.7499	.4062E-2	.9883
0	1	1	100	.2077E-1	.8048E-1	.3020E-2	.9469	.1019E-2	.7500	.7655E-3	.9862
0	1	1	1000	.3207E-2	.9877E-1	.4636E-3	.9355	.1556E-3	.7500	.1168E-3	.9831
0	2	1	2	.3692	.3114E-1	.3966E-1	.9585	.1388E-1	.7498	.1047E-1	.9893
0	2	1	10	.1781	.3414E-1	.1578E-1	.9547	.5398E-2	.7499	.4062E-2	.9883
0	2	1	100	.3833E-1	.4024E-1	.3020E-2	.9469	.1019E-2	.7500	.7655E-3	.9862
0	2	1	1000	.6091E-2	.4939E-1	.4637E-3	.9355	.1556E-3	.7500	.1168E-3	.9831
.01	.0101	10	10.1	.9990E-3	.8700	.9990E-3	.9931	.9990E-3	.8700	.9990E-3	.9931
0	b/999	1	1000	.5002E-3	.1824	.2056E-3	.9401	.9494E-4	.7545	.7593E-4	.9832
0	b/99999	1	1000	.5000E-5	.9689	.4947E-5	.9977	.4843E-5	.9703	.4791E-5	.9978
0	b/9999999	1	1000	.5000E-7	.99968	.4999E-7	.999977	.4998E-7	.99968	.4998E-7	.999977

.XXXXE-n means $0.XXXX \times 10^{-n}$

In Table 1 we show how "the reliability" of a product changes as a result of the different types of evidence that could be available. For brevity here we have chosen to present the mean of the distribution of P_4, and the reliability function evaluated at 10^7 demands (i.e. the probability of surviving this number of demands), in each of the four cases: given no data; given only evidence of failure-free operation of this product; given only evidence of failure-free working of earlier products; and given both these latter items of evidence.

The most interesting and important results concern the different predictions of future operational behaviour, expressed as the probability $R(10^7)$ of surviving 10^7 further demands without failure; the information from the perfect working of previous products makes only a modest contribution to our confidence in the current product when compared with actual evidence of failure-free working on that product itself (compare columns 8 and 10). Thus when we only have evidence from the previous products, although this is of extensive perfect working for each, it only allows us to claim, in the case of the rectangular priors, about 0.75 probability of similarly extensive perfect working (i.e. surviving 10^7 demands) for the new product[5].

The evidence from previous perfect working of the *same* product, however, is more informative. It allows us to be much more confident that the product will work perfectly in the future: the probability of it surviving 10^7 demands, given that it has already survived 10^7 demands, exceeds 0.9 in all cases.

On the other hand, the small increase in confidence that comes from experience of other products may be useful in the case of safety-critical systems, especially as it is likely to come with little or no cost to developers of the new

---

[5] We conjecture that some limiting result may be indicated here : perhaps the probability that product A_k will survive its first X demands, given that $k-1$ previous products have done so, tends to $(k-1)/k$ as $X \to \infty$.

product. Thus, in the first row of Table 1, the *a priori* belief of the 10^7 demand survival is .062, this increases to .96 after we have actually seen the product survive 10^7 demands, and to .99 when we are told, in addition, that three other products have also survived 10^7 demands. Putting it another way, this evidence of previous product survival has reduced the chance of a failure in the next 10^7 demands by a factor of 4 (from .04 to .01) compared with the result based only on the evidence from operational experience of this product.

We have shown the columns for the means of the various distributions for P_4 mainly as a warning that these can be misleading if used to represent "the reliability" of a product. Thus the mean probability of failure on demand can be quite large (0.24 in the first line prior distribution), but still the chance of surviving 10^7 demands may be non-negligible (0.063 in this case). The informal reason is that the distribution is such that the mean is not a good summary statistic, and in particular cannot be used in a geometric distribution to approximate to the more complex model that applies here.

In fact, decreasing values of $\mathbf{E}(P_4)$ do not necessarily imply increasing chance of surviving 10^7 demands, as might naively be expected: see, for example, columns 7 and 8 of rows 1 to 4. Imagine that we have two experts, let us call them James and Peter, represented by two different prior distributions (rows of Table 1), who observe the system to survive for 10^7 demands. They are then asked to tell us how reliable the system is. If the question is posed as "what is the mean of P_4?", then James is more optimistic than Peter; if, however, the question is posed as "what is the chance of surviving a further 10^7 demands", Peter is more optimistic than James. Such (only apparent) paradoxes underline the importance of using the right formulation for our purposes when we ask questions about the reliability of a system.

6 Conclusions and future work

A major motivation for research of this kind is to make the process of assessing safety-critical systems more open to analysis. Currently, particularly in those cases where complex software is involved, such assessments have a high degree of informality and rely a great deal upon expert judgement. Whilst this process is usually carried out responsibly, and with great rigour, it is difficult for an outsider to analyse how the final judgement has been reached, and much has to be taken on trust. Since there is some evidence of experts being unduly optimistic about their judgemental abilities [3], simply checking their honesty is insufficient. What is needed is a more formal means of argumentation, where the assumptions and reasoning processes are visible and can be questioned. This new model treats a small part of this problem by providing a representation, and means of composition, of two important types of evidence that are commonly used to make claims for the reliability of a product: evidence from testing of the product itself and evidence from previous experience of "similar" products.

Whilst we make no great claims for the realism of the example we have used, it does indicate the way in which a formal model of this kind could be used to question whether an optimistic conclusion drawn from past experience might be ill-founded. Essentially, if you were to claim that great trust could be placed in a particular system because of past experience of other systems, you would have to justify this by trying to claim that your prior distribution is reasonable within the model. It is clear that some of the examples of prior distributions we have used could be said to be "unreasonable" in the sense that they represent beliefs about the reliability, prior to seeing any evidence, that are very strong.

The particular numerical examples used here are meant only to be illustrative. Clearly further work is needed to identify classes of "plausible" prior distributions, even for the case in which the expert professes "complete prior ignorance". For example, rather than addressing the raw $\langle a, b \rangle$ parameters, it may be easier for the subject to think in terms of a reparameterisation - the mean and coefficient of variation are possibilities. Another area of future work concerns the impact of different kinds of evidence upon the conclusions. For example, the case here of complete perfection of operation of the previous products is the best news that it is possible to have, and it would be interesting to investigate the case where there have been failures in the earlier products.

The possibility that conclusions about the reliability of a system can be highly dependent upon the precise way in which they are formulated is somewhat surprising and needs further investigation. However, the results here support those obtained in a different context, concerning stopping rules for software testing [7].

Finally, all this modelling depends upon the reasonableness of notions of "similarity" between different products. In this we are merely making more formal the extremely informal claims that experts make when they argue that the behaviour of one product can be used as a means of inferring the likely behaviour of another. Justification of such assumptions of similarity in particular cases is, of course, outside the direct scope of our studies—in the case of software, from knowledge of the application domain (the problems being solved were similar), the development process (the methods used were similar), the design teams (they were the same or of comparable competence), etc. However, we believe that our model can be used to provide a curb on the enthusiasm of experts: specifically, the use of "similarity" arguments to make stronger claims than would be warranted via the model should be treated with suspicion.

Acknowledgement

This work, which was was previously published as [6], was supported by the ESPRIT PDCS2 Project 6362, the DTI/EPSERC Safety Critical Systems Research Programme's DATUM Project, and the CEC Environment Programme's SHIP Project. It has benefited considerably from numerous critical comments and suggested improvements by colleagues working on these projects and colleagues at the Centre for Software Reliability.

References

1. Butler, R.W. and Finelli, G.B. (1993). The infeasibility of quantifying the reliability of life-critical real-time software. *IEEE Transactions on Software Engineering*, **19**, 3–12.

2. DeGroot, M.H. (1970). *Optimal Statistical Decisions*, McGraw-Hill, New York.

3. Henrion, M. and Fischhoff, B. (1986). Assessing uncertainty in physical constants. *American J. of Physics*, **54**, 791–798.

4. Laprie, J.C. (1992). For a product-in-a-process approach to software reliability evaluation. *Proc. 3rd Int. Sym. on Software Reliability Engineering (ISSRE92)*, Research Triangle Park, NC, IEEE, 134–139.

5. Littlewood, B. and Strigini, L. (1993). Validation of ultra-high dependability for software-based systems. *Comm. Assoc. Computing Machinery*, **36**.

6. Littlewood, B. and Wright, D.R. (1995). A Bayesian model that combines disparate evidence for the quantitative assessment of system dependability. *Proc. 14th Int. Conf. on Comput. Safety, Reliability and Security (SAFECOMP95)*, Editor: G.Rabe, 173–188, Springer Verlag.

7. Littlewood, B. and Wright, D.R. (1995). On a stopping rule for the operational testing of safety-critical software. *Proc. 25th Fault Tolerant Computing Sym.*, IEEE.

8. Rouquet, J.C. and Traverse, Z.Z. (1986). Safe and reliable computing on board the Airbus and ATR aircraft. *Proc. 5th IFAC Worshop on Safety of Computer Control Systems*, Editor: W.J. Quirk, 93–97, Pergamon Press.